The Fictive World of
CONRAD
AIKEN

The Fictive World of

CONRAD AIKEN

A
Celebration
of
Consciousness

Catharine F. Seigel

NORTHERN ILLINOIS UNIVERSITY PRESS
DeKalb 1993

© 1992 by Northern Illinois University Press
Published by the Northern Illinois University Press,
DeKalb, Illinois 60115
Manufactured in the United States using acid-free paper ⊗
Design by Julia Fauci

Library of Congress Cataloging-in-Publication Data
Seigel, Catharine F.
The fictive world of Conrad Aiken : a celebration of consciousness /
Catharine F. Seigel.
p.   cm.
Includes bibliographical references (p.   ) and index.
ISBN 0–87580–172–2 (acid-free)
1. Aiken, Conrad, 1889–1973––Criticism and interpretation.
2. Consciousness in literature. I. Title.
PS3501.I5Z86   1992
818'.5209––dc20   92-3804
CIP

The Huntington Library, San Marino, California, and the Washington
University Libraries, St. Louis, Missouri, have generously granted
permission to reprint correspondence and material held in their
collections.
Research supported by National Endowment for the Humanities and
Rhode Island School of Design Faculty Development grants.

To Jules

Contents

The Fictive World of
CONRAD
AIKEN

Chapter One

INTRODUCTION

What is there in thee, Man, that can be known?
Dark fluxion, all unfixable by thought,
A phantom dim of past and future wrought,
Vain sister of the worm—

Coleridge, "Self-knowledge"

CONRAD AIKEN WROTE HIS AUTOBIOGRAPHY his entire life. From his first volume of short fiction, *Bring! Bring! and Other Stories*, in 1925 and his first novel, *Blue Voyage*, in 1927 to his professed autobiography, *Ushant*, in 1952 (and in most of the poetry before and after these dates), he sang variations on the same song. Saying this does not mean that Aiken, like all writers, merely drew on an imagination informed by personal experience; rather, it means that Aiken actually recycled a myriad of specific, often minor incidents (for instance, a walk with his mother to the post office) and the one major incident in his life (the shooting of his mother by his father and his father's subsequent suicide) over and over again. And just as Aiken had one story to tell, he wove the narratives on a single philosophical loom: a theory of expanding individual consciousness.

Any responsible study of the modern novel should confront the works of Conrad Aiken. Even the broadest survey of the psychological novel should use Aiken's fiction as a touchstone, and no study of the lyrical novel should neglect Aiken's singular contribution. Yet most criticism of the modern novel routinely ignores Aiken. Such contemporary critical indifference follows from Aiken's limited readership throughout his long career. While obviously nothing can be done about Aiken's neglect when he was writing most of his fiction, occasionally, as we know, a writer's reputation is established posthumously. Classic examples include Edward Taylor, Emily Dickinson, Herman Melville, and to some degree Malcolm Lowry—all marginally recognized in their own day; subsequently, through perceptive though belated criticism, they have assumed their rightful reputations. In each case, the role of the critic was to reintroduce the writers and to teach people how to read them, and this is precisely what must be done for Aiken. Almost forty years ago Aiken identified a similar problem with readers coming to the prose of William Faulkner. Writing for the *Harvard Advocate*, Aiken acknowledged that even the most devoted of Faulkner's readers (of which he considered himself) "must find, with each new novel that the first fifty pages are always the hardest, that each time one must learn all over again *how* to read this strangely fluid and slippery and heavily mannered prose, and that one is even, like a kind of Laocoon, sometimes tempted to give it up."[1] Advising readers on how to approach Faulkner grew out of a long admiration on Aiken's part for the Southern novelist, dating back to 1927 when Aiken's was the voice crying in the wilderness prophesying a literary career for the author of *Mosquitoes*![2]

. . .

An evaluation of Aiken's fiction written between 1925 and 1940 must have as its focus a thorough understanding and appreciation of Aiken's singular theory of evolving consciousness. Aiken's commitment to consciousness colors everything that he wrote: five novels, five volumes of short stories, twenty-five volumes of poetry, drama, autobiography, and even two volumes of criticism. Yet the importance that Aiken placed on consciousness and its evolution went virtually unnoticed by reviewers and has never been seriously studied by literary critics. Why this is so is as difficult to determine precisely as it is to be certain why, in general, Aiken was discounted. One could speculate that his "theory" was too simple to command attention, that it lacked philosophical pyrotechnics, or that it was too "romantic" for the intellectual climate of the 1920s and 1930s. However, such indifference to the philosophical concept at the heart of his work surely contributed substantially to Aiken's neglect.

The centrality of autobiography for plot and consciousness for theory will be the thread that runs through this study of Aiken's fiction. The criticism is undertaken with the expectation that such explication of his works might open up Aiken's fiction, making his singular philosophical insights—which remain undeniably relevant—and his innovative, complementary, often complex poetic prose style available to a new generation of readers.

. . .

For a writer who won almost every coveted literary award—the Pulitzer, Bollingen, the National Medal for Literature, and others— Conrad Aiken remained a very private person throughout his long life. He was the first of four children born to Anna Potter Aiken and Dr. William Ford Aiken, a Harvard-educated physician. Although Northerners on both sides, the family had moved to the South for reasons of Dr. Aiken's health, and Conrad Potter Aiken was born in Savannah, Georgia, on 5 August 1889 (in a boarding house, "and not a particularly distinguished one," he once boasted, enjoying the contrast with his *Mayflower* roots). The young Aiken lived in Savannah with his two brothers and a sister until he was dramatically and painfully orphaned in February 1901, when his father murdered his mother and then committed suicide. The children were immediately divided among several relatives, with eleven-year-old Conrad moving to his mother's native New Bedford, Massachusetts, to live with an aunt and uncle (who agreed to take "one male child"). Young Aiken attended Middlesex School in Concord and then Harvard, from which he graduated in 1912.[3]

As a child, Aiken insisted that he was going to be a writer, and he never digressed from that intention. He recalls at length in his autobiography his first encounter with the magical word *poet*, in the epigraph to *Tom Brown's School Days*: "The poet of White Horse Vale, Sir, with liberal notions under my cap." But Aiken's "liberal notions" were destined to hinder his literary recognition; they always kept him out of step with his contemporaries. I. A. Richards, for instance, acknowledged that Aiken's early application of Freudian principles to literary analyses was, unfortunately, far ahead of its time. Shortly before his death on 17 August 1973, Aiken remarked to an interviewer that one of the few things that he continued to read were the newspaper comic strips because they were consistently a "step ahead of public opinion." Aiken might well have been describing his own art.

One first thinks of "modern" in terms of technique: Woolf's and Joyce's stream of consciousness, Eliot's and Pound's elliptical lines, for example. Imposing itself, technique here is immediately apparent. But Aiken, in applying the term to himself in a BBC interview, defined it less in terms of the technique that made him "modern" and more in terms of a mind-set—moral or religious. In that sense, he saw, for instance, Donne—and by implication, himself—as far more "modern" than Hopkins, but he also allowed that a modern poet was

> apt to be a lonely one, lonelier, spiritually, than the poet whose advance, or invention, as in the case of Hopkins, was in the *texture* of poetry rather than in the nature of the statement for which the texture was designed. A poet like Hopkins might be likened to the bird who is embarrassed by the, as it were, anti-social conspicuousness of his plumage, especially if his lot is cast among sparrows; but a poet like Donne is unhappy because, willy-nilly, he flies himself right out of sight.[4]

The totality of Aiken's modern artistic vision constantly eluded reviewers, who would respond to a part of the novel and praise or damn the whole for the part. It is painful to see how frequently reviewers, when they bothered with his fiction at all, misread Aiken. For instance, a critic for the *New Republic*, in a review of Aiken's third novel, *King Coffin*, abhorred his negative attitudes, his "pessimism, his sense of a civilization past the age of belief or hope."[5] The critic clearly failed to realize that Aiken's insistence in that novel, as in all his writings, on the primacy of individual consciousness precluded any such categorical generalizations about civilizations and that "pessimism" was an impossible label for a truly realized Aiken character. For example, in *Blue Voyage*, Demarest, Aiken's own spokesman (by Aiken's admission and insistence), is aptly characterized by one of his fellow voyagers: "We ought to be sorry for him. More to be pitied than blamed. After all, he's an idealist: a subjective idealist."[6]

Then, too, Aiken's preoccupation with the evolution of the individual's consciousness frequently resulted in his being viewed as a passivist, a self-indulgent non-doer, caught up in his own mental labyrinth. Even so loyal a supporter of Aiken as

Malcolm Cowley chastised him for his noninvolvement. In reviewing *Bring! Bring! and Other Stories*, Cowley observed:

> This dangerous passivity, the neglect of logical thought, the distaste for action (growing into a contempt for action): all these are symptoms of the malady which afflicts the more intelligent writers of our time. Their books are concerned with people who drift, accept, surrender to their passions. A strain of inherited agnosticism, applied first to God, then to society, has finally centred in the self. They are palsied with doubt; afflicted, characters and authors, with an atrophy of the will.[7]

But the unpardonable sin of which Aiken was most frequently accused was ambiguity. Again this follows from reading an Aiken novel with expectations derived from more traditional paradigms. Such criticism misses the very point that for Aiken ambiguity was the most distinctive quality of the modern mind, and also that the ambiguity in Aiken's novels derived not from faulty writing, as was frequently suspected, but from his insistence that it was an essential condition of consciousness. Robert Linscott, Aiken's literary agent and good friend, wrote to him crystallizing his difficulties in placing Aiken's short stories by projecting an imaginary scenario with the editor of *Atlantic* when faced with considering Aiken's "Strange Moonlight" (incidentally, Aiken's favorite short story): " 'What's it all about' he'll bark and to a sorry task explaining to a hardboiled editor that it isn't an incident but an emotion in rhythm. 'But my subscribers' he'll say, 'want something solid and something tangible, something that can be laid hold of and bitten into——' " (26 November 1922, HHL MS. Aik 3766). Aiken should have been recognized as writing in a viable tradition that might well be called the continuity of American ambiguity, with its roots in Hawthorne, Melville, Dickinson, and Whitman (all of whom Aiken acknowledged as important to him), but the prevailing taste in American prose fiction of the 1920s and 1930s, when Aiken was writing most of his fiction, was for immediate accessibility.

Related to the criticism of Aiken's ambiguity was the impatience with his apparent inconsistencies. One fairly typical critic charged that Aiken obviously had not subjected his ideas to an "intellectually rigorous scrutiny. That is not to say that he is unintelligent or unthinking, but only that in the end his skepticism is not consistent. The result is a paradox: the 'philosophical' skeptic is also a poetic philosopher."[8] Aiken—echoing Whitman's "I contradict myself? I contradict myself"—would have added, "Of course."

Such apparent ambiguities and inconsistencies were not limited to his fiction but likewise characterized his literary criticism, where one might assume Aiken would have liked to suggest that his conclusions followed from some carefully and logically structured paradigm. Instead he cautioned the readers of *Scepticisms: Notes on Contemporary Poetry*, his first volume of criticism: "Our utterances are apt to sound authoritative and final. But do not be deceived! We are no surer of ourselves at bottom than anybody else is. We are, in fact, half the time, frightened to death." [9] Almost forty years later in his second critical volume, *A Reviewer's ABC*, Aiken candidly admitted: "The inconsistencies I could, indeed, have eradicated. They remain because it seems to me that in so relative a world they may have a kind of value. One is least sure of one's self, sometime, when one is most positive" (*ABC*, 34).

In only one realm was Aiken an unvacillating servant—in his priestly dedication to the pursuit of consciousness. His commitment to the theory coupled with his insistence on the redemptory role of the artist demanded that he teach a reader how to come to terms with his or her individual consciousness. This would logically follow from Aiken's painfully honest pursuit of his own consciousness in each of his novels. A thorough understanding of the place of consciousness in the Aiken canon should allay the most persistent criticisms of his novels: that, in addition to being inconsistent and ambiguous, nothing happens in them; and that they have no artistic unity. What for so long was seen as Aiken's lack of control over his form will come to be recognized *as* his form. Aiken's prose runs essentially counter to Francis Fergusson's definition of the dramatic form of the novel as one in which a situation leads to a decision that effects change. A partial explanation for Aiken's neglect was that he did not fulfill the reader's expectations for a novel within these traditional boundaries. Like the readers of Faulkner whom Aiken had early instructed, we must also be taught how to read Aiken's unique contributions to the emerging twentieth-century American novel. Such instruction must begin with the recognition of Aiken's theory of evolving consciousness, continue with a close observation of this theory at work in his fiction, and culminate in an examination of his strange and beautiful novel/ autobiography, *Ushant*, where the biographical, psychological, and philosophical forces that contributed to his Weltanschauung coalesce.

. . .

In 1932 *Nation* surveyed several American public figures to determine what they really *believed* in at the time. "To ask a man what he believes is perhaps tantamount to asking him why he lives," answered Conrad Aiken.[10] Since it was a Depression year, as well as one in which the war clouds were gathering on the international horizon, most replies were economic or political in focus. Edmund Wilson's was fairly typical: "I believe that the discussion of other matters must wait until the problems of the social classes, with the political and economic questions they involve, have been definitely settled."[11] But consistent with the pattern of his entire life, Aiken was listening to a different drummer and answered the survey with an outline of his belief in the primacy of the individual consciousness, essentially the philosophy by which he lived his entire life. To an age desperately seeking concrete "answers" from its literary prophets—for instance, the sorts of societal salvation suggested by Auden, Dos Passos, Dreiser, and Steinbeck, or the invitations to religious or mythic explanations offered by Eliot or Pound, Aiken only contributed the disquieting consolation of a celebration of consciousness: "If we begin by understanding ourselves, as far as we can, we progress thus toward an understanding of man and his potentialities. This seems to me a sufficient field for belief and will. Let us be as conscious as possible" ("What I Believe," 80). Some forty years later—after an international war of hitherto unimagined dimensions, after the nightmare of the holocaust, and after the surrealistic perfection of the means for the annihilation of the human species—when Aiken was interviewed on his eightieth birthday, he unhesitantly replied to the question about whether there was any longer a workable ethic for man, "Yes. The main thing is to know thyself."[12]

While many moderns struggled with the viability of any systematic epistemology, Aiken insisted that by virtue of being born one was initiated into a structure. "One is 'here,' " Aiken insisted, "simply, involved in a scene and sustained by it. We are born of a system, and into it, and our birth is our first act of acceptance" ("What I Believe," 79). Beyond that Aiken was uncertain about the choices of believing or not believing, living or dying, one could make, but he concluded, "Will it be safe to say that it is the function of the sane, or healthy, to live, or believe, and of the insane, or unhealthy, to disbelieve and die? And in this respect can we say that belief is perhaps a measure of energy, as courage is perhaps a measure of desire?" ("What I Believe," 79). Thus Aiken saw merely staying alive, even on the simplest plane of consciousness, as heroic, and for this reason he held all humanity in reverence.

Yet this does not suggest that Aiken was proposing a mere animal faith limited to satisfying primary instincts—to eat, to sleep, to keep warm. Rather as one moved up the scale of civilization, one inevitably ascended the scale of consciousness, moving into a world of ever-increasing ambiguities and abstractions. Aiken explained the steps:

> as he becomes more conscious, not only is he farther and farther removed from the level of simple animal faith, or the level on which he can quite simply accept it, but also his credulity is itself weakened. More and more his faiths must recommend themselves to reason; with each successive plane of awareness new terms for faith must be found—less concrete, more abstract, more comprehensive. From religion he perhaps moves to philosophy, from philosophy to science—and from science to what? In recent years we have seen that even when he has reached the realm of pure observation, he is still sometimes not content—here we have the extraordinary spectacle of the scientist endeavoring to force a shotgun marriage between science and mysticism. This is interesting, if only because it so conveniently proves how strong is our inherited will-to-believe in something vaguely "divine." ("What I Believe," 79)

Aiken was particularly sensitive to the growing expectation in his own day that science would provide relief—in the form of explanations—to man's metaphysical angst. He warned that one should not ask of science more than it can give: "the infinite everywhere precedes and succeeds the finite which is our little field of observation . . . the fact remains that the limits of knowledge are ultimate, not immediate . . . and we can never reach them. . . . The conscious life of man becomes therefore an absolutely unanswerable, but relatively answerable 'Why?' " ("What I Believe," 79).

While such a conclusion is less than comforting, Aiken was confident that once the individual realized, or, perhaps more to the point, would admit, that there were no absolute answers, he would gradually cease struggling to believe in formal systems: "I can see no reason why man will not presently give up all major beliefs . . . and simply surrender himself to what is perhaps the first principle of his own present state as a conscious creature—an inexhaustible curiosity" ("What I Believe," 79). About this time Aiken expressed the same conviction in a long poem, "Time in the Rock":

> Mysticism, but let us have no words,
> angels, but let us have no fantasies,
> churches, but let us have no creeds,
> no dead gods hung on crosses in a shop,
> nor beads nor prayers nor faith nor sin nor penance:
> and yet, let us believe, let us believe.[13]

It is on this final realization by the individual that within oneself are the answers—or the questions—which are finally one and the same—that Aiken insisted in each novel. The problem, however, never engaged the sensibilities of a wide-reading audience. A *New York Times* reviewer was certain that the novel *King Coffin* (1935), like the two that preceded it, *Blue Voyage* and *Great Circle*, would not be popular because Aiken was appreciated only by a "minority that is spiritually . . . attuned to him." The reviewer pinpointed why the writer was out of touch with most readers: "Aiken believes man is his study. Not man in love, man at work, man in hate or in grief, but that vast, dimensionless universe that exists within man."[14]

Aiken's "study" undoubtedly began early and unconsciously. Commencing with the violent death of his parents when he was so young, Aiken came to realize prematurely that he was absurdly a part of, and in many ways dependent on, a seemingly quixotic, perhaps even perverse and random, world. Therefore he came early to look into himself, both to assess what blame for events rested with him and to discover what resources there were within himself, so that he could depend as little as possible on the capricious external world and on the shallow systems that men had fabricated to explain it. Aiken's own internal voyage—his autobiography, then—is to a greater and lesser extent the subject of each novel—beginning with *Blue Voyage*. This first work, which treats the protagonist's lonely inward journey as he travels outward on an ocean liner, provides a textbook introduction to Aiken's whole philosophical world. By the end of the novel, William Demarest understands and even accepts all the "MISERY" (the word acts as a refrain) that he has touched upon. Through Demarest, Aiken attempts to fictionalize his conviction that there is, finally, only one explanation, and that is consciousness:

> Consciousness is our supreme gift. Not only does it contain—in every sense—all that we value, but also it is the fundamental and indeed the only means by which we are able to value. To see, to remember, to know, to feel, to understand, as much as possible— isn't this perhaps the most obviously indicated of motives or beliefs, the noblest and most all-comprehending of ideas which it is relatively possible for us to realize? To understand all is not merely to forgive all—it is also to accept all, and on whatever plane one wishes. If to be a genius is to be . . . an extender of man's consciousness, then there can be no monopoly of genius by the few; it is the common inheritance of all mankind. ("What I Believe," 80)

Such conviction led Aiken to believe that consciousness was the essential reason for writing. First, writing it all down—as accurately as one dared—was therapeutic for the writer, a medium through which he could come to terms with his existence. Second, what he wrote could become a handmaiden to the reader's pursuit of his or her own consciousness. To this end, Aiken was absolutely insistent about the proselytizing role of the writer through self-revelation. After reading a new collection of Malcolm Cowley's poetry in 1919, Aiken expressed disappointment in his friend's neglect of this primal obligation. He chastised him for being too preoccupied with technique and too little with self:

> Somehow you've forgotten to get down to the real business of the poet: *viz.*, consciously or unconsciously to give the lowdown on himself, and through himself on humanity. . . . The stuff is so good, and yet so (somehow) superficial! As if you'd adopted one palette after another and demonstrated your skill, but nevertheless avoided the final business of self-betrayal.[15]

Aiken made no attempt to disguise the fact that he took his own advice quite literally and throughout his life wrote variations on one theme: the particular pursuit of consciousness in the life of Conrad Aiken, writer—its peculiar risks, its exacting responsibilities. It is not surprising to find that the conflict in four of Aiken's five novels is within the mind of an artist. Demarest, the protagonist of *Blue Voyage*, is a playwright; in *Great Circle*, Cather is a tutor and a writer;[16] Noni, the central character in *A Heart for the Gods of Mexico*, is a musician, and Blomberg, the narrator, is a reader of novels for a publishing house; and in the last novel, *Conversation*, Kane is a painter. (The exception is *King Coffin*, in which Jaspar Ammen is a student.) Finally in *Ushant* the author and the persona—D.— totally merge; the mask is dropped, and the dimension of consciousness is exhaustively explored in the life of Conrad Aiken.

Chapter Two

FREUD AND THE PSYCHOANALYTIC FOUNDATION

IT WAS ONLY AFTER TWELVE VOLUMES of published poetry had established his modest reputation as a poet, after ten years of reviewing had earned him respect as an "advanced" if not always a popular critic, and after the publication of a volume of short stories that Conrad Aiken brought out *Blue Voyage*.[1] The transition from the poem to the novel was minimal: autobiography remained the subject, and the exploration of consciousness remained the prevailing theme.

Blue Voyage has a simple narrative structure; its power and complexities lie, instead, in its relentless probing into the psyche of the protagonist, William Demarest, a thirty-five-year-old writer struggling to assess his past, to speculate on his future, and, in short, to determine who he is. Aiken, thirty-three when he began the novel, freely admits the parallels between Demarest and himself, assuring us that they are by design, not accident. Years later Aiken made explicit the intended connection between this novel and his later "autobiographical essay," *Ushant*:

> I really wanted, sort of in mid-career, to make a statement about the predicament of the would-be artist and just what made him tick and what was wrong with him and why he went fast or slow. Just as *Ushant* was the other end of that statement, "D." of *Ushant* is Demarest of *Blue Voyage*, grown fatter and balder. That was always planned—that I should as it were, give myself away, to such extent as I could bear it, as to what made the wheels go round. Feeling that this was one of the responsibilities of a writer—that he should take off the mask.[2]

The romantic pursuit by Demarest of Cynthia, an elusive social snob, is the simple plot for the writer's complex journey into himself. In the narration of the superficial tale, Aiken explores several involved philosophical and aesthetic problems that become the interrelated themes of the novel: the nature of consciousness; the nature of the relationship between art and the artist; and the nature of male/female relationships with particular reference to the tensions between the secular and the ideal. If all that sounds more like philosophy than fiction, it is, nonetheless, a fair estimate of what engaged the sensibilities of Conrad Aiken in his first novel.

. . .

A realization that the major focus of *Blue Voyage* is a study of the phenomena of consciousness comes slowly to the reader. At the narrative level of the novel, very little happens: Demarest, a playwright, sails from New York to England, where he hopes to pursue a relationship with Cynthia Battilore, whom he met— and thought he loved—on a similar trans-Atlantic voyage the previous year.[3] He discovers to his dismay that Cynthia is on the same ship (though in first-class accommodations) returning from a stay in America (during which time she had never contacted Demarest) to England to be married. The bulk of the novel consists of conversations that Demarest holds with his fellow passengers, with himself, an analysis of his dreams, his extended reverie, and, finally, his writing of six—unsent— letters to his "lover." Unlike Cynthia, who remains a shadowy, ill-defined woman, there are three other characters who have slightly more than mere symbolic dimensions: Smith, a recently retired music store employee (a sad little man whose wife ran off shortly after their marriage) returning, after an absence of thirty years, to his birthplace; Silberstein, a bluntly realistic man, owner of a chewing gum business; and Mrs. Peggy Faubion, a seductive, dark-eyed beauty currently being sued for divorce on the grounds of infidelity.

The novel is essentially all talk, and one can understand the oft-repeated criticism that nothing ever happens in Aiken's novels. The author himself was acutely aware of this liability. Writing to Robert Linscott after completing the first four chapters of *Blue Voyage*, Aiken admitted being pleased with his manuscript: "But who except you will take the trouble (supposing him to have staggered through Chapter IV) to plough through this? Not even the publisher's reader" (8 February 1926,

WUL MS.). Few reviewers were as perceptive and sympathetic as Malcolm Cowley, who correctly observed that the arena of Aiken's action is elsewhere: "nothing is changed externally: a *situation* leads to an *emotion*, or else to *an exploration of self*, as a result of which the hero (or the reader, or both) achieves *a higher degree of self-awareness*. The only drama, if we can call it that, is the drama of the widening and deepening consciousness."[4] The reviewer for the *New York Herald Tribune* was more typical when she warned that most readers would have difficulties with Aiken's *Blue Voyage*: "Obviously this is no book for the reader who wishes to be borne along restfully on a 'good story.' It is swift, but subtle; rich, though confusing as smoking-room conversations, fragments of poetry, smut and brilliant colored memories shift brokenly like a crazy kaleidoscope, through the mind of William Demarest."[5] This apparent formlessness, however, was Aiken's form. In the manuscript notes to *Ushant*, Aiken muses on his simultaneous, nonlinear prose: "the important and the unimportant—Senlin is this, Festus is this, Great Circle is this, Blue Voyage—there is no *progress* in this sense, as in the usual work of art—it is a sort of static-dynamic—everything back is given (hypothecated) everything future is implied—in this kind of stillness is all motion the humming centre—"[6]

Blue Voyage is Aiken's first extended fictional exploration into his theory of consciousness, and, although the doctrine is not yet fully formulated, it does provide the philosophical focus of the book. Voyaging into the self is precisely the real journey on which William Demarest embarks. In the opening pages, Demarest goes to his cabin, confronts himself in the mirror, and sets the direction of this first novel as well as the focus for all of Aiken's art:

> He looked long into his own eyes, so unfathomable, as if in an effort to understand himself, and—through his own transparent elusiveness—the world. What was it he wanted? What was it that was driving him back? What was this singular mechanism in him that wanted so deliberately, so consciously, to break itself? A strange, a rich, a deep personality he had—it baffled and fascinated him. Everybody of course, was like this,—depth beyond depth, a universe chorally singing, incalculable, obeying tremendous laws, chemical or divine, of which it was able to give its own consciousness not the faintest inkling . . . He brushed the dark hair of this universe. . . . And this universe would go out and talk inanely to

other universes—talking only with some strange fraction of its identity, like a vast sea leaving on the shore, for all mention of itself, a single white pebble, meaningless. A universe that contained everything—all things—yet said only one word: "I." . . . Ah—thought Demarest, drawing on his sweater,—if we stopped to consider, before any individual, his infinite richness and complexity, could we be anything but idolatrous—even of a fool?[7]

While for Demarest, as for Aiken, the pursuit of consciousness was the only quest, it was one that demanded a constant diminution of what one positively "knows." Every step downward or inward into the unconscious jeopardized one's security, made one increasingly less sure of what one was absolutely sure of, and caused increasing fragmentation and dissolution of self. He who would find himself must lose himself. Aiken frequently expressed this journey into the unconscious in terms of a downward movement, often into water. The controlling metaphor of *Blue Voyage* is, not surprisingly, the journey over water by a protagonist whose name divides into "de-mar-est."

In 1915, before *The Waste Land* or *Ulysses*, Aiken wrote to a friend that he was haunted by a notion of " 'a single human consciousness as simply a *chorus*: a chorus of voices, influences. As if one's sum total of awareness and identity were merely handed to one progressively and piecemeal by the environment. As if one were a mirror. As if one were a vaudeville stage across which a disjointed and comparatively meaningless series of acts was perpetually passing. This flux being one's being.' "[8]

Demarest is threatened by the chaos about him. He longs for control at least over himself, to become a partially unified self. He is the modern persona experiencing the confusion of the modern sensibility. But Demarest has a particular need for some kind of convincing identity that would offer clues to an order or design in the universe in which he had a place: he had been catapulted into an awareness of the terrible chaos earlier and more precipitously than most. In *Blue Voyage* Demarest only obliquely alludes to the killings that shrouded Conrad Aiken's own child-world.

While the tragedy underlies the novel, the facts are only hinted at. It is somewhat disconcerting—and a justifiable criticism of the novel—that Aiken is unable or unwilling to be more explicit about the circumstances surrounding Demarest's shattered childhood. We must be satisfied with the shadow of some terrible early trauma. There is no way in which a reader can tell exactly how the father of Demarest "deprived him" of his mother. Instead one is simply told that his father "then" was thirty-seven, and now would be fifty-five:

> What would he think of me, I wonder. Would I be afraid of him still? . . . You see these plays? they come from the deep wound you inflicted on my soul . . . You see the unhappy restlessness with which I wander from continent to continent, this horrified and lacklustre restlessness which prevents me from loving one person or place for more than a season, driving me on, aimless and soulless? This is what you did to me by depriving me of my mother. (CN, 85)

This is the fullest treatment that the actual event directly receives, but veiled references are everywhere. For instance, a few pages earlier there had been an initial factual reference to the Aiken tragedy in Demarest's reverie, which continues for the entire chapter: "You have seen, in Mount Auburn cemetery (beautiful isn't it), that tombstone of white marble . . . upon which, annually on a certain day, two drops of blood are found? Those drops of blood are mine. Expiation. On the twenty-eighth of February each year, in the evening, I go there and cut my left wrist, letting two drops fall on the stone. Twenty-eight is my fatal number" (82). Dr. Aiken had actually committed the double murder on 27 February 1901, when he was thirty-seven. In another instance, Demarest walks at night on the deck and touches lifeboat number fourteen. He immediately thinks of the number as being half of twenty-eight, and his mind wanders: "The Number of the house had been 228—228 Habersham Street." Only a reader familiar with Aiken's biography would know that 228 was the number of the house where the fatal shooting in Savannah, now echoing in the mind of Demarest, occurred.

The drive toward an ever-widening consciousness, though having strong stimuli in Demarest's childhood, is spurred on by approaching middle-age restlessness—dissatisfaction with his professional life as well as with his personal relationships—all crystallized in his rejection by Cynthia. But Demarest has methodically constructed his conventional defenses. No one sees him for the tormented man that he is. Shy and intensely insecure about social relations, he is particularly sensitive to class differences.[9] His social diffidence is projected into a nightmare (the first of several dreams in the novel) that frightens

Demarest just before he awakes the first morning on board. He dreams that he has inadvertently walked into a garden party, and as he frantically tries to escape he is spotted by a group of society women. He then notices that his shoes are covered with mud and that his trousers are torn; he hears their derisive laughter and sees their hard eyes upon him. On waking, Demarest identifies this as simply a variation on a recurring motif: his absurd " 'inferiority complex.' "[10]

It is not surprising, then, that Demarest views his own social inferiority as a major barrier in his relationship with Cynthia. The first reference to her in the novel comes while Demarest is rethinking this same dream: "It was precisely this damned inferiority complex that had put him at such an initial disadvantage with Cynthia" (*CN*, 30). Of course, the problem of communicating with her is complicated by her traveling first class and his traveling second-class. When he finally summons the courage to walk on the upper deck and meets Cynthia, Demarest becomes frantically preoccupied with how he is going to let her know that he is not traveling first class: "He must, somehow, mention that he was not in the first cabin—that he was a sneaking interloper; just what he had always been afraid of seeming!" (70). And not having found a way to tell her, he imagines Cynthia looking over the first-class passenger list and chuckling with her mother over the absurd conduct of the silly man.

But the most painful portrayal of social failure is in chapter 6, the long fantasy chapter in which Demarest has a waking dream of a meeting among the other main characters in the novel: Smith, Silberstein, Faubion, and Cynthia. He imagines that he hears one of them talking about him: " 'He came to me with a shabby chessboard under his arm! And he had forgotten to button—' " (141). But the unkindest cut is made by English-born Cynthia: " 'And do you know what he said when I asked him if he would like to come one afternoon to hear my brother William play Bach on the piano? Do you know what he said, delicious provincial little Yankee that he is and always will be? . . . *"You bet!"* ' " (141).

Demarest, in a relentless pursuit of self-understanding, seeks the reasons for his acute sense of inferiority and finds them rooted in his childhood relationship with his parents. In his serious examination of the profound influence of childhood experiences, Aiken makes one of the earliest and best uses of Freud in American literature. He always acknowledged a significant debt to the founder of psychoanalysis. "Have you been influenced by Freud and how do you regard him?" was a question asked by the editors of *New Verse* in 1934 of forty poets. Aiken unhesitantly replied, "Profoundly, but so has everybody, whether they are aware of it or not. However, I decided very early, I think as early as 1912, that Freud, and his co-workers and rivals and followers, were making the most important contribution of the century to the understanding of man and his consciousness; accordingly I made it my business to learn as much from them as I could."[11] It is to Aiken's credit that he so early recognized the importance of Freud to modern thought.[12] In addition to being an avid student of Freud, Aiken throughout his life numbered several psychologists, psychoanalysts, and medical doctors as his closest friends.[13]

Although both Freud's insistence on the permanent effects of childhood experiences and his views on religion as illusion were important to Aiken's intellectual development, it was Freud's exploration into the significance of the unconscious that was central to Aiken's theory of evolving consciousness. His lifelong friend, psychologist Henry A. Murray, summed up the far-reaching effect Freud was to have on their generation:

> [Freud's] findings constituted a complex block of knowledge lying athwart the path of intellectual advancement in the West. From then on philosophy would have to proceed with a fresh set of postulates. It was not possible to reach the new world of thought by going around Freud's work, giving it a wide berth or skimming its surfaces; one had to go through it.[14]

Far from wishing to skirt Freud, Aiken embraced him, finding, in part, a foundation for a psychological ordering of his existence. Murray isolated the singular significance of Freud to Aiken's thought: "Aiken's abettor, the psychopompos who illumined his pilgrim-rake's progress through the seven circles of the mind, inward, downward, and backward, was quite obviously Sigmund Freud."[15] Aiken freely admitted that the quintessential use he early made of Freudianism remained with him through the years. In 1944, he insisted that Freud "still fits admirably in such philosophic order as I find necessary—a belief in the evolution of consciousness, awareness, as our prime gift and obligation and a Socratic desire to get on with it at all costs."[16]

It is not surprising, then, that Demarest seeks clues to his identity in his childhood and looks to himself for meaning rather than to any systematized orthodoxy. Nor is it surprising to find that Demarest frequently calls into play the technique of self-psychoanalysis, nor that the novel draws heavily on the prose techniques of stream of consciousness, free association, and interior monologues, and emphasizes dreams and waking reveries. Demarest remarks that Tompkins, his psychoanalyst friend, had urged him to relinquish his writing career in favor of a career as a psychologist or as a psychological critic of literature.

Demarest gradually traces his quivering, diffident adult personality, his general failure as an artist, and his inability to win Cynthia all to his early relationship with his parents and especially to his serious conflict with his father. There are direct authorial statements such as the one characterizing Demarest as a man "whose fear of his father has frozen him in the habit of inaction and immobility, as the hare freezes to escape attention" (*CN*, 136). But more stylistically subtle is the bizarre transference by Demarest of Smith, the older passenger, into a father figure whose death he then projects. It starts as a kind of shipboard jest in answer to an inquiry as to whether the two men are traveling together. Demarest responds that they are father and son, giving an absurdly humorous explanation for why they have different last names. Smith, although he enjoys the joke at the outset, signals the other dimension of the relationship as he later admonishes Demarest: " 'Don't call me father. *Brr.* Makes me shiver. I feel my coffin . . . ' " (42). Subsequently, a clairvoyant on board predicts that someone will be murdered on the journey, and Demarest, in relating the story to Smith, says that although the clairvoyant did not know who it would be, he knows that he will " 'recognize the man when he sees him . . . Father!' " (62). To Smith's angered response, " '*Don't* call me father!' " Demarest thinks to himself: "Why conceal it? He had suddenly thought—and thought vividly, with absurd apprehension—that it was *Smith!* Ridiculous, both to entertain the thought and to suppress it . . . Nevertheless, he had seen Smith, with shattered forehead, blundering into the dark stateroom" (62).

Again, in explicitly Oedipal terms, Demarest tries to transform his beloved Cynthia—of whom he is so unworthy—into the mother who was forever lost to him. In a long reverie, Demarest cries out to Cynthia: "Let me bury my infant's face against you and weep! . . . I am looking everywhere, for my mother. Is it you, perhaps? . . . You remind me of her. Let me be your child, Cynthia! . . . Who is it that has that theory of compulsory repetition. Freud, is it?" (103). The first unsent letter to Cynthia, mainly a long narrative account of a childhood experience one morning on a New Bedford whaling ship (lifted directly from Aiken's biography), is prefaced by Demarest's confession that in moments of Sturm und Drang he feels a powerful desire to talk to her about his growing up:

> I found myself constantly . . . babbling to you my absurd infantine confidences and secrets, as if you were—ah!—my mother. Exactly! And isn't that the secret of your quite extraordinary influence upon me? For some reason which I cannot possibly analyse, you strike to more numerous and deeper responses in me than any other woman has done. It must be that you correspond, in ways that only my unconscious memory identifies, to my mother, who died when I was very small. (CN, 144)

If *Blue Voyage* suffers the labor pains of an apprentice novel, it is particularly apparent in the clumsy use of—even indulgence in—Freudian dream analyses. Aiken uses a variety of dream types. There is the previously mentioned dream of Demarest entrapped in the garden party, the projection of his inferiority complex. There are prophetic dreams: Demarest tells his shipmates about how he had had a recurring dream about the sinking of a ship on which he was once about to sail and how the ship actually did sink before he boarded. And finally there is a masturbatory dream in which Demarest finds an asphyxiated baby abandoned in a train station: "Horrible and strange; for as he worked over it . . . pressing with merciful palms the small back to induce breathing, regarding the small blue neck and wondering at the parents who had so casually abandoned it on a railway platform, he suddenly noticed that the head was not a head but——A spasm of disgust" (49).

A Freudian critic might well suggest that this dream was prompted by Aiken's not having been honest in *Blue Voyage*, not admitting that Demarest-Aiken was a married man with several children whom he "abandoned" while pursuing beautiful Cynthia across the ocean. That this suppression bothered Aiken is apparent in *Ushant*, where *Blue Voyage* appears as a drama, *Purple Passage*, and Aiken chastizes himself: "Why have suppressed, for example, the fact that the philandering D. was married, and had children? Why throw away, and at the outset, the very element in the situation that made for tragedy, and thus irremediably rob the poor play of any possible extension towards the classic, or power?"[17]

Although Aiken feared that he thereby flawed the whole work, he sensed that it was necessary in order to make Demarest respectable. The omission was also prompted by his fear of offending the real woman (Jessie McDonald) to whom he was married at the time, as well as by a concern for his children, and finally because of "a deep fear of public opinion" (*Ushant*, 142).

Aiken also put Freud's observations about fetishes to narrative use: Demarest, for instance, has a slipper fetish. (Freud had identified the foot, from its particular use in ancient myths, as a primitive sexual symbol.) He admits in his reverie that he "collected slippers—a hundred and sixty-three. The fifty-seven varieties were child's play to me, and the sixty-nine, and the one thousand" (*Cn*, 91). Undoubtedly, too, Smith's voracious sexual appetite, which we see through his absurd pursuit of Faubion, has its Freudian dimension in his constantly holding, swirling, fondling, and smoking expensive cigars.

In addition to the more obvious Freudian influences such as dreams and fetishes, the basic psychological impulse to return to the womb (Aiken mercifully spares us the phrase) runs throughout the novel. Early, in a casual manner, Silberstein mentions that Smith wants to die and doesn't know it; Demarest concurs that so also does he. Silberstein concludes that desiring death represents something in both of them that is constantly "scheming for oblivion. It's the something that remembers that nothingness which is our real nature, and desires passionately to go back to it. And it *will* go back to it" (133).

There can be no question about Freud's marked influence on Aiken's first novel or on his second, *Great Circle*. Aiken, in fact, came very close to visiting Freud for the purpose of being analyzed. Apparently H. D. and Winifred Bryher were so impressed with *Great Circle* that they sent Freud a copy "which he is *said* to have called a masterpiece."[18] In a 1963 interview, Aiken elaborated on the possibility of his visiting the famous analyst:

> I damn near was sent to him as a result of knowing H. D. and publishing *Great Circle*. H. D. was then acting as a kind of amanuensis and biographer to Freud, and she was very close to him in Vienna. She had the idea that she should publish a small book on his method, with biographical background, and the result was that she proposed to me, after reading the *Great Circle*, that I should take on the job as her successor on this project. For reasons of health she wanted to give it up. I agreed temporarily, but I had no money to go to Vienna. How was I to get it? She said she could get the money. But I was going to Boston, and I decided to see Freud's disciple, Hanns Sachs, who had settled there, and who was editor of *Imago*. It was thought that I should see him first and then go on to Freud.[19]

Aiken subsequently met Erich Fromm, who suggested that if Aiken's work were going well he should not go to Vienna. Fromm's advice, coupled with Aiken's instant dislike of Sachs, led him to drop the journey: "And this I regret," Aiken later admitted.

Despite Aiken's extensive use of Freud, his world view was never limited to Freudianism, unlike many of Freud's other disciples; never overwhelmed by it, the novelist maintained a distance. His was an inquiring, sympathetic, even enthusiastic attitude, but it was an attitude tempered by restraint and by innate skepticism. Aiken welcomed the extending of the human psyche that Freud made available, but he was sensitive to the limitations of any system. Yet, ironically, Aiken was repeatedly dismissed as being "merely a Freudian."[20] This is regrettable especially in light of Aiken's own acute awareness of how seductive Freud could be and how tempting it would have been to take refuge in Freud.

But even amid the euphoric heyday of Freudianism in America, Aiken wrote a review in 1919 brashly titled "Dam Up Your Libido! Be A Poet!" in which he chastised Albert Mordell, author of *The Erotic Motive in Literature* for swallowing Freud "a little too whole and [having] temporary indigestion."[21] As Aiken remarked in "A Letter from America," a regular column that he wrote for the *London Mercury* between 1921 and 1922: "Our present generation has a passion for the diagnostic. The appearance of Dr. Sigmund Freud was for this generation that of a *deus ex machina*—nothing could have been more profoundly satisfactory. But this has served only to stimulate our young appetites for the corrosively analytic" (*ABC*, 48).

Aiken likewise saw the disservice that enthusiastic but undiscriminating discipleship of Freud could do to his unique contribution to the study of the psyche. He was aware of the ease with which erroneous philosophical conclusions could be deduced from Freud's profound psychological insights. One such false assumption was the exclusion of free will. It was widely held that subscribing to Freudianism meant a submission to the tyranny of prenatal or at best early childhood experiences. The eminent critic Frederick Hoffman so concluded: "The pessimism of the naturalist assumed that external forces left no room for individual free will; man was a plaything of these forces. The pessimism of the psychological novelist is an extension of this same naturalism."[22] But Aiken denied that Freudianism necessarily led to pessimism or to the denial of free will. On the contrary, Aiken enthusiastically endorsed the thesis of E. B. Holt in *The Freudian Wish and Its Place in Ethics*, which stated that only the whole Freudian truth could make one free. Aiken praised this "brilliant little book" because it developed "a kind of potential *ethics* of the whole Freudian concept."[23] Holt's theory posited that only by having all information available—conscious and unconscious—could an individual operate with real "free will." Aiken, like Holt, found in Freud cause for celebration, not reason for the despair, resignation, or fear felt by many.

While Aiken's grandfather had provided him with the proper predisposition toward a healthy skepticism of any accepted "reality," Freud suggested to Aiken the actual existence of a dimension beyond the conscious world, a realm, then, of another, perhaps more "real" world. It subsequently became Aiken's lifework to construct a philosophical order—in its loosest meaning—to live and die by, a theory of consciousness that he was still engaged in understanding at the time of his death. In 1929, when Aiken was forty, he confided to a reporter, "All this [his philosophical attitudes] has been an experiment which hasn't yet come to an end." On the occasion of his eightieth birthday, he commented to a journalist on the number of young people who continued to seek him out; he concluded that they must be "interested in my free wheeling attitude to life, my skepticism, my preceptualism, my belief that there are no final solutions, that things may have no meaning and that we've got to face that possibility. Everything is in a sense reversible."[24] Thus, at the end of his life, Aiken was philosophically at the beginning of it—though with much more knowledge of himself and consequently of the world.

Blue Voyage, however, is the introductory text, frequently sacrificing narrative progress for the necessary structuring of the philosophical framework. It is an apprentice text filled with exclamation points and dominated by the persona of the author (Robert Linscott wrote to Aiken that he liked the book, but, as a whole, it was "too much a personal document" [2 July 1927, WUL MS.]) The subsequent novels emphasize different aspects of the philosophy of consciousness; they construct a more viable narrative on which to build the philosophical thesis; and they express it all with a less doctrinaire rhetoric. But while the following novels differ in the expression of consciousness and the extent to which it dominates each book, never does Aiken desert the teleology of consciousness introduced in this first novel. Consciousness, to greater or lesser degrees, remains the subject of his fiction as well as of his poetry.[25] Richard P. Blackmur, in reviewing *The Coming Forth by Day of Osiris Jones* and *Preludes for Memnon*, was one of the very few critics who ever saw precisely what Aiken was about philosophically. He was particularly sensitive to what Aiken called his "preceptions" (which copyreaders, to his annoyance, were always correcting to read "perceptions"):

> More interesting is the predicament of the consciousness that knows. Consciousness seems always to stop short of its object, and is defined by its limitations. There is a gap, a chasm, all round it, which is the gap between what we know and our knowing. As our knowing shifts, grows, diminishes—as we know more or differently or know that we know less—we proceed through disillusion. Knowledge is the terrible key to that ignorance in which, if we turn the key, we shall lock ourselves; and there is no unlocking. Yet a mind may not use its ignorance; ignorance is a condition to be achieved, like grace, and is not a weapon; the weapon is knowledge, a sharpening, a definition, of the fragments of consciousness. The

pursuit is full of victory and assertion, the most formidable sensa-
tions are vanquished. The end is denial and annihilation; the abyss
surveyed by consciousness widens, consciousness topples and is
engulfed. In our ends are our beginnings. Between-times we are
conscious of more or less.[26]

Blackmur's excellent summary of Aiken's themes in the two
books of poetry indicates how Aiken insisted on precisely the
same philosophical order in his poetry as in his prose. Much
has Demarest, a Divine Pilgrim, traveled in the realms of consciousness by the end of *Blue Voyage*. He is not necessarily wiser
in the ways of the world, and he is certainly not happier for his
journeys—though his unhappiness is no longer linked exclusively to the loss of Cynthia. He has become uncomfortably
aware of his metaphysical discontent. Though he has experienced more of himself during the trip, he finds himself philosophically restless, plagued by questions as he tries to sleep that
last evening on board: "One . . . became startlingly conscious of
the fact that one was at sea; alone with the infinite; alone with
God. These rows of white marshmallows on the ceiling—these
little painted bolts that held the ship together—these were one's
faith! But it all seemed ridiculous, unreal. What was a ship? . . .
What were human beings? . . . What was a world?" (*CN*, 166).

Chapter Three

THE EVOLUTION OF CONSCIOUSNESS
The New England Roots

REVIEWING CONRAD AIKEN posed problems for critics; they found it difficult to identify precisely the philosophy that informed the art of the writer. Frustrated by the elusiveness, ambiguity, and inconsistency of Aiken's beliefs, they would have done well to heed his warning in the preface to *The Jig of Forslin*:

> The critics who like to say "this man is a realist," or "this man is a romanticist," or in some such way to tag an author once and for all, will here find it difficult. For my intention has been to employ all methods, attitudes, slants, each in its proper place, as a necessary and vital part of any such study as this. Consequently, it is possible to pick out portions of this poem to exemplify almost any poetic method or tone.[1]

Aiken goes on to say that the explanation for such inclusiveness lies in the poem's reflection of the poet's idea of consciousness—though Aiken, in 1916, does not yet employ the term as such: "This eclecticism, or passage from one part to another of the poetic gamut, has not been random or for the sake of a mere tour de force: it has been guided entirely by the central theme. This theme is the process of vicarious wish fulfillment by which civilized man enriches his circumscribed life and obtains emotional balance" (*CP*, 1018). As Forslin plays at various roles—that of the youthful clown, the old man, the murderer, Christ, and Judas—he is variously expanding his consciousness. The experiences detailed in *Forslin*, however, are those only imagined as he sits in his room, alone, with evening approaching. But dream experiences will constitute only one phase—that of wish fulfillment—in man's struggle toward self-knowledge.

Just two years later, in 1918, Aiken defined for the first time the specific term *consciousness* in his preface to a volume of poetry entitled *The Charnel Rose*: "The attempt has been made [here] to divest the successive emotions dealt with of all save the most typical or appropriate physical conditions, suggesting physical and temporal environment only so far as the mood naturally predicates it. Emotions, perceptions,—the image-stream in the mind which we call consciousness,—these hold the stage" (*CP*, 1017). Aiken's novel use of the term *image-stream* in 1918 suggests the vocabulary about to enter literary parlance with stream-of-consciousness fiction.

A further elaboration on "consciousness" was provided by Aiken's own review of *Charnel Rose* for *Poetry*. Speaking of "Senlin," a long poem in the collection, Aiken identifies the theme as illustrating "the problem of personal identity, the struggle of the individual for an awareness of what it is that constitutes his consciousness; an attempt to place himself, to relate himself to the world of which he feels himself to be at once an observer and an integral part."[2] Aiken expanded on his theory when he explained the explicit *process* of the evolution of consciousness in prefatory remarks to the *House of Dust* in 1920 and illustrated just how this system of belief would satisfy man's intrinsic inclination toward religious faith. Readers of the poems in the collection would discover that the movement was

> intermittently but steadily from simple to complex, from physiological to psychological; and, in the end, from the relatively simpler levels of consciousness to those in which it attempts to see and understand the world, or macrocosm, on the one hand, and the consciousness, or microcosm, that *sees* the world, on the other. Implicit in it, therefore, is the theory that was to underline much of the later work—namely, that in the evolution of man's consciousness, ever widening and deepening and subtilizing his awareness, and in his dedication of himself to this supreme task, man possesses all that he could possibly require in the way of a religious credo: when the half-gods go, the gods arrive: he can, if he only will, become divine.[3]

Though Aiken insisted on this priority of consciousness, the term had slightly different meanings, or at least different emphases, at various times in his career; one hesitates, therefore, to settle for the simple definition of it that Aiken once gave: "the evanescent bubble of awareness which is all that we know of ourselves." Instead it is incumbent to look at consciousness chronologically in the development of Aiken's art. His artistic declarations of his credo will rescue such a survey from tedium.

It is at first tempting to look at consciousness as Aiken's personal religion substituted for the traditional creeds that appeared to be disintegrating in the twentieth century before the advances of skepticism. It was Aiken who, in fact, coined the phrase "religion of consciousness," though F. O. Matthieson was the first to use it in print—with Aiken's permission—in *Henry James: The Major Phase.*[4] But the religious complexion of the age seems to have had less to do with Aiken's emerging belief than did an insistent New England transcendental family tradition. That is, it is likely that Aiken would have moved in this philosophical direction even if he had come to maturity in the midst of a powerful religious revival rather than in the tumult of religious fragmentation. In an interview for the *Paris Review*, Robert Wilbur asked Aiken specifically if his "teleology of consciousness" was a search for a " 'new religion not based on conventional dogmas or conventional God,' " and Aiken hesitantly replied,

> "I don't know whether I'd put it quite like that. Of course I do believe in this evolution of consciousness as the only thing which we can embark on, or in fact, willy-nilly, *are* embarked on; and along with that will go the spiritual discoveries and, I feel, the inexhaustible wonder that one feels, that opens more and more the more you know. It's simply that this increasing knowledge constantly enlarges your kingdom and the capacity for admiring and loving the universe."[5]

This association between an expanded consciousness and an expanded capacity for "admiring and loving the universe" must not be minimized; herein Aiken's ideas on consciousness differ dramatically from some other important writers who use the term. Two such essentially different thinkers as Nietzsche and Kierkegaard both use the term *consciousness*, but they draw conclusions from it not shared by Aiken. Although Aiken was indebted to Nietzsche for many of the philosopher's observations on the superior man (especially when writing *King Coffin*), he did not subscribe to his conviction that consciousness developed only as man became more communal, a "social animal" yielding up his individuality; nor did Aiken agree that increased consciousness encouraged man's "averageness," reducing him, superficially, to a generality. Aiken's insistence that consciousness also makes possible one's divinity ("he can, if he only will, become divine") is alien to Kierkegaard's Christian evolution of consciousness that led him to insist that despair is bred by consciousness of self unless the self is measured in the sight of God.[6] The roots of Aiken's understanding of consciousness were neither in traditional Christianity nor in a reaction to it, but were, instead, in the tradition of nineteenth-century German-English romanticism and American transcendentalism.

In *Ushant*, Aiken insists that the real wellspring of his ideas was his maternal grandfather, William James Potter.[7] Though born a Quaker, Potter found Unitarianism more compatible with his liberal religious attitudes, and in 1859 he became minister of the New Bedford Congregation, where he preached Darwin and Humboldt rather than Christianity. He eventually found even the relatively casual bonds of Unitarianism too restraining, and in 1867 he led his congregation out of Unitarianism and into the Free Religious Association that he founded along with Emerson and Colonel Thomas Higginson. This was a transcendental, mythically unencumbered "religion." Aiken was proud of his grandfather's "complete liberation from dogma; and a determined acceptance of Darwin and all the rest of the scientific fireworks of the nineteenth century."[8] But the note that struck the most responsive chord in the grandson was Potter's elaboration in a sermon, "God in Humanity," on the individual's divinity: "People are gradually learning that the grand providential resources for insuring human progress and happiness are stored within the keeping of human beings themselves,—that sufficient of Deity is naturally incarnate in humanity to endow humanity with the power of being a Providence and a savior to itself."[9] The echo is loud in Aiken's phrase, "he can, if he only will, become divine."

In *Ushant*, D.—that is, Aiken—relates an early memory of sitting in the park with his grandfather, a scene that calls to mind the old prophet sharing ritual secrets with the neophyte. It is an essential scene in Aiken's ongoing autobiography; in one form or another it appears in *Blue Voyage*, *Great Circle*, numerous poems, and essays. The *Ushant* sketch is significantly ladened with religious metaphors:

Was there not, in that blessed scene under the trees . . . when the teacups and saucers had been made out of the little green acorns, grandfather tenderly stooping over them to work with the tiny pearl-handled penknife, was there not in this scene a kind of dedication, could he not remember it still as profoundly just that? Had grandfather not been saying, the white beard saying, "Thee must now—always remember this, little D.—thee must now and hereafter do *my* thinking for *me*, thee must be the continuance of me, thee will forever, even if intermittently, or if only every so often *consciously*, stand in the ghost of a pulpit, in the ghost of a church, in the ghost of our beloved New Bedford. Our little sacrament, see, is in these beautiful green cups, green because living; and in my hand upon thy head." Yes, this was true. Something like this had really happened—wordlessly, but it had happened. And this implicit and transcendental exchange, subtle as aether between them, was, when one considered it justly, one of the profounder forms of the process of inheritance.[10]

While Aiken never heard his grandfather preach (he died in 1894 when Aiken was four), the importance that Aiken placed on his grandfather's sermons is attested to by his insistence that throughout his life he never traveled anywhere without both volumes of Potter's sermons.[11]

The philosophical debt that Aiken owed to his grandfather was owed as well to Emerson and New England transcendentalism in general. Certainly the idea that as one ascends the evolutionary scale of individual consciousness, one is becoming more and more divine, a god, is Emersonian. And the roots, of course, are in English romantic poetry and, beyond that, in nineteenth-century German philosophy.

But Aiken's metaphorical framework rises from particularly American—and, even more specifically, New England—philosophical foundations. The importance he places on historical inheritance is high. The Aiken-Emerson parallels are so persistent that Martin in *Conrad Aiken* could safely say that Aiken inherited the Emersonian transcendentalist philosophy "more directly than almost any other modern poet."[12] In sentiments echoing Emerson's "Divinity School Address" (in which Emerson has Christ advise: " 'Would you see God, see me; or see thee' "), Aiken writes in a 1931 poem, "Preludes for Memnon":

> —And this alone awaits you, when you dare
> To that sheer verge where horror hangs, and tremble

> Against the falling rock; and, looking down,
> Search the dark kingdom. It is to self you come,—
> And that is God.
>
> (*CP*, 515).[13]

Equally important both to Emerson's transcendentalism and to Aiken's evolution of consciousness is the correspondence between the tangible world and the mind of the individual. In "A Letter from Li Po," Aiken observes:

> We are the tree, yet sit beneath the tree,
> among the leaves we are the hidden bird,
> we are singer and are what is heard.
>
> (*CP*, 905)

Consciously or unconsciously, Aiken is echoing Emerson's "Brahma":

> They reckon ill who leave me out;
>   When me they fly, I am the wings;
> I am the doubter and the doubt,
>   And I the hymn the Brahmin sings.[14]

In addition to acknowledging the centrality of the work of Freud and others in the early psychoanalytical movement to framing his evolution of consciousness, Aiken also professes a considerable debt to Darwin (as well as to Nietzsche):

> Out of this [discussion about Freud at Harvard] and the reading at the same time of *The Origin of the Species*, and Nietzsche's *Zarathustra* and *Beyond Good and Evil*, was to evolve (since one spoke of evolution whether of worlds or morals), but so imperceptibly and slowly that he found himself possessed of it before he knew he had been thinking about it, his own late concern with the evolution of consciousness . . . : as being, for *homo sapiens*, or *homo incipiens*, the only true teleological "order of the day," his share in the great becoming *fiat* in the poietic of the great poem of life, his share—if one preferred to call it so—in the self-shaping of godhead, or the only thing we knew it by, the mind of man. (*Ushant*, 174–75)

While Darwin spoke of the physiological evolution of the species, Aiken, excited by Freud's investigation of the preconscious and the unconscious, began to speak in specific terms of the evolution of consciousness. The individual's philosophical intention must be progressively toward ever greater, ever widening consciousness, or the end of all must be total self-knowledge:

> *Gnowthi seauton*—that was still the theme, the open sesame, Freud had merely picked up the magic words where Socrates, the prototype of highest man, had let them fall, and now at last the road was being opened for the only religion that was any longer tenable or viable, a poetic comprehension of man's position in the universe, and of his potentialities as a poietic shaper of his own destiny, through selfknowledge and love. The final phase of evolution of man's mind itself to ever more inclusive consciousness: in that, and that alone, would he find the solvent of all things. (*Ushant*, 220)

Aiken's persistent inquiry into worlds other than the one immediately apprehensible necessitated his calling upon a metaphysical vocabulary that often included such words as *God*, *divinity*, and *being*; at the same time, he became exasperated with having to deny again and again a belief in an orthodox God with which so many wanted to burden him. He replied rather abruptly to an Italian student writing a thesis on his poetry: "Which brings me to your question about god. . . . I would have thought *Ushant* answered that pretty extensively. . . . I was brought up with No religion. . . . And as I say in USHANT and elsewhere my credo could be put as a belief in the evolution of consciousness: this is all we know of god, and perhaps in this sense we are a *becoming* god."[15]

While Aiken could sympathize with the inherent longing of individuals for comfort in their spiritual malaise, he could not understand their settling for "half gods," for orthodox, institutionalized religious systems. Aiken's temporary alienation from T. S. Eliot, with whom he had a close friendship dating back to their Harvard undergraduate days, stemmed largely from Aiken's inability to accept Eliot's embracing (in 1927) the dogmas of Anglo-Catholicism. In *Ushant*, Aiken refers several times to Eliot's (or "Tsetse's," in this roman à clef) conversion. Aiken chastises him for resigning from the pursuit of awareness and for being seduced by the security of conforming to a myth:

> The thing, of course, was not to retreat, never to retreat: never to avoid the full weight of awareness, and all that it brought, and above

all never—and this was the undaunted grandfather, speaking from his . . . church in New Bedford—never to seek refuge from it in the comforting placebos of religious or mystical myth or dogma. The pressures would become, for some, too great to bear: the temptations, too, would be insidious. The security in conformity, in joining and belonging, was to prove to be too seductive for many a better mind than D.'s. Including that best of all, the Tsetse's. (*Ushant*, 168)

Later, while praising Eliot's brilliantly analytical undergraduate thesis on epistemology and acknowledging its influence on his own thinking, Aiken—in an elaborately metaphorical paragraph—reiterates his keen disappointment over Eliot's final acceptance of orthodox Christianity:

Thenceforth, like the salmon, leaving behind him the outrages of ocean, together with its wilder freedoms, he [Eliot] would ascend the ancient river of a more peaceful culture, where the banks were trim, and the views symmetrically landscaped; and, mounting from cataract to cataract, or hierarchy to hierarchy, of accepted order, would at last achieve what no American ichthyolater had achieved before him, and find himself, at Canterbury, after the pilgrimage of pilgrimages, in the very presence of the Ichthos itself. That the achievement was unique and astounding, and attended, too, by rainbows of creative splendor, there could be no doubt. Indeed, it was in the nature of a miracle, a transformation. But was it not to have been, also, a surrender, and perhaps the saddest known to D. in his life? (*Ushant*, 215–16)[16]

While Aiken and Eliot remained friends throughout their lives, Eliot's "conversion" or "submission" marked a permanent hiatus in their relationship. Although at first genuinely unhappy about Eliot's enrolling in the Church Militant, Aiken could eventually joke about it: he named his wife's portrait of Eliot, with its background of the stained-glass windows of Canterbury, "Fallen Arches." There is little wonder, though, why his conversion left Aiken with a heavy heart, since he looked upon it as a diminution of Eliot's consciousness; he had abandoned his individual divinity. Eliot had not, finally, created out of his own consciousness a viable relationship between the known and unknown worlds. Anything less expansive than the pursuit and celebration of consciousness was ultimately ignoble.

The loss of Eliot to the Church had ramifications for Aiken beyond Eliot's own diminished consciousness, since Aiken had strong convictions that a writer had a particular responsibility to cleanse the windows of perception for his less evolved readers. This altruistic aspect of Aiken's philosophy, with its roots in his grandfather's humanitarianism and reinforced by his Harvard mentor, George Santayana,[17] is expressed precisely in Aiken's preface to "Changing Mind," a poem he published in 1925, just two years before his first novel:

> The wholly anonymous hero of "Changing Mind" . . . is not only particularized, he is also shown to be the willing participant, and perhaps to some extent even the instigator, in the process of seeing himself resolved into his constituent particles: and this with a purpose, that his increased awareness may be put at the service of mankind. . . . he . . . inherits the complete private situation of a highly complex and self-conscious contemporary individual whose neuroses have made it necessary or desirable that he should be an artist. He must make his experience articulate for the benefit of others, he must be, in the evolving consciousness of man, the servant-example, and in fact he has little choice in the matter. He is himself simply a part of that evolution. (*CP*, 1024–25)

The writer, then, has the expressed obligation to record his doing battle with the demons; he thereby transmits some kind of vatic knowledge. The ideal reader, as imagined by Aiken, was someone like Malcolm Lowry, who wrote to him after writing his own first novel, *Ultramarine*, to explain away its heavy reliance on *Blue Voyage*:

> *Blue Voyage*, apart from its being the best nonsecular statement of the plight of the creative artist with the courage to live in a modern world, has become part of my consciousness, and I cannot conceive of any other way in which *Ultramarine* might be written. . . . Nevertheless I have sat and read my blasted book with increasing misery: with a misery of such intensity that I believe myself sometimes to be dispossessed, a spectre of your own discarded ideas whose only claim to dignity exists in those ideas.[18]

Such a role for Aiken would have to be played out through his fiction and poetry. It was inconceivable that Aiken would follow in his grandfather's steps as a formal preacher of the gospel of consciousness. On the contrary, Aiken had a lifelong predisposition to avoid the mainstream. In a *New Republic* article, "A Plea for Anonymity," Aiken argued for the importance of circumventing the increasing assault on a writer's privacy, especially in America, which had a predilection for commodifying writers: "From the moment that a young writer has, let us say, turned out a 'promising' or brilliant first book, his doom is practically sealed. In a hundred ways, he is drawn into the whole hideous literary and journalistic and publicity racket." Aiken continues that it is not enough that a writer has produced a first-rate piece of literature: "no, like a movie star or a heavyweight wrestler or a prima donna, he must also prove to the public that he is interesting or peculiar as a *person*. He finds immediately that his career is not merely, as he thought, to write books, but—and more importantly—to appear, book in hand, in public." Finally, Aiken expressed the real cause for alarm: "The individual is being submerged, the clear notion of his value to society precisely *as* a nonconformist is being lost."[19]

Instead Aiken saw that the first task of the writer-priest of consciousness was the Herculean one of knowing oneself, and that was best pursued offstage. His frustrations with stalking self-knowledge are expressed by the hero of *Blue Voyage* as he cynically says to himself: "*Know thyself!* That was the best joke ever perpetrated. A steaming universe of germ cells, a maelstrom of animal forces, of which he himself, his personality, was only the collective gleam. A hurricane of maggots which answered to the name of Demarest."[20]

Yet, through his belief in consciousness, Aiken remained certain that man contained within himself all that was necessary for his "salvation"—if only he would save himself. So we find that each of Aiken's five novels is framed by his theory, but each pursues a different part of the whole; *Ushant* examines the entire biography against the backdrop of Aiken's evolving consciousness.

The emphasis in *Blue Voyage* is on the relationship between consciousness and the particular life of the artist. William Demarest must come to terms with his personal suffering to determine whether there might not be an aesthetic prohibition against minting art from suffering—or neurosis. In *Great Circle* the emphasis shifts to the influence of early family life in contributing to the formation of the individual's consciousness.

Andrew Cather slowly realizes that the roots of his faltering marriage go deep into a tragic childhood experience. It becomes increasingly apparent to Cather that he will not be able to come to terms with his wife's unfaithfulness until he both confronts his haunting and confused memories of his deceased mother and recognizes his own role in the marital infidelity. *King Coffin* examines the consequence of cultivating one's individual consciousness to the exclusion or intolerance of any other reality— that is, what follows from an individual's assertion of his superior consciousness and his consequent alienation. Ammen's egotism is the counterpart of Demarest's characterizing himself as a "forked radish," a "carrier of germs and digester of food," and, finally, the "momentary host of the dying seed of man." In Jaspar Ammen's superior, fatal isolation from the world, Aiken lays the groundwork for the final two novels, with their emphasis on the importance of one's humanity. In both *A Heart for the Gods of Mexico* and *Conversation*, the protagonists are caught up in the relationship between individual consciousness and the consciousness of others. These last two novels, though artistically flawed, are successful in extending the construct of consciousness beyond the individual.

Undeniably one of the principal problems posed by the term *consciousness*, as used by Aiken throughout his life, is that it is a word used both casually in common parlance and more specifically in the disciplines of philosophy and psychology. But while the nuances and emphases are slightly different, the term, as employed by Aiken, was generally inclusive. At the risk of being reductive, he meant primarily that process of reflecting on or being conscious of what goes on in one's mind. It is what gives rise to an understanding of states of thinking, reasoning, perceiving, and so forth. Aiken would have been comfortable with Locke's definition of consciousness in *An Essay Concerning Human Understanding* as "the perception of what passes in a man's own mind." Aiken, however, would have put his emphasis on the introspection and selfknowledge that follow such perception. Further, while some philosophers, such as Auguste Comte, denied the very possibility of a person's being able to divide himself into that part which is perceiving and that which is observing the perception, such belief is absolutely essential to Aiken. This was, as mentioned, Senlin's fundamental struggle, "an attempt . . . to relate himself to the world of which he feels himself to be at once an observer and an integral part" (*ABC*, 130). Finally, while philosophers speak of "states of consciousness" as those conditions in which one is thinking of something, imagining something, believing something, or feeling something, Aiken would put his emphasis on those conditions in which the mind is acutely open to the "image-stream" that is nonjudgmental, nonrational, nonhierarchical. Although individual poems, short stories, or whole novels emphasized different aspects of consciousness at different times in Aiken's long career, they all subscribed to his early description of consciousness as "the evanescent bubble of awareness which is all that we know of ourselves."

In the last analysis, however, Aiken's intent in all his works was to understand his own consciousness (as he comes to do in *Ushant*) and, by creating out of it, to extend the consciousness of others by inviting his readers to voyage inward. The extent to which Aiken insisted on the writer's own personality candidly informing the work of art was philosophically contrary to the more popular literary position expounded in Eliot's "Tradition and the Individual Talent." Aiken's place in American literature would have been secured if only he had had more readers as sensitive to what he was about as his friend, the poet John Gould Fletcher. In reviewing *Senlin*, for instance, Fletcher knew immediately that Aiken himself was the subject of the work and saw clearly Aiken's total philosophical intention: "He looks beneath the surface of age-old compromises and sees the body of Everyman poised on an unstable helpless planet, carefully arranging his tie, while his soul, darkened and without knowledge, humbly seeks to penetrate to the cause of all things. The cruel clarity of such perception as this startles and horrifies. But none the less it is both beautiful and true. In this mind we find all minds mirrored."[21]

Chapter Four

THE DILEMMA OF THE ARTIST
Blue Voyage

WHILE AIKEN IDENTIFIED an ever-evolving consciousness as part of the general human condition, the drama, he realized, was peculiarly complicated in the life of a writer. Aiken's many anxieties about consciousness and its relationship to art are evident in *Blue Voyage* in the protagonist, Demarest, who worries about *how* to integrate this all-consuming and fairly idiosyncratic philosophy into his creative work and whether one *should* do it at all. This initial novel stands as a working philosophical statement by Aiken the writer. Here he touches on all the significant questions a writer must ask himself before consciously dedicating his life to art. In light of this, *Blue Voyage*, as Aiken's philosophical foundation, is far more significant than the simple plot would suggest. Demarest reflects: What exactly is a tenet of consciousness? Morally, should one proselytize such a belief? Artistically, what are the risks? At the same time there are for Aiken—and in turn for Demarest—two other important, and not necessarily compatible, forces exerting pressure on his work: the dictum of his greatly admired Santayana that the greatest poetry (and here, by extension, prose) must be the poetry of ideas; and the insistence by Freud that art is a product of neurosis. On the one hand, Santayana maintained in *Three Philosophical Poets* that the philosophic vision of great poetry must also satisfy "rational scientific standards of truth"; on the other hand, Freud saw art as a substitute gratification and as such an illusion in contrast to reality. Aiken spoke to the dilemma created for himself: he had learned from Santayana that poetry had to be philosophical, that it "must have at its center some sort of world view, or *Weltanschauung*. But how, in the fragmented world of the psychologists—not only Freud, but

Jung, Adler, Ferenczi, Holt, and all the rest—was one to shape this?"¹

Of course, both Santayana and Freud, though for quite disparate reasons, placed great value on art. Santayana, starting from the premise that religion was a creation of man's imagination—no more or less valid than other creations—placed poetry on the same level of truth and felt that good poetry could be one's most useful and noble contribution to the interpretation of existence. Denying the absolute validity of any organized religion and paying homage only to man's spirit and imagination, Santayana appealed to young Aiken's inherited skepticism. A mantle of responsibility fell on the shoulders of the artist; without a philosophical dimension, one could not create great art. As Aiken admitted in a personal interview with Robert Wilbur, " 'Santayana's insistence that the greatest poetry was *philosophical poetry* . . . fixed my view of what poetry would ultimately be. . . . That it really had to begin by *understanding*, or trying to understand.' "²

In *Blue Voyage* Aiken tries to reconcile this dilemma of the artist who subscribes to Santayana's directive on the supreme and even holy power of art and at the same time believes in, or at least suspects, the validity of Freud's suggestion that art has as its source neurosis; that is, it satisfies the artist in a therapeutic manner and appeals primarily to wish-fulfillment desires of the reader. Demarest sheepishly admits to a "sneaking feeling . . . that the arts—and perhaps especially the literary arts—are a childish preoccupation which belong properly to the infancy of the race, and which, although the race as a whole has not outgrown, the civilized *individual* ought to outgrow."³

Demarest explains to Silberstein this notion that art's primary function is to fulfill man's childish longings. He insists that we do not want to grow up, do not want to admit our ignorance about our beginnings or our fears about our endings, and, consequently, we seek refuge in literature:

> Reading a novel, we become the hero, and assume his importance as the *center of the action*—if he succeeds, we too succeed; if he fails, then we can be sure it is against overwhelming odds, against the backdrop of the colossal and unpitying infinite, so that in failure he seems to us a figure of grandeur; and we can see ourselves thus

with a profound narcissistic compassion, ourselves godlike in stature and power, going down to a defeat which lends us an added glory . . . Art is therefore functionally exaggerative. (CN, 117)

Demarest's didactic explanation is almost a paraphrase of Freud's "The Relation of the Poet to Day-dreaming."

The whole conflict for the artist is further complicated for Aiken/Demarest—by his realization that if one's art appeals to the fulfillment of the dreams or wishes of the readers, then might not the most vulgar work that appeals to the most prurient imagination be as valid as any more sophisticated creation? Aiken addressed himself to this aesthetic dilemma in an essay, "A Basis for Criticism," published shortly before *Blue Voyage*. His recognition here of the importance of what is now labeled "popular culture" was quite in advance of his time and deserves to be read in detail:

And this is a fact that the critic cannot ignore: he cannot, with a sneer, dismiss the tastes of the vulgar. Those tastes are important. They give us, in clearest view, the common denominator of art, the factor of wish-fulfillment without which art would not exist. The dime novel or shilling shocker, the lurid melodrama and explosive farce, the cosmetic musical comedy and the "movie"—these we have no right to designate simply as bad or inferior art. They are the art of the people for whom they were created; they give these people illusion, escape from themselves—and that is beauty; and if we wish to bring this sort of art into relation with the sort of art we consider finer, the *The Golden Bowl* or *The Brothers Karamasov*, we shall most accurately define the relationship by saying that the latter sort of art, while in principle the same as the former, is designed for people in whom credulity has been weakened by intelligence or self-awareness: the desire for escape, for illusion, is as strong in them as in those others, perhaps even stronger, but as they are most conscious they require more persuasion, that is, a greater wealth of documentation. For these people a simple unqualified statement of a thing or action has no longer sufficient magic. It must be elaborated.[4]

These sentiments suggest just how out of step Aiken was with the contemporary literary climate that Richard Poirier, in an essay, "The Difficulties of Modernism and the Modernism of Difficulty," described as the period of "grim reading," one in which spontaneous reading was precluded by the inherent difficulties of the work (Joyce, Faulkner, Eliot, Pound, among others): "Modernism in literature can be measured by the degree of textual intimidation felt in the act of reading."[5] Nonetheless, Aiken's singular democratic judgment is reiterated almost verbatim by Demarest as he and Silberstein stroll along the deck. Demarest confesses that he is a fairly unsuccessful writer of plays, an unfinished novel, and a few poems. He suggests that perhaps his failure is related to his basic misgivings about the value of what he does. In order to clarify this for Silberstein, who seems unconvinced, he poses one of the problems that he says has tormented him:

> "if we take a functional view of art, as we must, then everything becomes relative; and the shilling shocker or smutty story, which captivates Bill the sailor, is giving him exactly the escape and aggrandizement, and therefore *beauty*, that *Hamlet* gives to you or me. The equation is the same. What right have you got, then, to assume that *Hamlet* is 'better' than *Deadeye Dick*? On absolute grounds, none whatever. They are intended for different audiences, and each succeeds." (*CN*, 117–18)

Demarest is aware that admitting this to be true only ushers in another whole set of questions: For which audience should a writer write? Even more fundamental, if writing itself is only the feeding of illusion, should one write at all? Taken a step further, does one, perhaps, have a serious, even moral, obligation *not* to write? Demarest imagines what it would have been like if Shakespeare had come to this same conclusion and had then determined—even with Hamlet and Lear and the others all waiting in his imagination—that "for the good of humanity" he would not write a single play. Or, taking his argument to another level, what would it have been like if Christ, for that matter, had only understood the real nature of his neurosis and how it was about to impede the next four thousand years of man's development and had then chosen not to participate in the drama? This latter idea so engages Demarest's imagination that he speculates on it as a subject for a play, *The Man Who Was Greater Than God*.[6] Yet the oppressive futility drives Demarest to the next step, the logical conclusion: he wonders if, instead of writing that play, he should live it; that is, his problem becomes "to write, or to commit suicide" (*CN*, 119).[7]

In addition to this fundamental artistic dilemma, Aiken/ Demarest faces the complications of being an artist-critic, fully realizing how one role can undermine the other. Both in *Blue Voyage* and in its gloss, *Ushant*, Aiken looks on criticism as "pot-boiling" or at best as "ephemeral," though frequently also as an economic necessity. But in *Blue Voyage* he examines the idea more fully and sees not only that the threat to the creative artist doubling as a critic is the impure motivation or the demands on his time but also that the philosophical dissection of art, necessary for good criticism, cripples the artist, drives him into inactivity. Demarest admits to Silberstein that he is beginning to resist writing criticism and then relates to him a relevant dream he has had that Tompkins, the psychoanalyst, assured him reflects his Samson-complex. Demarest dreamed that he was a messenger in ancient Greece running feverishly to a temple where the high priests were about to perform some serious ritual but were waiting at the altar for the news he was to bring. When he arrived, however, he realized that the run had exhausted him and that he was about to die. As he stretched himself on the altar of stone, he looked up at the massive temple and thought: " 'If it should fall—if it were only to fall—would it not destroy—not only myself, already dying—but also these hateful priests and their mysteries? the temple?' " He continues, " 'And suddenly, then, with a last spastic effort of body and soul, I cried out in terrific command to the ceiling 'FALL! FALL!' . . . 'and it fell' " (*CN*, 120).[8]

A problem more common to writers about which Demarest also complains is the impossibility of saying what one means and having it understood precisely. Near the end of the novel Demarest longs for "some subtler medium than language" (*CN*, 157). For him, though, the problem is intensified by his insisting on the teleological dimension of all his art. In one of his abortive letters to Cynthia, for instance, Demarest admits that his propensity for complicating things, for seeing everything from numerous angles, all refracted, fragmented, and qualified, carries over into his art, which ends up " 'a melancholy *cauchemar* of ghosts and voices, a phantasmagoric world of disordered colors and sounds; a world without design or purpose; and perceptible only in terms of the prolix and the fragmentary' " (153).

But, while he allows that the critics are right in recognizing this excessive inclusiveness in his prose, he insists that they are wrong in not appreciating that it is intentional, that it grows out of his frustration with traditional narrative techniques for expressing the complex consciousness of the modern world. Demarest has come to accept that he is destined to failure as an artist, but he still wonders if his failure stems from a failure of genius, or from a neurosis, or even from a failure of technique, a " 'mistaken assumption as to the necessity for this new literary method' " (153).

Demarest is finally tormented by the fear that maybe this highly fragmented, dissociated, tentative, ambivalent mind is *not* one that is universal but is, instead, some highly singular, peculiar, maverick one that relates to nothing and from which nothing can be deduced—one, then, that is *not* in harmony or sympathy with other minds. "I frequently suspect," he admits, "that I am nothing on earth but a case of *dementia praecox, manqué*, or arrested. Isn't all this passion for aspects and qualifications and relativities a clear enough symptom of schizophrenia?" (153). This final fear haunts William Demarest throughout the novel as it did Conrad Aiken throughout his life.

Houston Peterson, in the first full-length study of a twentieth-century poet, says that Aiken's disappointment over his public reception as a poet in part precipitated his writing *Blue Voyage*, which allowed him to "examine in prose his own mind and be better prepared for an unsung future."[9] Peterson goes so far as to suggest that Aiken suspected that he would fail as a writer and that "it was time to take up a new career." But *Blue Voyage* stands as testimony that a novel ending in ambiguity, with large unresolved philosophical speculations, and in which the protagonist as a writer remains in doubt about the very value of writing, nonetheless commands the attention of the conscious reader.

· · ·

Aiken knew that a philosophical diatribe was not synonymous with a novel, and therefore *Blue Voyage* calls on a fairly commonplace plot: the pursuit of the goddess by the spurned lover. However, Aiken turns the plot into the traditional conflict between the spirit and the flesh, and that idea in turn becomes symbolic of the conflict between art and nature. Assuredly, the number and variety of complex philosophical issues worked into the text of one short book mark this as a first novel. As the story develops, Cynthia becomes less and less credibly human and more and more a symbol that sheds light on the artistic problems weighing heavily on the mind of Demarest. At the same time, *Blue Voyage* becomes a less compelling novel as Aiken gradually sacrifices plot and character to aesthetic and philosophical speculations.

Aiken scrupulously examines the tensions between secular (that is, sexual) and ideal (that is, spiritual) love. He makes extended use of a classical allusion to the details in the life of Caligula, as recorded by Suetonius in the year 120 A.D. On first reading *Blue Voyage*, one is likely to read quickly through a number of seemingly passing references to Caligula, but it soon becomes apparent that, for Demarest, Caligula is a paradigm for the ambivalent nature of the individual—his spiritual or extrahuman potential posed against his animalistic reality. Gradually Caligula moves from being the brilliant administrator toward being a sexual pervert, a symbol for man's voracious sexual drives. Finally Caligula becomes Demarest's jaundiced view of his own sexual temperament. But the allusion is first casually precipitated by Smith's trite remark that fleshly Faubion can "put her slippers——," which touches off a surrealistic daydream by Demarest in which the provocative woman puts her zebra-striped slippers under the coffin of elderly Smith, whom Demarest imagines as a bearded, toothless old wizard who extends his claw over the edge of his coffin, drags the woman in, and eats her alive. Demarest concludes: "Caligula. King Caligula and the immortal daughter" (*CN*, 45).

It is in the midst of a chess game that Demarest's interior monologue provides a complete scenario of Caligula. At first the kings and queens trigger reminiscences about the life of King Caligula; then the next several pages of the novel are taken almost verbatim from Suetonius. The account emphasizes Caligula's growing rampant sexual wantonness and its attendant cruelty. At the same time Demarest recalls what a gentle and temperate ruler Caligula had once been. But the focus remains on the King's sexual appetite for both men and women. Demarest recalls Valerius, who Suetonius identified as "a young man . . . [who] publicly proclaimed that he had violated the emperor and worn himself out in commerce with him."[10] Demarest next imagines Caligula calling for Pyrallis, a concubine for whom, according to Suetonius, Caligula had a "notorious passion." But Caligula's love and cruelty coalesce in Demarest's "Ah, Pyrallis—a throat so lovely,—to cut when I like! Shall I cut it, to discover the secret of its loveliness? I have told Caesonia that I will vivisect her, so as to find out why I love her" (*CN*, 50).

Although Demarest has labeled Smith in his relations with Faubion "a Caligula" and has called Silberstein "Caligula," it is the Caligula in himself that most troubles Demarest. He remembers, for instance, all his "horrible furtive years of adolescence": the time he invited a little neighbor girl to a vacant lot, the time he peeped through the shutters to watch a Negro couple embracing, the time he watched the Swedish sailor watching the two dogs. Demarest suspects and fears that he has gradually become ever more "a Caligula with strange festered recesses in his mind, with wounds in his body. Love (he had been taught) was sensuality, sensuality was evil, evil was prohibited but delicious: the catechism of the vacant lot. But how, then, had beauty come in? How had it so managed to complicate itself with evil and sensuality and the danks and darks of sex?" (65). It is, finally, this aspect of Caligula that commands Demarest's attention—the strange wedding of evil and beauty, lust and love, coalescing in the same man: "It is Caligula, who nevertheless has the rainbow wings of a seraph" (65). Demarest flagellates himself for his own seeming corruption, "my filthiness," but at the same time he knows that, in part, his "filthiness" gives birth to his art. These thoughts bring Demarest back full circle to the problems that Freud had posed for him. Was he, finally, an artist or a neurotic? Could he ever hope to write convincingly and clearly, given the peculiar nature of his consciousness? Should he create illusions for others or seek professional therapy for himself?

Aiken reinforces the philosophical argument between the pure and the sexual by playing the two major female characters, Cynthia and Faubion, against each other. On the one hand, Cynthia—on the threshold of a respectable marriage—is rhetorically associated with the moon, with the East, and with chaste Diana; with litany-like rhetoric, Aiken chants her praises: "Orbed maiden with white fire laden! Moon-daughter, snow-cold and pure, but fiery at heart!" (93). On the other hand,

Faubion, early in the voyage named "Fleshpot Faubion," is described as a "heliotrope," is associated with the West ("Faubion, coming out of the West, unperturbed, darkly walked eastward on the dark waters, Napoleonic, sardonic, ironic, Byronic" [49]) and is in the process of being divorced by her husband for infidelity.

Although Aiken repeats the refrain, "Blest be the marriage betwixt earth and heaven," throughout the novel, it does not convince Demarest, who is making a three-thousand-mile pilgrimage in search of the undefiled Cynthia and who is at the same time wildly attracted by a "small impudent brazen baggage of a vaudeville queen" (36). His problem is the timeless one—torn between virgin and whore, the ideal and the real—but he is almost Augustinian in his self-flagellation, in his utter disgust with his sexuality while in pursuit of purity. Demarest, reminiscent of the Red Crosse Knight in his admiration of Una, writes to Cynthia about his expectations for their relationship:

> What I had hoped was that at last I had found a love which somehow *transcended the flesh.* Yes—I actually persuaded myself that I had captured the chimera; and that in Cynthia and poor William the phoenix and the turtle were met anew. A beautiful, a divine illusion! One of those heavenly beliefs which, in intensity of being, makes the solidest of our realities seem insubstantial as a shade. I am not a believer in souls, nor in immortality; I have no sentimental conception of God, no religion from which to extract, for my daily needs, color and light; yet in encountering you I felt that I could only explain what was happening to me by assuming at least a *symbolic* meaning and rightness in the treacherous word "soul." (154–55)

Aiken projects Cynthia's holiness against Demarest's vulgarity in language and in situations drawn from courtly love or, more specifically, from Dante, whom he had studied with Santayana and whom he was rereading while writing *Blue Voyage.* For instance, Demarest is momentarily interested in the invitational knocking on his cabin wall by the beautiful Irish girl in the adjoining room, but the spirit of guardian-angel Cynthia rushes to intervene, a fortification against temptation: "Tonight so great is your heavenly influence upon me, so permeated is my gross body by your beauty that I pay no attention" (75).

At other times Demarest casts Cynthia in the ecclesiastical role of Father Confessor. He imagines himself prostrate and contrite before her: "I have been misunderstood,—I have blundered,—I have sinned,—Oh, I have sinned" (75). His words seem punctuated by blows to his chest. On another imagined occasion he tells her of his youthful voyeuristic experiences and tries to justify them to her—and to himself—by portraying them as having had a certain beauty about them, but his superego will have none of it. "Beauty? Beauty in that lascivious life of yours? No—it's quite impossible" (92). Demarest in his imagination persists in trying to enlighten Cynthia about the legitimate kinship between the sexual and the beautiful, but he can picture her reducing all of his arguments: " 'Poor little William— I recognize in you this imperative impulse to confess' " (93).

The final spiritual triumph of Cynthia—which calls to mind Beatrice and the *Paradisio*—is her transfiguration into a stained-glass window at the end of the extended fantasy in chapter 6. Demarest readily admits that a cynic might suggest that the whole scene resulted from imbibing too heavily, but he insists that the whiskey served simply to break down certain inhibitions and permitted his unconscious greater freedom. Demarest, on the hurricane deck for a walk before bed, states: "as I stood in the marvelous darkness, alone in the world, alone with my ridiculous transitory little unhappiness, I indulged myself in a fantasy. I was then, suddenly, no longer alone" (157). He is joined by Cynthia, Smith, and Silberstein, but they are all transformed. He sees them as part of a perfectly harmonious scene, exchanging quotations from the Greek anthology and then holding a beautiful, intimate conversation. They are like actors in a play, and it dawns on Demarest, the outsider, that he has written the musical score "Caligula" for the production. This fantasy chapter ends with a transfiguration: "The whole night had become a Cathedral. And above Demarest, faintly luminous in the cold starlight that came from beyond, was a tall Gothic window, where motionless, in frozen sentimentalities of pink, white, and blue, Cynthia was turned to glass" (142).

Demarest, however, with his predisposition to complications, enters an unsettling note of ambivalence into this idyllic, symbolic scene; three times the Freudian slip occurs: "stained-glass widow." It should also be noted that the stage directions for the play call for "Miss Battilore . . . several times engaged, virgin in fact but not in thought" (141).

In an earlier exchange with Silberstein, Demarest has disallowed even "the slightest *conscious* sensual attraction" (122) to Cynthia, insisting on the spiritual nature of their relationship. But as we are invited into the recesses of Demarest's mind we find another whole scenario that rapidly expands in its sensuality. Demarest, reflecting a little later on the Silberstein conversation, realizes that it was good that they had stopped talking when they had:

> "I'd have told him everything. I'd have told him about——why did I lie to him about her physical attraction? But I only recognized the lie as I told it. So did he. She was pure as the snow, but she drifted, PURE as the snow, but she drifted. And the next time I met her she was all dressed in black. Back. Smack. Crack. Golden engine and silver track. The golden engine on the silver track. I am wounded with a deep wound." (127)

Demarest's stream of consciousness descends to a sophomoric prurience. He recalls once having heard that a Mexican girl could be returned to her parents if her husband found her virginity in doubt. This prompts Demarest to remember bits of smutty songs, then classic dirty jokes: " 'Hey! How do you expect me to find my ring when there's a guy in here lookin' for his motor bike!' . . . And mama, she say, 'Well, I ought to know! It's the same way I fooled your old man!' " (128). Demarest continues in this vein until he is interrupted by a greeting from a fellow passenger. All of this, however, brings Cynthia's virginity into question, which, in turn, lends an ironic, comic overtone to the entire transfiguration scene.

· · ·

Our credulity, though, has earlier been strained by the extremes of Demarest's dissatisfaction with his sexual nature as reflected in the Caligula corollary as well as by the purity of the abortive relationship with Cynthia. Consequently, the suggestion of irony in the transfiguration scene leads one into the realization that both situations are moving simultaneously on yet another plane; they are not merely reflecting the tension between the spiritual and the sensual. In addition, events have meanings that color the philosophic fiber of the novel as a whole in relation to the nature of consciousness and to the role of the artist.

One can, for instance, put Demarest's crucifixion complex in its larger context; that is, it is related to his pursuit of consciousness. Demarest thinks that if he can only be purified of his terrible lust—yes, even crucified for it—he would be moving toward subjugating his individual will, and he might then be able to move beyond the limited self toward some ideal selflessness.

> "Crucifixion. Why do we all want to be crucified, to fling ourselves into the very heart of the flame? Empedocles on Etna. A moment of incandescent suffering. To suffer intensely is to live intensely, to be intensely conscious . . . Passionate, perverse refusal to give up the unattainable—dashing ourselves blindly against the immortal wall. I *will* be crucified! Here are my hands! Drive nails through them—sharp blows! . . . He looked long into his own eyes, so unfathomable, as if in an effort to understand himself, and—through his own transparent elusiveness—the world. What was it he wanted? What was it that was driving him back? What was this singular mechanism in him that wanted to deliberately, so consciously, to break itself?" (23–24)

Later, in measuring the nature of the sacrifice that he would be willing to make for Cynthia, Demarest's mind again wanders to his crucifixion: "And how even more horrible was it to come thus to you, before whom I so passionately longed to stand with something of Parsifal's mindless innocence, bearing on brow and palms the stigmata of that crucifixion" (80). But the quintessential use of the crucifixion metaphor is to explain a step in Aiken's theory of consciousness—that only by crucifying the self can Demarest progress beyond a consciousness limited by self. All the world's misery that Demarest has reviewed throughout his reverie in chapter 4 could be expiated through his crucifixion; he could thereby redeem the world:

> MY SELF. I will destroy my individuality. Like the destruction of the atom, this will carry in its train the explosion of all other selves. I will show them the way. The Messiah. They will pursue me, mocking and jeering. They will crowd closer about me, stoning. And at this moment I will destroy my SELF out of love for all life,—

my personality will cease. I will become nothing but a consciousness of love, a consciousness without memory or foresight, without necessity or body, and without thought. I will show mankind the path by which they may return to God; and I will show God the path by which he may return to peace. (104–5)[11]

Still another way in which Demarest can redeem the world is through what he calls a "miraculous communion" with Cynthia. Such a communion, once again dependent first on an annihilation of the self, would be a foreshadowing and a first step toward a communion of humanity: "Was it possible to guess, from this beautiful experience, that ultimately man would know and love his brother; that the barriers of idiosyncrasy and solipsism, the dull walls of sense, would go down before the wand of Prospero?" (CN, 155). Demarest sees this not only as something to be desired but also as something that is absolutely necessary. He sees further that the only obstacles between the individual and this divine understanding are the Will: "When we sufficiently *desired* this communion, when at last we realized the weakness and barrenness of the self, we could be sure that we would have sufficient wisdom to accomplish the great surrender" (155). This community of mankind is not given such attention by Aiken again until his penultimate novel, *A Heart for the Gods of Mexico*.

The culminating and pivotal symbolic action in *Blue Voyage* is Cynthia's transfiguration into the stilled figure in a stained-glass window. It becomes apparent that her metamorphosis from a warm human being into a cold church window is symbolically a move from the frank truthfulness of nature to the untrue ornamentation of art. Her purity suggests the consequences of sublimating sensuality and animal vitality into a spurious world of art, which finally Demarest must denounce, even though he finds it compellingly seductive. He admits that just before waking back into consciousness from this fantasy he had been contemplating the very question of "sublimation versus immersion" and had asked himself: "How can we possibly decide which is the better course to pursue? Shall we take the way of art, and lie, and try to make life as like the lie as we can— remold it nearer to the *child's desire*—or shall we take the way of nature, and *love*? Love, I mean, savagely with the body!" (158). He recognizes that it might not be so much a choice between art and nature as between two aspects of nature, the one more primitive and the other less so.

Cynthia's refusal of Demarest has made him acutely aware of this schism in his nature and has forced him to confront it. Consequently, in one of his unsent letters, he tells her that he will no longer go on as this " 'half-civilized liar' "—that is, adding " 'a few more reefs of flowery coral to my already disgracefully massive production, and thus help deluded mankind to add delusion to delusion' " (158)—but he will, instead, work to destroy this terrible superstructure of hypocrisy, the world of art that Cynthia has come to symbolize. " 'I think, Cynthia, I . . . must turn my back on you. I think I must decide, once and for all, that though you are beautiful, and though I have fixed my heart on you as on nothing and no one else, you are a sham, a fraud, an exquisite but baseless, or nearly baseless, work of art. A living lie. A beautiful betrayal of nature. A delicious fake' " (158).

Such an argument would appear to sound the death knell for Demarest and, as the author's counterpart, for Aiken as an artist, but so deep is the schism in the nature of Demarest that on the last page of the novel, as he lies awake, his thoughts turn almost instinctively to Cynthia. And, although the knock on his door is that of Faubion, the "blood beating painfully in the side of his throat" comes from wishing for Cynthia. In short, Demarest knows the impossibility of categorizing the artist as an instrument of God or of the devil; he knows also that he is to live not in an inferno of life or a paradise of art but to "struggle and fluctuate in the Limbo between—saving ourselves now and then from an art of life too fine-drawn by a bath of blood; or from an awareness and control too meager by a deliberate suppressing of our lusts, a canalization of those energies . . . And never, at any time, knowing exactly where we stand, what we believe in, or who we are" (158). It is here—with the acknowledgment of the dilemmas, the schisms—that *Blue Voyage* ends. There was to be no easy solution, no panacea, for Aiken for some time. But a resolution was inherent in Aiken's theory of evolving consciousness.

The precise relationship between art and sex will be explored exhaustively again in *Ushant*. One passage in particular gives such insight into Demarest's precise philosophical morass that it deserves to be quoted in full with the reminder that here

Aiken is speaking directly autobiographically in what constitutes a gloss of *Blue Voyage*:

> Sex and art, art and sex: the twinned and ambiguous voices chimed harmoniously or discordantly everywhere, denied each other only then to embrace each other, or so naughtily mimicked each other as to be at times quite tantalizing, indistinguishable. If the dream was all sex, rooted all in love, was art therefore, too, nothing but an instinctive love-song, a song of glory, a praise of the life-force in its very essence, the becomingness of sex? Could it be anything but a compulsory—if infinitely elaborate—celebration of the will to live? and in that case, had the individual, the artist, any say in the matter, any freedom at all? Bewildering questions, one was for a long time to be caught in that logical predicament, and to feel that there were only two possible alternatives: either the individual was a "healthy" or true child of nature, of the *natura rerum*, in which case he was automatically and helplessly her servant, her unconscious spokesman and celebrant, her predetermined victim, her slave, and incapable therefore of assuming any pride of identity or originality or virtue; or he rebelled, and ascended magnificently into the empyrean, out of time and space, like Lucifer in starlight, for a treasonable and independent view of the *primum mobile*, in which case he was forced to admit that he was *ipso facto* unhealthy, and from nature's point of view defective. D. was not for many years to see beyond this somewhat specious "either or" dilemma, with its fine use of logical exclusion, although the comprehensive vision of an evolving consciousness in an evolving world—a synthesis which could accommodate healthy and unhealthy alike, finding use in all—was already implicit in his very awareness of the problem.[12]

Blue Voyage occupies a central position in the Aiken canon as the introductory text to the entire philosophical perspective. It identifies the limitlessness of consciousness in general; it attempts to define the particular consciousness of the artist; and it examines the tensions between art and nature, hinting at the resolution through an appreciation of evolving consciousness. Aiken's four other novels reflect in various ways on what is first offered in *Blue Voyage* through the labyrinthine mind of William Demarest.

· · ·

In reading *Blue Voyage* now, more than a half-century since its publication in the spring of 1927, one is immediately struck by its modernity both in conception and execution—in its singular and compelling attention to the theme of consciousness and in its special use of the stream-of-consciousness prose technique. Yet it was precisely the modernity of *Blue Voyage* that frightened or confused or angered its contemporary reviewers. Aiken himself was sensitive to the limits of readers' patience. In anonymously—and candidly—reviewing his own *Nocturne of Remembered Spring and Other Poems* for the *Chicago News*, he sighed, "Can anyone remain interested for forty pages in the protagonist's vacillations between flesh and sentiment—except the protagonist himself?" (*ABC*, 122). However, it should be remembered that only five years had passed since the publication of *Ulysses* (many more years passed before the novel was readily available in America), only two years since *Mrs. Dalloway*; *Remembrance of Things Past* was not to be completely translated until 1932. Among American novelists, only John Dos Passos in *Manhattan Transfer* had consciously experimented with the stream-of-consciousness novel. So *Blue Voyage*, with its interior monologues, its fantasies, its manipulation of chronology, and so forth, was truly an unfamiliar kind of work.

When attacking the prose technique of the novel, reviewers often saw it as a lesser *Ulysses*, but at least one reviewer, Robert Lovett for the *New Republic*, suggested that Aiken out-Joyced Joyce in his exercises of consciousness: "Aiken is more plausible than Joyce at this sort of thing; for while we are inclined to wonder at the way in which the characters in *Ulysses* invariably reduce their mental operations to words, in the case of Demarest we understand that he is literally trying to talk himself into unconsciousness."[13] More typical, however, was the anonymous reviewer for *Outlook*, who predicted that in reading this novel, "Only those skilled in the method of Joyce will be able to determine which are conversations, which are thoughts, which are thoughts about conversations, and which are thoughts, about thoughts. . . . The old-fashioned reader of novels will put it down as 65 per cent lunacy."[14] But for those readers who did not put *Blue Voyage* down, it was usually admiration of technique that made them Aiken admirers. After admitting that the novel is too ponderously philosophical and has too heavy a Freudian overlay, readers find that its technique continues to command attention. The first three chapters are fairly conventional in that they provide the expected exposition. By the end of chapter three we have isolated Smith, Silberstein, and Faubion as the ancillary characters in Demarest's internal voyage, the accomplices in his resolution of the Cynthia conflict. It is in the fourth chapter, a seventy-two-page interior monologue, that the nonconventional begins to dominate: Demarest descends into his unconscious and reviews his whole life, particularly his childhood and then his various affairs with women—all projected against recurring references to a painting by Goya and lines of romantic poetry from Shakespeare, Keats, Coleridge, and Poe. The entire chapter is punctuated by a child's crying and by the word MISERY. The solution appears in the reverie, a call for the crucifixion of Demarest.

In the fifth chapter Demarest, chastened by his monologue, assumes his role as ship's passenger and momentarily stands outside the action, watching the mundane shipboard events: he listens to conversations; he watches the card games; he enters into the dinner-table banter. But with a wave-like recurrence, chapter 6 moves again into reverie. This time Demarest goes up on deck after midnight and engages in the wish-fulfilling fantasy in which all four major characters participate in the idyllic communal scene; their voices are barely distinguishable; a harmony prevails—Prometheus and the vulture are one: "It means not only the past and future we have in common, but the past and future that each of us has separately. And this, of course, is precisely what blesses us. It is this diversity in unity that makes the divine harmony" (CN, 134). But the scene changes, and the others attack Demarest as a disruptive force, failed dramatist, self-devouring egotist, coward, sadist and froterer, voyeur, onanist, exploiter of women—and they conclude that they should pity him because, "After all, he's an idealist: a subjective idealist" (141). In a style anticipating Bellow's Herzog, Aiken's chapter 7 is a series of letters—never to be sent—to Cynthia, and in chapter 8 Aiken returns his novel to a traditional conclusion.

Offended as most reviewers were by Aiken's prose style, they had no more sympathy for his subject matter, his exploration of the artistic psyche. While often giving lip service to Aiken's metaphysical speculations, the contemporary critical establishment—as well as subsequent literary historians—persisted in reading Blue Voyage fundamentally at the level of a love story, a shipboard romance between Demarest and Cynthia. Starting from the assumption that the novel had a fairly traditional plot, the critics then rightly found it confusing, cluttered, or superficial. Misreading the novel in this way, Kenneth Burke concluded: "By way of happy ending, the book closes characteristically with Demarest entering for the first time the illicit [Faubion's] cabin. It is a dingy homecoming."[15] In addition to this being a simplistic reduction of the novel, it is factually untrue. Demarest is in bed in *his* stateroom, and Faubion knocks on *his* door (*CN*, 166).

Other reviewers, reflecting the moral disputes of the day, lined up behind Aiken's being too sexually liberated or too puritanical, though he was primarily accused of the former. The reviewer for *Outlook* suspected that Aiken was trying the limits of literary permissiveness: "Like many other ultra-modern productions, [*Blue Voyage*] occasionally flirts with indecency, and seems to out-Cabell Cabell and out-Vechten Van Vechten in getting unprintable things into print."[16] The repugnance toward the novel's sensuality was not limited to the American reviewers; the novel received no kinder treatment from the *Times Literary Supplement*: "The fundamental inspiration . . . seems to be disgust at the fleshly corruption in which the spirit lives on earth. . . . [Aiken] presents a Narcissus alternately ogling and cursing his image reflected, not in clear water, but in a muddied pond. This attitude, though it may be typical of our time, is not important."[17] Aiken, however, insisted on the importance of the sensory dimension of fiction. In his preface to *Three Novels*, he acknowledged that while form was very important to him, just as important was putting down on the page "the taste, touch, sight, smell, immediacy and rankness, and sheer appallingness, of the living world itself, in its inevitable and daily appearance: the brutal and beautiful here-and-now of it, its absurdity, the inexhaustible comicality of it, its cruelty, even its lunacy. . . . In short the purely *sensory* impact must be of high-frequency and never forgotten for a moment."[18] Not surprisingly, Aiken's first novel achieved the dubious distinction of being "banned in Boston."

A final objection to the novel was that the author was too much a part of the tale. Little realizing that this was exactly Aiken's intention, the *Spectator* reviewer lamented: "Mr. Aiken has not dissociated himself from his characters sufficiently to give them roundness or objectivity."[19] As Aiken explained later in his preface to *Three Novels*, what he had wanted above all was to make of *Blue Voyage* "a statement of the position and nature of the poet or novelist or critic at that particular moment in time, and then to make it palatable, in terms of a novel" (n.p.). But always the form was secondary. He continues that his main concern was the idea, not the vehicle; that while it must appear to be a novel—that is, have enough action, plot, character, or design to hold it together—of greater importance was that it make "as complete a psychological statement of my own moral and social and aesthetic situation as I could possibly make" (n.p.). For this reason Aiken chose "Self-knowledge" for the epigraph. *Blue Voyage* is essentially the apprentice chapter in the autobiography that Aiken would write his whole life. In the preface he insists that every bit of it was true, including the fantasy chapter. Writing to Malcolm Cowley, he explained that he was very interested in "the autobiography turned novel, given shape and distance. And it seemed to me a useful thing to do, at this point in my life: I mean, to give myself *away*, for the benefit of any stray psychologist of literature who might be interested in diagnosing the case of the author of Forslin et al."[20]

Of course, Aiken had been "giving himself away" since he began writing and consistently chose—though there seemed to be little real choice in the matter—as his subject no less a theme than self and reality. The record of Aiken's struggle to understand his own consciousness is in everything he wrote. His poetry can be read as a gloss to his fiction, his fiction as a gloss to his poetry, and both as a gloss to *Ushant*. Thus art is only possible through the voyage into self, which was indisputably the theme of *Blue Voyage*; but Aiken extends the theme even further: living is only possible through the ironic voyage toward self-knowledge—ironic because impossible ("Ay, there's the laugh"). It is not, finally, the arrival that is important in the voyage but the voyaging. As Aiken was to speculate in *Ushant*,

Would they arrive—now or ever—at anything in the least resembling what they had hoped for? Would anyone? Or did it matter, provided one had at least set out on that voyage, made the endeavor? Or did it matter if what one arrived at wasn't *quite* what one had envisioned? Well, they were all heroes, everyone of them; they were all soldiers; . . . all of them engaged in the endless and desperate war on the unconscious." (362)

Aiken sensitively and exhaustively explored mammoth themes in this first, fairly short novel by laying bare the complex mind of only one character, William Demarest. As Aiken remarked in his preface, Demarest, the artist-hero-servant, was faced with a problem: to understand his neurosis and then go on to create with it, while simultaneously analyzing both the neurosis and himself away. The full disclosure of Demarest's innermost thoughts and feelings sometimes embarrasses us but always informs us. Aiken was willing to undress, to examine himself in public, to take such a risk not only because he was an artist driven to expand his own demon consciousness but also because he was an artist with a conviction that, in the true vatic tradition, he must make available to his fellow pilgrims the way to personal redemption.

Chapter Five

THE RECURRING BETRAYAL
Great Circle

SEVEN YEARS AFTER PUBLISHING his first novel, Aiken continued his autobiography in *Great Circle*, which is *Blue Voyage* written more directly, more intensely, and, finally, more successfully. It is as though Aiken suspected that he had not made himself clear. He was certain that he had not been honest about the profound effect his parents' death continued to have on his life. He was also certain that such dishonesty resulted in flawed art. He was, at the same time, uncertain whether "truth" was really possible to know and, if known, whether language was sufficient to communicate it: "That eternal problem of language, language extending consciousness and then consciousness extending language, in circular or spiral ascent."[1] It had all been hinted at in *Blue Voyage*, but the profound relevance of the tragedy was lost beneath the narrative surface. Reluctant to risk being oblique once again, Aiken in his second novel writes four clearly defined chapters about loss or desertion, betrayal, and reconciliation—the great circle. In his writing of a passionately intense novel that makes exhausting demands on the sensibilities of the reader, Aiken was writing to understand better his childhood experience—although he never did write about it absolutely directly until *Ushant* (and even there he called on an assumed persona, D.). But *Great Circle* comes closest to meeting the obligation that Aiken set for himself, the imperative of writing about the tragedy in a fitting way—a memorial:

> He was retaining all this, and re-enacting it, even to the final scene of all: when, after the desultory early-morning quarrel, came the half-stifled scream, and then the sound of his father's voice counting three, and the two loud pistol-shots; and he had tiptoed into the dark room, where the two bodies lay motionless, and apart, and finding them dead, *found himself possessed of them forever* [italics

mine]. . . . he knew that he was irrevocably dedicated to a life-
long—if need be—search for an equivalent to it all, in terms of his
own life, or work; and an equivalent that those two angelic people
would have thought acceptable. (*Ushant*, 302–3)

The cathartic nature of *Great Circle* is playfully reflected in the
protagonist's name, Andrew Cather, and the biographical dimension is sounded in his initials, which are the reverse of
Aiken's own. This, then, is Aiken's most specifically autobiographical novel; it is also, not surprisingly, the novel most
reflective of Aiken's sustained interest in psychology and psychoanalysis. Preceded by *Blue Voyage*, which laid the theoretical
groundwork—the viability of the evolution of consciousness—it
was followed by *King Coffin*, which reverted to Aiken's theoretical emphases.

Although biographical criticism has fallen on hard times, it
would be willfully perverse to deny the biographical intention
of *Great Circle*. Richard Hauer Costa, among so many interview-
ers of Aiken, remarked that he "neither could nor wished to
separate his life from his work. Aiken told this writer with a
pride undiminished by forty years that everyone in *Blue Voyage*
was drawn from actual life, that everything happened as recorded. The pattern of *Blue Voyage*, as well as that of its succes-
sor, *Great Circle* . . . is wholly autobiographical."[2] This is as it
should be in light of Aiken's theories on the relationship between life and art as presented in *Blue Voyage*. Art was blatantly
therapeutic and self-sustaining—that is, writing helped the author live with the recurring traumas of existence by allowing
him to sift through the details, look at the pieces, and translate
them with aesthetic and ideological revision and commitment
into a narrative—a fiction. It placed the artist in the fragile dual
role of observer and object of observation.

By reliving particular experiences, especially painful ones,
the artist was able to inch ever closer toward an understanding
of his own unconscious and to expand his consciousness beyond the immediate experience. When just starting *Great Circle*—having written a mere fifteen hundred words—Aiken wrote
to his psychiatrist friend G. B. Wilbur (who, incidentally, as a
fellow Harvard undergraduate had begun translating Freud for
Aiken in about 1909) saying how the book was both amusing
and disturbing him:

Odd, how these damned things get to digging into one's unconscious on their own hook. I thought I'd pretty well analyzed myself with B[lue] V[oyage], but now I begin to see that I'd only scratched the surface by way of a little exhibitionism. The new thing has taken the bit in its teeth, and rides me blind. It has come to an end, pro tem, largely because it has uncovered so many infantile blocks and such that it has momentarily paralyzed me. And very curious too to observe how my dreams have gone back many stages. Night after night I've revisited my father and mother; alternately replaced my father and accepted him; death and birth inseparably interlocked.[3]

Since Aiken's very reason for existence was to persist in the ongoing struggle to establish a tenable reality (the pursuit for him was never some idle metaphysical exercise to be whimsically indulged), the centrality of biographical experiences cannot be underestimated in his fiction.

It is, therefore, significant that *Great Circle* was published in 1933, just four years after Aiken had divorced Jessie McDonald, the woman he had married seventeen years earlier on his graduation from Harvard, the mother of his three children. It is not surprising that the major theme that Aiken explores so relentlessly here is that of betrayal and abandonment, between both husbands and wives and parents and children. Before their divorce was final, Aiken had already begun seeing Clarissa Lorenz, whom he was to marry a few months after the divorce. Significantly, before he initiated divorce proceedings, Jessie announced that she was going to marry his good friend, writer Martin Armstrong.[4]

But Aiken, ever insistent that nothing exists except in its relationship to something else, must situate the infidelities of his fictive couple, Andrew and Bertha, in a wider context. That is, first he must consider the extent to which their betrayal and abandonment of each other are a retelling of the infidelity of Andrew's mother with his Uncle David; and second he must consider the parallels to the breakdown of the relationship between Aiken's own parents as witnessed by himself as a boy. This coming full circle, then, constitutes a second theme of the novel: an exploration of the philosophical pattern of simultaneity and timelessness. In Aiken's notes for a tribute to his grandfather Potter to be called "Dead Letters" (but never finished), Aiken wrote "——for it became important for both of us to emphasize, in the diagram of our lives, the extraordinary extent, from this point onward, to which pattern was to repeat pattern, and sometimes, as in my own case, without the slightest awareness that it was being repeated, or that there was, in fact, any pattern to repeat."[5]

Finally, Aiken finds that through the painful opening up of old wounds, scrutinizing the nature of human motivation, shamelessly exploring the breakdown of human relations and of institutions such as marriage, he simultaneously exposes what is common to the general human condition. This leads Aiken logically into his third and concluding theme—the same thematic conclusion as in *Blue Voyage*: wisdom through suffering, an arrival at a more integrated level of consciousness through psychic pain.

. . .

Just as *Blue Voyage* was preceded by a trial-run volume of short stories, *Bring! Bring! and Other Stories*, Aiken had already examined the theme of marital betrayal and its ramifications in a well-received volume of short stories, *Costumes by Eros*, before publishing *Great Circle*. As the title suggests, twelve of the fourteen short stories published in 1928 deal primarily with male-female conflict, usually sexual. It is particularly relevant to *Great Circle* that in a significant number of the stories ("Your Obituary, Well Written," "Farewell! Farewell! Farewell!" "The Necktie," "The Professor's Escape," "I Love You Very Dearly," and "West End"), the protagonist is involved in an extramarital (though not always sexual) relationship. Frequently the marriages have been flawed in a serious way, and the husband, more often than the wife, becomes restless and seeks diversions outside the marriage. In every case we know very little about the other married partner. Aiken is not interested in getting caught up in the legalistic division of faults or the assignment of guilt in the failed marriages. So it is not surprising that in *Great Circle* we come to know little about Andrew's wife, Bertha. One of the few faults that Cather mentions is her sloppiness, even a tendency to be dirty: "The upright soul indifferent to filth." Instead Bertha assumes her importance as one of a number of women—and men—who have betrayed Cather, thereby reinforcing his keen sense of abandonment, which has haunted him since childhood. However, Andrew does believe his chauvinistic rationalization that " 'a woman can share a man, but a man can't share a woman. And that's all there is to it.' "[6]

Similar to *Blue Voyage*, which had been restricted by location and by time—the first three-and-a-half days of the trans-Atlantic crossing—the drama of *Great Circle* is intensified by its taking place in a day and a half. The novel begins with the rumored betrayal of Andrew by his wife and by his good friend, Tom; chapter 2 is a flashback to young Andy's watching the betrayal of his father by his mother and his Uncle David, his father's brother; in chapter 3 Andrew drinks and talks through the night with his psychoanalyst friend, Bill, about betrayals in general and specifically the betrayal of the artist Michelangelo by his best friend; chapter 4 constitutes the working out of a resolution or at least an understanding of the relationship between the several betrayals and Cather's growth of consciousness.

The novel begins its exploration of Bertha's infidelity with the jealous husband, who, having been alerted by a friend, rushes home to Boston three days early from a New York trip intending to catch the adulterous couple in bed. Almost immediately the familiar Aiken ambivalences are sounded. Andrew wonders about his own responsibility in the affair; perhaps he has precipitated, even encouraged, his wife's involvement with his best friend. He imagines himself walking into his sitting room and surprising the couple: "But supposing there *should* be some one? Ah. This is what you really want. You really want to find some one there. Do not deny it—do not pretend. You are deliberately seeking a catastrophe—you are yourself in the act of creating a disaster" (*CN*, 171).[7]

Next Andrew begins to draw comparisons between himself and Tom, to his own disadvantage, thereby proffering, by implication, a reason for Bertha's unfaithfulness. He sees himself as the dull, middle-aged tutor and compiler of Spanish textbooks, while the adversary is an adventurous, hell-raising biology professor. Andrew is thirty-eight in the novel; Aiken was forty-one when he was divorced the first time.

It soon becomes apparent that Andrew has, indeed, reasons for feeling guilty. He has had a number of affairs and realizes that he spiritually deserted their marriage at least a year earlier. Consequently he has been drinking heavily for the past six months in a determined effort to avoid consciousness: " 'I get drunk because I don't want to be wholly conscious. Because, I admit it, I'm partly a coward, and don't want to know, or to have you and Tom know, exactly how many volts of pain I'm carrying' " (*CN*, 194).

Slowly we get an insight into the complexities of the betrayal. On the first level Andrew is truly hurt by his wife's infidelity, especially since her partner is a friend whom he had implicitly trusted; on a deeper level, he is confused and saddened by his own need to betray the marriage, by his misgivings about his ability to love. He is also perplexed about the nature of love and its proximity to cruelty and even death. He looks on his marriage as "the whole prolonged obscene and fecal grapple in steadily deepening darkness, year after year of it, the burden upon his consciousness becoming hourly more foul and more frightful" (195). A mistake commonly made by critics is to ignore the complexity of Cather's problem and to assume that Aiken is once again writing about the Freudian wife/mother dilemma only. David M. Rein, in an article entitled "Conrad Aiken and Psychoanalysis," passes this rather simplistic judgment on the first two novels: "In *Blue Voyage* Demarest wanted Cynthia because she was, unconsciously, a symbol of his mother. In *Great Circle* Andrew didn't want Bertha because, after marriage, she failed as a symbol of his mother."[8]

Of greater importance than Bertha's failure is Andrew's failure, as well as the possibility that love itself is a chimera. He sadly suspects that he is incapable of loving or of sustaining love; he worries that love is too hazardous and that love is finally to be feared. Certainly with his mother's infidelity never far from his mind, it is not surprising that Andrew concludes,

> Love is cruelty. Love is hate. Love is a desire to revenge yourself. It's a bloody great butcher's cleaver, that's what it is. It has eyes of a ferocity known only to comets, its hands are red, its feet are claws, its wings are scythes of jealousy. Its will is destruction: it tears out the heart of the beloved, in order that its own heart may break. Love is murder. It's a suicide pact, and all for what? All for death. (*CN*, 267–68)[9]

The novel settles into an exploration by Andrew about his growing doubts that he could ever trust love. He traces his fears to two sources. First, the experiences in his childhood, his betrayal by the people he most trusted (his parents) and the final loss of his mother through death (which has contributed to his seeking her in lovers),[10] undermine the very structure of trust on which love is built. Second, he worries simultaneously about his rampant sexual appetite. We know the biographical source of the first fear, and as to the second, Aiken tells us in *Ushant* about a clairvoyant Unitarian minister-prophet he once met in London who predicted that he would waste much of his talent by gratifying his baser appetites: "You will be devilled by sex, and will not, will *never*, learn to control it; and for its sake you will disgracefully, over and over again, betray or sacrifice all that is dearest to you" (131).

The reader of *Great Circle* readily agrees with Cather that in the present case—in the Bertha-Tom affair—his suffering and subsequent mental imbalance is excessive. We also suspect the wellspring of grief is elsewhere and are not surprised when Cather suggests to Bill that perhaps looking back to his childhood might shed some light on his present suffering. This leads to the original betrayal. In the rantings of the first chapter there is one passing reference to Duxbury, the town where Andrew spent his summers as a boy. Standing in the rain outside his Boston apartment before confronting his wife and Tom, he lectures himself, " 'Retreat, you idiot. Go back to the Harvard Club. Get your bag and drive to Duxbury. Duxbury? Why Duxbury?' " (*CN*, 188).

It is in chapter 2 that we witness the initial Duxbury betrayal, that involving Andrew's mother and his Uncle David. Mother and children had gone ahead to spend the summer with Uncle Tom, Aunt Norah, and Uncle David, while Father remained working in Boston, intending to make periodic weekend trips to the family. But young Andy quickly becomes aware of a strange relationship between his mother and his uncle, whom he instinctively dislikes: "Brothers looked very much alike, Uncle David looked like Father, but with red mustaches, like a Visigoth; he was taller too, and stronger, but his face was long and funny; I didn't like it, and he looked at you with narrow blue eyes as if he didn't like you" (220). The young boy is upset by his mother and uncle's early morning tennis games, their walks, their sailing trips in the uncle's boat, their attempts at eluding the children ("Why was Mother always trying to get rid of us like this" [211]).

One afternoon Andy's father, anxiously expected by the three children for a promised clambake, surprises him on the path to town. He has come from Boston and is staying—unknown to his family—at a rooming house. He makes his son promise not to say that he has seen him. The boy is further confused when later that same night he overhears his father's voice downstairs engaged in a heated conversation. The following day the father again confronts the son on his way to the library, entrusts him with a letter for his mother, and tells Andy that he is leaving for Boston on the noon train. Andy hides and reads the message, which is written in the old Quaker dialect of his forebears. It suggests that his mother is hopelessly attracted to his uncle's *"racy side of life."* As if this were not damaging enough to the neglected and confused child, he then reads his father's shocking offer to abandon the children altogether if by so doing he might save his wife from a tragic mistake:

> *Forgive me for entertaining for a moment such an idea, Pussy—but I must recognize it just long enough to tell thee that deep as my concern is for the needful reorganization of our home life and home relations, for the salvation of the children, I must, nevertheless, tell thee that rather than that thee should be exposed to even the remotest possibility of such a risk, I will gladly give up every consideration of them. . . . For in my heart and life, thee comes before everything else: and that one thing thy crown of purity, is to me so precious that even the moral loss of the three children would be a small sacrifice!* (227)

The autobiographical parallel is strikingly seen in *Ushant*, when Aiken recalls the pain of his own divorces and desertions and the prediction of his Beloved Uncle:

> Not for nothing the succession of Loreleis [general name for his wives] . . . and the abandoned children, the little D.'s, and the suffering inflicted alike upon them and himself; look, he would be able to say: see what happened to me: remember, now, what excellent advice you gave *me*, when, in this very room, after the fatal interview with Lorelei Two [Clarissa Lorenz], I announced that I had fallen in love with her . . . and that I would leave Saltinge [Rye, England] and the children in order to live with her! You were the first to say . . . that I loved the children too much, the three little D.'s, and they me: it would cause hideous suffering, but most of all for myself. (*Ushant*, 80)

The rounding out of the domestic tragedy for the child follows soon after, when, on a dangerously stormy night, Uncle David and his mother recklessly take a boat out in a gale and are drowned.[11] Andy listens through the night for some message about them; he hears the telephone ringing; he sees Uncle Tom and two men go off toward the Point. But it is Andy who takes his dory out at five the following morning and finds the sunken boat. It is Andy, too, who answers the police inquiry: "I could see some brown cloth quite close to one of the portholes, and I knew it was my mother's dress, the one she had on yesterday" (*CN*, 237).

The role played by twelve-year-old Andy in the discovery of the boat and its drowned passengers and in the reporting to the police inspector closely parallels in fact and in tone that of eleven-year-old Conrad Aiken reporting the double death of his parents to the Savannah police in the early morning hours of 27 February 1901. It is not accidental that Andrew's marital disaster surfaces in February or that the hotel room in which he receives the note advising him of his wife's infidelity is "218"—Aiken's Savannah house number.

The Morning News (28 February 1901), quoted extensively here since it is the scene that dominates Conrad Aiken's entire fifty-volume canon, gives the following graphic account:

A few minutes before 7 o'clock Patrolman Harry Lange, on duty in the sallyport, was walking from the sergeant's office to the station house, when he heard behind him the patter of bare and boyish feet. He turned to face Conrad Aiken, Dr. Aiken's 12–year-old [sic] son.

"Papa has shot mama and then shot himself," said the boy.[12]

"Who is your father?" the policeman queried.

"Dr. Aiken." . . . With a degree of calmness and self-possession beyond his years and that under the tragic circumstances was almost weird, the lad indicated the room of his mother. Lange pushed open the door and entered. The room was in almost total darkness, as it was then scarcely broad daylight, and the shutters of the windows were closed. The policeman had a single match, and striking it, a flickering and uncertain light shed itself over the room. By its rays the grim details of the tragedy were revealed. The bed was just to the left of the policeman as he entered the room and stretched on this, lying in an easy and natural position on her left side, was the body of Mrs. Aiken. A pistol wound, ghastly and gaping, in her right temple, explained too well the cause of her death. On pillows and bed-clothing, and on the walls of the room near the head of the bed, were further evidence of the short distance from which the fatal shot had been fired.

On a rug at the side of the bed, face downward, was the body of Dr. Aiken, a like gaping wound in his right temple and the revolver from which the shots had been fired still clasped in his right hand. The position in which he had fallen showed that death had been instantaneous. . . .

It was a scene to touch and melt the hardest heart. The eldest boy, Conrad, lingered outside the door, while the other children, Elizabeth, Kempton and Robert, the last named but 6 years old, scarce realizing the extent of the awful calamity of which they were the innocent victims and from which they would be the greatest sufferers, cowed in terror and sorrow unrestrained, in the adjoining room which they occupied. The two younger peered wide-eyed from the bedclothes in which they were huddled.

Surely Aiken was forcing himself to work through this memory in *Great Circle*. There is, however, no evidence of Mrs. Aiken's infidelity, although in *Ushant* Aiken recalls that there were terrible quarrels over his mother's social, party-going nature (302) and that Dr. Aiken had grown increasingly suspicious of her. But the usual reason given for the shooting was the doctor's irrational fear that his wife was preparing to have him committed to a mental institution.

In addition to the central tragedy, there are a host of minor biographical similarities in *Great Circle*. In chapter 2, for instance, we find that Andy's father is an avid photography buff who had given the boy a camera "and took me on walks and showed me how to take pictures" (*CN*, 211). Dr. Aiken's obituary notes that he had been president of the Savannah Camera Club and had been a member of the Barnesville Corps, which had successfully photographed the sun's eclipse the previous May.

Again, when young Andy is unable to deal with thoughts of his mother and Uncle David's clandestine meetings, he stretches out on the grass and tries to induce sleep by chanting a rhyme: "the rhyme Mother always said for Porper when she blew out the light. One—two-three! Out. Goes. She" (232). It is a rhyme taken directly from Aiken's childhood. In "Prologue to an Autobiography" Aiken remembers his mama, "clasping the little flat valve of the gas jet, just before she puts us to bed, and reciting the magic words: One—two—three—out—goes—she! and timing the word 'she' quite miraculously and alarmingly with the sudden extinction of the light, the terrifying extension of the dark."[13]

Young Andy and young Aiken also share an enthusiasm for the same books. In Andrew's all-night associative ramblings, he remarks to Bill that his favorite stories as a child were *Jackanapes* and *Twenty Thousand Leagues Under the Sea*. In *Ushant*, Aiken tells us that Cousin Maud had sent *Jackanapes* as a Christmas present, and, in listing the pleasant memories of his move to New Bedford, Aiken mentions "the books from grandfather's library, most notably *Twenty Thousand Leagues Under the Sea*" (85).

Then, too, the cups made out of acorns, which figured significantly in the ritual between young Demarest and his grandfather in *Blue Voyage*, reappear in *Great Circle*: "We sat on the doorstep of the playhouse, and made cups and saucers out of green acorns for Porper.—Look, Porper, we're having tea, this is what Grandfather showed me how to do" (*CN*, 221). The scene receives its fullest treatment in *Ushant* (111–12).

There is, then, no question that the desertion of Bertha by Andrew (or Andrew by Bertha) is a reenactment of the desertion of Andy's father by his mother, which is, in turn, a reenactment of the desertion of Aiken by his parents. As he says in *Ushant*, "Translation—it was all translation" (31). It is important to notice, however, that in recasting the autobiographical account into the mother–Uncle David relationship, Aiken's sympathy is with his father. In *Ushant*, Aiken tells us that while he was at Harvard his paternal grandmother allowed him to see the leather portfolio that included his father's letters and poems, as well as the newspaper accounts of the tragedy, and that, as a result, "A singular, and slightly naughty, alliance had grown up between them: they had become accomplices in what was admitted was a sort of private vice—the illicit re-appraisal and exoneration of father, and the tacit admission—against the family taboo—of his genius" (103). Aiken remembers in *Ushant* how he even tried deliberately at this time to make himself look like his father, to tighten the muscles around his mouth to overcome the "narcissistic fullness" he had inherited from his mother. Along with this attempt to fashion himself physically after his father was the "taking over of the father's role as a writer" (107).[14]

Just as in *Blue Voyage* Aiken moved beyond consciousness in the life of Demarest to the role of consciousness in the life of artists in particular, there is a widening of the circle of betrayal in *Great Circle*. Chapter 1 initiates the theme with the betrayals of Bertha and Andrew; chapter 2 takes it back to Andrew's mother and uncle; in chapter 3 Andrew considers the betrayal of Michelangelo by his best friend. Obviously, the purpose of this betrayal is to mark how the artist transmuted his suffering into his paintings and sculpture. His suffering became a legacy; it passed into the consciousness of others.

. . .

A second, though related, theme in *Great Circle* is the relationship of time and timelessness to reality. Aiken wrestles with speculations on the nature of time and tries to bring his conclusions into harmony with his thoughts on the principle of recurrence. He deals with different aspects of these philosophical problems at different times in the novel, frequently attempting to clarify them through his metaphor of the great circle. Although the circle is a natural symbol for infinity, Emerson's specific use of it was undoubtedly important for Aiken, especially in light of Aiken's general admiration for him.[15] The transcendentalist consistently explained the unity that he saw underlying all existence in terms of a circle. In *Nature*, for example, to clarify his idea that every universal truth expressed in words implies all other truths, he illustrated, "It is like a great circle on a sphere, comprising all possible circles."

On one level—the thematic—the title *Great Circle* refers to the circles of betrayal: Bertha and Tom, Andrew and assorted women, the mother and Uncle David, Michelangelo and a friend, on back to the quintessential autobiographical betrayal. On another level—the structural—the novel moves full circle from adulthood in Boston (chapter 1), to a flashback to boyhood in Duxbury (chapter 2), to adulthood in Boston (chapter 3), and ends with Andrew's deciding in chapter 4 to drive back to Duxbury—thus coalescing the experiences of the boy and the man. But the circle is much more philosophically intrinsic than that: there is the essential underlying tenet that each of the horrifying experiences of the novel culminates in a kind of death that gives birth to a wider expanse of consciousness. As one, then, approximates an understanding of the circular nature of existence, one simultaneously widens one's consciousness. Just as the proverbial pebble that is dropped into the lake defines itself by the formation of a circle and at the same time sends out concentric circles, so also the individual, through separate experiences, becomes more aware—for instance of the nature of betrayal or of time—thereby sensing patterns of recurrence and further extending his consciousness.

Aiken also considers in *Great Circle* the comparison between the illusion of timelessness in youth and the reality of being time-bound in maturity. Andrew, as narrator, opens the novel blaming himself for living so narrowly and completely in a world dominated by time:

> Why be in such a hurry, old fool? What good is hurry going to do you? Wrap yourself in a thick gauze of delay and confusion, like the spider; hang there, like the spider, aware of time only as the rock is aware of time. . . . Must you always be running desperately from minute to minute?" (*CN*, 169)

But Andrew must keep reminding himself throughout the novel, "Permit yourself to be sifted by time, slowly,—be passive,—wait. Learn to rot gently, like the earth: it is only a natural rot that is creative" (169). Yet it is a lesson that will come hard for Andrew, whose very nature is precipitous. He is, instead, bound up in time. He even personifies the train he takes as running from New York to Boston: "Hurry—hurry—hurry—everything was hurrying. The train was hurrying. The world was hurrying. The landscape was hurrying" (170). He notices as soon as he gets to the Harvard bar that there is no clock in the room. He remarks on leaving that it is 9 P.M., and as he walks toward the encounter with Bertha, he urges himself on: "Hurry—hurry—hurry—everything was hurrying. The world was hurrying" (187). Arriving at their apartment at 9:30, he immediately notices the "damned little gilt clock, ticking subtly and complacently to itself, for all the world as if it were Tom's own pulse. Break it. Dash it to smithereens on the red-brick hearth. Step on it, kid—let time be out of joint" (189). Later, when Andrew is trying to fathom for his friend Bill some conceivable reason for continuing to live, he guesses that maybe it's for hot dogs and western sandwiches or for "the sound of the clock. Step up, ladies and gents, and see the fellow who lives with his left eye on the almighty clock" (258). He comments also on the clock in Bill's living room as it strikes the hour and then goes on ticking "as if in no astonishment at that sudden comment on division of time" (286).

In contrast, the sense of timelessness that existed in one's youth is projected against this time-hounded maturity. Andrew remembers longingly the seeming timelessness of his Duxbury boyhood, when "time held him green and dying though he sang in his chains like the sea." In deciding to return to Duxbury at the end of the novel, Andrew reconciles adult's "time" and youth's "timelessness" by calling on the theory of eternal recurrence (which, in part, he owes to Nietzsche). By making himself travel the full circle, Andrew takes part in the ritualistic rounding-out of the experience. He forces himself to face the reality of Duxbury both as locus for the timeless, pre-betrayal, halcyon days associated with youthful abandonment as well as locus for his mother's infidelity and death. Andrew suspects that only by returning to "that agony" will he be able to exorcise it and finally grow through it, to lose himself in order to create himself: "The end that is still conscious of its beginnings. Birth that remembers death" (295).

While Andrew Cather's circular return to Duxbury, scene of the first betrayal, makes it possible for him to come to terms with the second betrayal, Conrad Aiken, through the act of writing a novel about betrayals, expands his consciousness in respect to his personal tragedy.[16] The pattern of recurrence constitutes the essential structuring of all Aiken novels as well as of *Ushant*. Cather, within the course of the *Great Circle*, comes to the necessary realization that his present unhappy condition is intimately related to the accumulation of experiences that make up Andrew Cather—beginning, in one sense, in his Duxbury childhood but yet, in another sense, predating his birth, that is, growing out of his relationship to the very cosmic order itself. This is as close to a resolution of the novel as Aiken can come: the eternal pattern exists.

In 1963, while recovering from a heart attack, Aiken found himself writing limericks at a great pace (he remarked that the psychologist would probably explain his "seizure of limericks" as an attempt by the unconscious to keep him amused), and one of these is a humorous restatement of the same philosophical doctrine of the great circle treated so seriously in the second novel:

> Said a curve: I'm becoming hysterical,
> It is hell to be merely numerical.
> I bend and I bend,
> But where will I end
> In a world that is hopelessly spherical.[17]

In *Great Circle*, then, Aiken first insists that his readers become acutely time-conscious as he clocks Cather's scurrying from train to taxi to restaurant to apartment, and so forth. Then he encourages them to recall the timelessness of youth, realizing that the heedless abandonment of youth in a time-free world is only understood retrospectively, from the perspective, ironically, of time-charted maturity. Finally Aiken insists that there is a sense in which time does not really exist—that is, that ultimately there simply is no beginning or end. All things recur. One realizes by the end of the novel that the further one travels into the lonely realm of cosmic consciousness, the closer one is to meeting oneself.

. . .

In addition to the prevailing themes of betrayal, abandonment, time, timelessness, and recurrence is an additional theme common to the Aiken canon: wisdom through suffering. Andrew Cather realizes that Duxbury was, in a sense, unreal because it existed only by virtue of paradisiacal ignorance and was at best tenuously ephemeral. As he—like Aiken—learned sooner than most, "To be aware is to suffer" (*CN*, 265). Andrew painstakingly details to Bill that life is unavoidably one with suffering, but he also suggests the use (reminiscent of William Demarest) to which he, as an artist, can put the pain and the neurosis. Drawing on his own past (also Aiken's), Andrew explains to Bill that it doesn't help at all to tell the child crawling around in the dark that he shouldn't cry, that he doesn't need his mother, that she never belonged only to him. That won't alleviate the suffering. All he can do is to "translate" it into other terms—and he must retain that right: "The right to suffer in our own way—that's what we demand by God" (266).

Suffering, then, becomes a catalyst for evolving conscious-ness, the *felix culpa*. Andrew asks himself rhetorically, "Was suffering one's nearest approach to an acute realization of life? Of existence? And therefore desirable?" (288). Certainly this is the only way that the near-optimistic conclusion of the over-whelmingly pessimistic novel can be explained. As Andrew drives alone toward Duxbury, he concludes, "Life was good— life was going to be good. Unexplored, unfathomable, marvel-ous and terrible. Filthy, and incalculable. Cruel, and inexhaust-ible. . . . The wonderful nightmare, the wonderful and acceptable nightmare!" (295)

As the novel draws to its close, Aiken places his emphasis on this central point. He specifically explores in *Great Circle* the extending of human consciousness, first, through experiences— especially painful ones—and, second, through dreams—a num-ber of which are related in extensive detail. For instance, one of Cather's dreams takes up the first fourteen pages of the last chapter and is entirely set off in italics. The dream provides insights into Cather's suffering, but Aiken's interest in it ex-tends even beyond its content and into the mechanics of the process of returning from the dream world, from contact beyond the borders of the known experience. Again, as in *Blue Voyage*, Aiken chooses the metaphor of a swimmer ascending from some primordial watery depth to suggest one's return from the dream world. This emergence in *Great Circle* is one of the most explicit and extraordinarily beautiful descriptions in literature:

> To come upward from the dark world, through the mild shafts of light, as a swimmer in long and curved periphery from a dive; from the whirled and atomic or the swift and sparkling through the slower and more sleekly globed; effortless, but with a drag at the heels of consciousness—to float upward, not perpendicularly, but at an angle, arms at sides, turning slightly on one's axis, like a Blake angel, through the long pale transverse of light—with the sounds, too, the bell-sounds, the widening rings of impalpable but deep meaning, as if someone far off with spheral mouth said, Time—and the goldfish-mouth released its bubble, and closed, and then again opened to say, Time—to come upward thus slowly revolving, thus slowly twisting, the eye scarcely opened and almost indifferent to light, but opening more widely as the light with obscure and delicate changes teased at the eyelid, teased at the sleepy curiosity—and the textures too, the warm or soft, the wrinkled or knotted, those that

caressed whitely and obliquely, and those also that withdrew, or focused slowly in a single sharp point and pressed—to float upward like this, from plane to plane, sound to sound, meaning to meaning—the attitudes changing one into another as the hands shifted, the feet shifted, the breathing altered or the hearing cleared—from turbulent to troubled, from troubled to serene—but with the bell-sound nearer and nearer, as if the head were emerging into a glistening ring, and as if over the edges of this ring came the words like bubbles, at first meaningless, and then with half-meanings, and at last—not with meanings precisely but with gleams, as of fins that turned away in a flash and vanished—. (282)

The magic of this passage stems in part from Aiken's choice of Blake's angel as his controlling image, an angel so often pictured emerging from a wave, ascending at an angle, long hair flowing about the body and blending into the wings and soft folds of a gown. Here the angel seems to coalesce with a fish breaking water, releasing bubbles, puffing out the word "Time." Aiken's prose in the passage is indistinguishable from his poetry—the visual, aural, and tactile imagery, the repetition, the alliteration, the assonance: "focused slowly in a single sharp point and pressed—to float upward like this, from plane to plane, sound to sound, meaning to meaning." Since the entire account is a single sentence, one is drawn hypnotically into the chantlike words and unconsciously joins the dreamer in his slow, reluctant return to consciousness.

Whether the insights about the nature of suffering emerge from the waking or the dream world, there is still the necessity for Aiken to find the means by which the individual consciousness, thus heightened, can be made available to others—thereby extending the collective consciousness. To this end Aiken has Cather see a parallel between himself and Michelangelo, who was also betrayed by his best friend.

Michelangelo's rich, homosexual artist-friend, unable to involve the painter with himself as completely as he wanted, "took the next best course—viz., to wit., i.e., he took Michelangelo's mistress. . . . And so we have a rare kind of incest . . . a sort most painful to the heart" (246). That Andrew associates this tale with his own betrayal is indicated by the frequent references to the artist throughout the novel and by direct parallel passages: "he [Michelangelo's friend] left his hat in the hall, and his sword too, and his scarlet-lined cloak," which corresponds to Andrew's finding Tom's hat, stick, fur-lined gloves, and galoshes in the hall.

With the realization that art could be mined in the shafts of suffering, there comes a partial resolution of the problem that Demarest had found so perplexing in *Blue Voyage*: if art were in large part the product of a neurosis, should it be encouraged or repressed? Here Cather seems to suggest that suffering, though it causes much anguish and even leads to neuroses, may be a condition for great art. In *Ushant* Aiken says as much: "Perhaps the agonies and injuries were in some sort a necessity, if the individual was to accomplish an even partial originality of shape and purpose. As the tiny pine-tree is cunningly wounded and dwarfed by the Japanese gardener, in order that it may become a masterpiece worthy to be contained in a Ming bowl—!" (44). The implied extension of this metaphor is that art for which such a price in human suffering has been paid need not or should not be repressed; suicide is no longer the alternative. Such an aesthetic conclusion moves *Great Circle* a step beyond *Blue Voyage*.

Aiken had seriously considered the alternative. On 7 May 1927, following the publication of *Blue Voyage*, distraught over juggling a disintegrating marriage to Jessie McDonald and a burgeoning affair with Jerry (Clarissa) Lorenz, Aiken wrote to George Wilbur that he was in a "baddish hole. I've played feebly with the idea of suicide, but when it came to a showdown, pistol in hand, I discovered that I didn't have the nerve" (*SL*, 135). Then, just two months before sending off the final chapter of *Great Circle*, Aiken made his most serious attempt on his life. Again he confessed to Wilbur, in a letter written on 21 September 1932: "Last week I reached my peak or neap or nadir of discouragement and attempted suicide" (*SL*, 191).

It follows from moving beyond suicide that Aiken has Andrew toast Michelangelo, Shakespeare, and Melville as fellow sufferers whom he has inherited and who have created him: "They taught me how to suffer. They taught me how to know, how to realize, gave me the words by which I could speak my pain. They gave me the pain by giving me the words. Gave my pain its precise shape, as they gave me their consciousness. As I shall give my pain, my consciousness, to others" (*CN*, 285).

However, Andrew's acceptance of the value of suffering is undermined by his gnawing fear that his suffering may not be entirely honest or pure; that he is, in part, being self-indulgent, self-dramatizing; that the tale he relates through the long night is an unholy combination of fact and fiction that discredits the whole. He moans aloud, " 'But, my God, Bill, how sick it makes me to mix so much that's fraudulent with all this—at one moment what I say to you is genuine, at the next it's almost deliberately a fake' " (246). Andrew, again displaying the ambiguity of self-consciousness, also fears that his truth-telling may be vitiated by alcohol. And, finally, he wonders at what point his spirited dramatization of himself might have become drama for the sake of drama.

Cather then comes to the final realization, one essential to his whole metaphysical construct, that there undoubtedly was something dishonest in his painful, introspective reverie—a dishonesty that filled him with a fearful distrust of himself (just as Demarest had had ambivalent thoughts about his role as artist). Cather concludes that perhaps pure truth was impossible because "consciousness itself was a kind of dishonesty." That is, once something was made conscious, was entered into the realm of thought, it had already undergone a translation, a bastardizing, and was forever removed from pure truth. Also, the fact that it had to be thought through words, which were by definition metaphors, truth had to be diminished. Such conclusions greatly unburdened Cather:

> Could it be true—and if it was, what a relief! what an escape!—that consciousness itself was a kind of dishonesty? A false simplification of animal existence? A voluntary-involuntary distortion, precisely analogous to the falsification that occurs when consciousness, in turn, tries to express itself in speech? As the animate, then, must be a natural distortion of the inanimate. Each step a new kind of dishonesty; a dishonesty inherent in evolution. Each translation involving a shedding, a partial shedding or abandonment, and an intention of a something new which was only disguisedly true to its origins, only obviously true to itself. (285–86)

Was the suffering, then, simply a failure at translation?—"An inability to feel what one is, to say what one feels, to do what one wills? A failure, simply, to know? A failure of the historical sense?" (286).

To illustrate the contrasting, ideal state of preconsciousness, where presumably truth exists in a pure state, Aiken calls upon a metaphor that he frequently uses in his poetry, the rock. Cather consoles himself with the suspicion that unadulterated honesty can only exist in this rock stage, never in the intrinsically mutable "real" world:

> The fluidity of life, as long as it is life, can never have the immobile integrity of the rock from which it came. It will only be honest rock again when it is dead. And in the meantime, if it suffers, if it is aware that it suffers, if it says that it is aware that it suffers, and if it is aware that it cannot say completely *why* it suffers, or in severance from what, that's all you can ask of it. In sum—idiot!—it is only unhappy because it is no longer, for the moment, rock. (286)

After enjoying these flights of philosophical inquiry, Cather is brought abruptly back to his present unhappy reality. He is confronted with an unfaithful wife and friend as well as with an awareness of his own unfaithfulness and his own role in their unfaithfulness. But he comes to a resolution: if all the consequent suffering were a fake, "it was a genuine fake: suffering, even if it is only a transition, is genuine" (286). Further, the expression of the anguish, though often faulty, has never been false: "Speech, even if it must be only incompletely loyal to its subject, incapable of saying all, is genuine" (286).

Cather, the observed, and Aiken, the observer, must accept such a conclusion lest they render themselves powerless to create by their philosophical scrupulosity.

. . .

As a literary critic reviewing extensively throughout the 1920s, Aiken was sensitive to the contemporary interest in form in fiction. As a novelist committed to pursuing the complexities of the individual human psyche as well as the general chaos of human existence, he was fearful of writing what appeared to be a chaotic and perhaps meaningless piece of fiction; at the same time he was cognizant of the singular relationship between form and matter. In many ways Aiken was faced in the second novel with precisely the same technical problems he had confronted in the first, but by *Great Circle* he had gained considerably more structural control without consequent loss of the looseness of form necessary to the technique of free association, the basic structure of the novel. R. P. Blackmur called this feature of

Aiken's style "pre-morphous," noting that Aiken deliberately prevented his work from reaching more than minimal form: "He attempts to preserve the chaos he sees and he attempts to woo the chaos he does not see. The limit of form which attracts him is the form just adequate to keep the record with grace. . . . He has the sense that as things are finally their own meaning (as he is himself), so they will take up immediately their own forms."[18]

Yet, almost in defiance of Blackmur's perceptive and seemingly accurate description of his technique, Aiken provided a tight outline of a rather contrived plot structure for *Great Circle*. He denied in an interview with Ashley Brown that the book was worked out along lines suggested by *The Sound and the Fury*, claiming that, instead, it had a " 'symphonic form' " reflecting the influence of one of his favorite composers, Richard Strauss.[19] In his preface to *Three Novels*, Aiken elaborated on this statement, pointing out that the book had four distinct parts, like a symphony, each section with a different key and movement of its own. Chapter 1, the return of Andrew Cather to Boston to discover his wife's infidelity, is the " 'fast' movement, full of latent violences, and tragic-comic in tone." The second chapter, the flashback to Andrew's youth, constituting a "poetic evocation of that early paradise," is the slow movement. Chapter 3, Andrew's long pouring out of his life "as in psychoanalysis," is the third movement. Chapter 3 culminates in a catharsis that leads to the fourth and final movement of the last chapter, "now lighter and happier in tone," taking its key from Mozart's "The Magic Flute": "The *eclaircissement* is now at last in sight, the great circle to a conclusion can now be completed."[20] Aiken had even considered giving the four sections symphonic descriptions: "Part I, Presto, Part II, Andante in modo di fuga (or something suggestive of the fugue), Part III, Largo, Part IV , Allegro assai." But he wondered if such naming might be "a shade artificial and distracting."[21] Graham Greene, reviewing the novel for *Spectator*, read the four parts as thought, memory, speech, and action.[22] Still another psychological reading of the parts is suggested in a recent book by Ted Spivey, *Writer as Shaman*. He sees the first chapter as Adlerian: Cather is overcome by powerlessness. The second and third chapters are Freudian: in the second, Cather plumbs his unconscious for the repressed childhood memories of his mother's adultery, and in the third, Cather realizes that his "own sadistic wounding of his wife springs from his hatred of his mother." The last chapter is Jungian: Cather admits that his cure entails not only confessing his problem and rehearsing his dreams but also undergoing a ritualistic—that is, Jungian—act of returning to the scene of his mother's initial infidelity and subsequent death.[23]

While there clearly are musical parallels in the novel, one should be cautioned against overemphasizing them. Much critical attention has been focused on the musicality of Aiken's prose,[24] but it might adjust the perspective to know that Aiken's widow, Mary Hoover Aiken, once remarked to me that she thought her husband's musical interests were being inflated. She recalled that Aiken could not read music. Soon after they had first met, she noticed as he played the piano that he used only the black keys, and to her inquiry, he responded, "They're easier to see."

Further, although Aiken's symphonic reference explains the four-chapter division of the novel, it does not touch on the amorphous interior of the chapters that is the heart of the work, which projects its fine sense of the subtleties of human consciousness. But within each chapter Aiken remained sensitive to the necessity for imposing order on the frequently fragmentary, often unclear, disconnected labyrinthian processes of Cather's mind. The problem is intensified by Cather's drunkenness, his talking to himself after Bill, his auditor, has fallen asleep, and by his dreaming. To make Cather credible, Aiken called on a variety of techniques of the emerging stream-of-consciousness novel, but he did so with an awareness of the inherent hazards. He had, for instance, earlier reviewed H. D.'s *Palimpsest* and had qualified his otherwise positive response by remarking that

> one notes again, as one always notes of the "stream of consciousness" method, that one now and then flounders a little in the fragmentary and chaotic and repetitive welter of the interior monologue. One would have preferred . . . a little more stiffening—more of the direct narrative (retrospected or vatically projected), and less of the obsessed round-and-round of the heroine's mind, which sometimes, in its endless repetitions of certain leit-motifs, goes beyond the limits of the credible, as also of the aesthetically endurable.[25]

Therefore Aiken makes a number of artistic choices in the service of clarity and unity. He maintains, for instance, a primarily third-person point of view that allows him in what is essentially another chapter of the ongoing autobiography to give himself away in a seemingly objective manner while providing fictional coherence. Aiken was extremely pleased with the contrapuntal style provided by the long dialogue between Andrew and Bill. He felt he had stumbled on a new prose form with great potential, as he wrote to Linscott:

> and now I've done 15000 words of the novel, Linsk, and all of it dialogue between two gents, no comments, plain talk, a psychoanalytical session. . . . Don't, please mention the thing to anyone, least of all the fact that it's psychoanalytic in form: the notion is too easy to bag! and it's a damned good form. Why hasn't it been done? the question and answer gives one an ideal contrapuntal medium. (1 June 1931, WUL MS.)

Of course, the third-person narration is suspended during the lengthy interior monologues, thereby giving the reader a sense of first-person verisimilitude.

Great Circle is further unified by the tragicomic tone that Aiken sustains while taking some big risks. For example, in a novel that springs from the necessity to exorcise a horrendous personal memory and that ultimately speaks to the author's most profound philosophical convictions, Aiken names his hero—struggling through an emotional purgation, "Andrew Cather," with his villain Thomas Lowell Crapo![26] Probably Aiken was drawing on what he knew Freud had said about the cathartic uses of humor in *Wit and Its Relation to the Unconscious* (translated in 1916), a work of particular interest to Aiken because of the connection Freud makes between "dream-work" and "wit-work." The novel draws heavily on wit-work. There are, for instance, a host of puns. Cather imagines a conversation between Tom and Bertha as they play the piano together: " 'We'll start at G in the second bar. Haydn duet, hide and do it' " (*CN*, 172). Aiken plays in asking, "Was this the guy that went to New York with bells on and now returns with horns?" (176), and again in the statement, "He's made his bed, let his friend lie in it" (177). Aiken also employs surrealistic humor, as he had done primarily with the Caligula allusions in *Blue Voyage*.

Andrew, for example, imagines himself having committed suicide and his doppelgänger confronting Bertha and Tom in bed and questioning them: " 'Did you both brush your teeth before you went to bed, like good little children? Papa spank. Naughty naughty. You should never, *never* go to bed without first brushing the teeth. There's a new toothbrush with black bristles, I especially recommend it for smartness, particularly in cases of mourning' " (183).

That the nearness of the subject matter to Aiken's own tragedy demanded in part this tragicomic distance is specifically suggested by Andrew's heated reply to Bertha's objection that he is treating the whole situation as a "disgusting farce." He angrily retorts that no one is more aware of the tragic implications than he is, that he has come back to a "stinking void," to a part of himself that is dead. Yet he insists, "If I want to make a joke of it, for the moment, so as to avoid cheap sentimental dramatics . . . you might at least have the intelligence to see why I do it" (194).

Again, as in *Blue Voyage*, Aiken uses the prose technique of the direct interior monologue. In chapter 3, for instance, Bill, the auditor, sleeps on and off through most of Cather's commentary and is sound asleep for the last eleven pages of the chapter. At one point he advises Andrew, " 'When you get tired of addressing yourself you can have my bed' " (272). The reader, then, moves freely through the conscious and dream minds of Cather becoming totally immersed in his psyche. The remarkable part of Aiken's extensive interior monologues is their compulsive, mesmeric effect; they are long and uninterrupted, yet they do not bore us. Aiken was aware of the possible dangers of allowing Cather's narcissism to become oppressive, remembering, no doubt, that he had suggested that H. D. "overdoes a little the interpolative method, with its interjections, qualifications, parenthetic questions, parenthetic reminiscences—one feels, in the midst of this burning subjectivism, this consuming Narcissism, that it would be a relief to come oftener upon a simple narrative statement or a connected bit of dialogue" (*ABC*, 155).

Finally, the stylistic technique that Aiken uses more imaginatively in this novel than in any other is symbolism. He draws his symbols both from the conscious levels of Cather's mind and from an elaborate dream reserve. Robert Humphrey, in

Stream of Consciousness in the Modern Novel, observed the particular psychological use of symbols in the stream-of-consciousness novel, noting that symbolization is the most elementary mental process. From simple perceptions and feelings come symbols, and this symbol-forming process, he says, precedes association or ideation. Rooted in psychological experience, this theory has been analytically explored by such contemporary philosophers as Cassirer, Whitehead, and Langer and has been documented by a host of novelists. But Humphrey points out that, contrary to much opinion, *Finnegans Wake* and *Great Circle* are the only stream-of-consciousness novels in which there is a considerable Freudian influence.[27] While Aiken uses the traditional symbol of the voyage and the personal one of the stained-glass window in *Blue Voyage*, his symbolization in the second novel is far more exhaustive, controlled, and perfected; *Great Circle* is essentially a symbolic novel.

The careful, slow evolution of a symbol can be seen in Aiken's building on the hero's having only one functioning eye, his other eye being glass. We first become aware of Cather's loss in the opening pages when Jitters Peabody casually hails him in the Harvard bar as "One-eye." But the epithet keeps playing in Andrew's mind as he thinks to himself, "And when you cry, you cry with two eyesockets, but one eye. How much had this affected Bertha? And that heartless nickname! Jesus. It was no wonder. She had probably heard of him as One-eye Cather long before she had met him. . . . Have you heard how he lost it?" (*CN*, 178). We are never to learn precisely how he did lose it, but it is hinted that it was the price he paid for spying, for seeing too much. The symbol of the lost eye is closely related to the theme of the relationship between knowing and suffering. In the long dream that opens the final chapter, Andrew meets a friend he had known at Harvard who reminds him, "We played tennis once on Soldier's Field the ball hit you in the face is that why you are blind or was it because you were looking through a peephole" (280).

As a child young Andy frequently spied on his mother and Uncle David, once rowing out to watch them through the cabin window of his uncle's motorboat. His accounts of his spying, however, move ever closer to the account Aiken gives elsewhere of spying on his parents and his subsequent anxiety about their relationship. In addition to remarks scattered throughout *Ushant* about D.'s eavesdropping, there is the account in *The Morning News* (28 February 1901, 1) of young Aiken's listening to his parents quarrel during the night preceding their deaths:

> "Conrad, his son, the lad who brought the news of the double homicide to the station house, said that his father and mother were quarreling through the night and that he heard them from his room. As the morning dawned, he heard the quarrel renewed. The sound of their voices died away at last, and there was quiet, but the lad's strained nerves kept him awake, listening breathless for the next sound that was to break upon the stillness of the morning air. It came; it was his father's voice."

Andrew as an adult can accurately recall to Bill the penalties of his painful curiosity. He remembers as a child clinging to his mother's skirts and crying at the coming of the dark. "I hear my father going to bed with my mother, hear them talking together tenderly, and in the horror of the night I become once more a crawling little inspectionist." He laments about how he had wanted to know what they were doing and saying and why they had hidden from him. He wonders whether he had a right to know or whether knowing would be less painful than imagining. "How can you decide not to know, or not to imagine? It can't be done. If you don't know, you imagine; and once you've imagined, you want to know. One of the penalties of consciousness" (*CN*, 265). Andrew's partial blindness had allowed Bill earlier to make the obvious professional comment, "None so blind as those who see and doubt it" (256).

Knowing Aiken's commitment to the theories of Freud, Jung, and Adler, Andrew's partial blindness has psychological significance in its association with the castration complex. In his *Interpretation of Dreams* (which Aiken had in his library), Freud had discussed the Oedipus complex and its relationship to the castration complex, symbolized by blindness. A clearer explanation appears in *An Outline of Psychoanalysis* (also in Aiken's library), in which Freud explains how a child entering the phallic stage becomes his mother's lover: "In a word, his early awakened masculinity makes him seek to assume, in relation to her, the place belonging to his father, who has hitherto been an envied model on account of the physical strength which he displays and of the authority in which he is clothed. His father now becomes a rival who stands in his way and whom he would like to push aside." Freud then makes the relation between castration and the Oedipus complex quite direct: "Castration has a place, too, in the Oedipus legend, for the blinding with which Oedipus punished himself after the discovery of his crime is, by the evidence of dreams, a symbolic substitute for castration."[28] Andrew, relating a dream in which his mother seems to have replaced his wife in bed, concludes: "Everyman to his own interpretation. . . . Oedipus complex, castration complex, anything you like" (CN, 256).

This particular dream merits close examination because it incorporates two more of Freud's frequently mentioned dream symbols, ladders (or stairs) and rooms, and suggests the direct use Aiken made of the psychoanalyst. Ladders, steps, staircases, or the walking up and down them represent the sexual act, according to Freud in "The Interpretation of Dreams." He also observed that in dreams "Rooms . . . are usually women; if the various ways in and out of them are represented, this interpretation is scarcely open to doubt."[29] Andrew dreamed that he and Bertha were asleep, and she woke him, insisting that they go upstairs. He followed her, and at the top of the stairs they entered a dark bedroom where there was a double bed and a single bed. Bertha walked to the single bed in which his father slept, while Andrew "crept softly into the wide bed with my mother, who was asleep. . . . Could consciousness go further in deliberate self-torture? I lay on my side, facing my sleeping mother, drew up my knees" (assuming the fetal position), and "by accident touched her flank with one of my hands." Suddenly filled with horror, he called to Bertha somewhere in the dark that he was going, and she answered, " 'Do you call this a MARRIAGE?' " (CN, 256). He then ran down the stairs and found them strewn with the family silver, which, he later confides to Bill, had been given to him by his mother. There is little wonder that *Great Circle* interested Freud!

Earlier in the novel Aiken uses the symbol of the ladder in a less detailed way to suggest Andrew's sexual imaginings. He confides to Bill that the nightmares he has been having for the last half a year are of climbing, falling, and "desperate efforts to carry monstrous loads up broken and rotten ladders, fantastic scaffoldings which fell always beneath me as I climbed—night after night" (244).

Another image that Aiken develops symbolically is the sea, which appears from *Blue Voyage* to *Ushant* as a comprehensive, pre-experiential womb state to which one longs to return. It is not inappropriate to think here in terms of the prenatal amniotic sac, because elsewhere Andrew has explained to Bill: " 'I'm always dreaming about the sea. We all know what that means, don't we? I'm going to be born again one of these days. Oh, yes, we rise again. Back to the womb, and forth once more we swim, like the mighty hero of the *Kalevala*, after nine months in submarine caves' " (245). As mentioned earlier, frequently in an Aiken novel or poem one comes up into consciousness as out of the water. Andrew, for instance, questions Bill as to whether Michelangelo ever saw the sea and whether he, too, wanted to return to it. He pays elaborate poetic tribute to the sea:

> I want the sea and the moon. Above all the sea. Did you ever think of it. Did it ever really terrify you and delight you. You know, at midnight, under a brown wild moon, with a warm south wind, and a surf running. So that the surf is all of sinister curled bronze, and the sound fills the whole damned night, and the beach looks like a parchment on which nothing has been written. Nothing. (257)

While these symbols, basically psychological or conventional, recur throughout the novel, they are not as intricately developed as two private symbols, the skeleton and the pig. Following his usual narrative pattern, Aiken introduces both these symbols casually, giving no inkling of their future development. In the dream about the Harvard Club that ends the first chapter, Andrew sees little sparrows with broken wings and bones sticking out flying off to a star "or to God," but then as he watches them with one eye

> he picked up the skeleton and began to eat it; first the feet, then working slowly up the legs; and dry going it was, what with no sauce, no mustard, no Worcestershire, and the bones getting bitterer as he crawled right up through the pelvis, devouring all, and crunched the ribs. The spine tasted like the Dead Sea, like ashes in the mouth, getting worse as he crawled nearer to the skull; and the skull itself was a black mouthful of charcoal, which he spat out. (200)

The dream then drifts off in other directions, but the skeleton symbol, set in motion, reappears throughout the novel, each time taking on incremental significance.

In the third chapter, for instance, Andrew relates a dream in which he is on a boat that comes upon a sunken ship, *Everest*, filled with precious shells, gems, and gold, a treasure trove from childhood. But when he is about to reach for some of the treasure, he is dismayed to find that it is guarded by a skeleton standing upright with a rusted musket! Andrew identifies it for Bill, saying, " 'Oh, yes, I know what it means, I daresay the old fellow is my father—' " (245), and undoubtedly drawing on Freud's insistence that the young boy, in trying to assume his father's place vis-a'-vis his mother, is thwarted by his physically dominant father. At a point in the novel when Cather is filled with self-condemnation, he tallies the price he has paid for his mother-love and identifies it as the root of all his problems: "I'm dead. I've eaten my father's skeleton and I'm dead. I shall never love again, any more than I'll ever be able to stop loving" (268).

The most complex private symbol is the crucified winged pig. The animal carries both negative and positive connotations, once again reflecting the characteristic ambivalence of the author. The symbol calls on the traditional prejudice of assuming the pig to be dirty (here equated with sexuality), but since the pig is winged, it also suggests a transcendental idealism, the secular/spiritual tension echoing *Blue Voyage*. A pig with wings, as so many of his symbols, had a specific source in Aiken's past. He remarks in "Prologue to an Autobiography" that among his earliest and fondest memories was a drawing of a pig made by his mother: "the one thing she could draw with something like verisimilitude: her one vanity, her one trick. . . . she would draw, on any scrap of paper . . . the six-cylinder pig, with the corkscrew tail, and the smiling eyes, small as buttons" (625; also *Ushant*, 37). This historical account merely reinforces the association in the novel between the pig and the mother. Just as the father was symbolically figured in the skeleton—suggesting self-constriction, sexual prohibition, and classic reserve—so also the pig is associated with the female principle. The pig, in contrast to the skeleton, is self-expansive, sexually free, and desirous of union. But the pig is also a source of guilt and anxiety for the son.

However, Cather gradually identifies himself with the pig. The first few times that Andrew equates himself with a pig, it is only by way of allusion to his sexual appetites. For instance, early in the novel, speculating on whether he has, indeed, desired Bertha's affair with Tom, he tells himself that if that were so, the affair can't really hurt him; he shouts, "Step up, ladies and gents, and see the unwoundable pig" (*CN*, 195). A few pages later he chastises himself for crying and calls again on the pig equation, but already the symbol has expanded and become more personalized; now it has wings and a glass eye: "Disgusting. Step up, ladies and gents, and see the weeping pig: the pig with wings, the pig with a glass eye. Look at the little red veins in his nose, heritage of six months' drunkenness" (196). Shortly after, in his confrontation with Bertha, she cries out at him to stop taunting her and accuses him of being heartless. Cather responds, "Step right up, ladies and gents, and see the pig without a heart" (198).

The pig symbol reappears in the rambling, revelatory third chapter, but here the pig has entered Andrew's dream consciousness where he can free associate:

> Step up, ladies and gents, and see the trained lunatic, the miching mallecho Michelangelo, the pig with wings. Here lies the winged pig, feared and befriended by many, loved and betrayed by one.[30] Why do I always dream about pigs? Last night I hit one in the snout with a walking stick—I thought he was attacking me, but it turned out I was mistaken. He merely wanted to attract my attention; but by that time I had fallen down in the mud, and my stick was dirty. (*CN*, 240)

This leads to a comical Freudian exchange between patient and analyst as Bill responds:

> —It would be. Ha, ha.
> —Don't make me laugh.
> —Anal erotic, what.
> —Scatological too. Step up and see the scatological hebephrene, watch him weep pig's tears into his snout.
> —He eats them all.
> —The pig with wings was a much smaller pig—a tiny pig, and such a little darling, as clean as clean could be. His wings were transparent and opalescent, lovely, and oh so tender—they were just unfurled, and scarcely dry, and imagine it, Bill, a dirty little bastard of a mongrel dog chose just that moment to attack him, biting at the wings! (240)

Aiken has carefully expanded the pig symbol from casual, initial referents to women—to Cather's mother and even to Bertha in her carelessness about cleanliness—to a fully integrated symbol for the dual nature of the protagonist, with his warring secular and ideal selves.

The culmination of the pig as symbol for Andrew Cather's consciousness appears naturally enough in a very detailed dream, where it exists as pure symbol freed from any reality context. Andrew has the dream following his confrontation with Bertha and Tom. He relates it the next night to Bill: " 'I will start with the simple premise of the actual and delicious dream, that one, the one of the crucified pig, my old friend the bleeding pig . . . whose wings were bitten off in childhood' " (272). In the dream Andrew is in Spain and has sent a wire to Tom and two other friends that he will join them at some familiar inn. He takes an all-night train (clearly reflective of his New York–Boston ride) and then walks a long way to the inn through the mud. He realizes then that Tom, "burly and athletic," and the others are about to leave—immediately—in order to see the beautiful waterfall by sunrise. Andrew asks them to wait for him, but they tell him that they can't; he should have his tea and come along later. But when Andrew tries to follow, he finds the route knee-deep in mud, making passage almost impossible. Significantly, a peasant tells him that if he goes into the barn up ahead and out the other side, he will find another path that will lead to the waterfall. But when he enters the gloom of the barn, he hears the most terrifying, dreadful screams of an animal in agony and sees in a dark corner, enclosed in something like a pen, the pig:

> "It was the huge naked pig—supported upright, with arms outspread, as on a cross, by a devilish machine, an affair of slowly revolving wheels and pullies, with an endless belt which was attached by steel claws to the flesh of the pig. But my God there was practically no flesh left on the pig; none, except on the breast over the heart; the belt had torn the rest away, and as I went a little closer, appalled by the screams of the pig—whose head was flung back in a final ecstasy of anguish, turned to one side, the mouth wide open—as I went a little closer, and watched the endless belt slowly moving down the red breast of the carcass, between the ribs of which I could see the entrails, the steel claws fetched away the last strip of flesh, the pig was automatically released, and with a

final scream of pain rushed out of the pen. It was nothing but a skeleton full of guts, but it was alive and sentient. Sentient. It whirled madly about the floor of the barn, driven by such a demon of suffering as compelled it to translate the consciousness of pain into the widest energy." (274)

There are undoubtedly several possible interpretations of the brutal wounding of the pig but certainly foremost among them is the tragic experience that shattered Cather's (and Aiken's) childhood. And as the pig is "compelled to translate . . . the consciousness of pain into the wildest energy," so also must Cather (and Aiken).

The pig dream continues. Andrew follows the running pig down the road and comes on a monk with a brass bell standing on a scaffolding. The pig gallops up beside the monk, who announces to the ladies and gentlemen that they are about to witness the farewell performance of the dying pig, which will first give them an example of his acrobatic prowess. After the pig goes through a stunt routine, he begins a musical performance: "Ladies and gentlemen . . . the dying pig will now play the Chinese whole-tone scale on an arrangement of coins, with his hoof" (274). Following a number of musical acts, it becomes increasingly apparent that the pig is truly dying. The monk rings the bell again and announces to the spectators that "the dying pig will now give you a demonstration of the fact that the death-agony can be transmuted into pure genius of consciousness" (274–75). Andrew cannot stand it another minute because he does not want to see the pig die, knowing full well that the pig is himself. He tries to run away and find the others, but he realizes that in the meantime he has missed seeing the waterfall by sunrise: "Christ, yes—they've seen the ideal, I've been seeing the real. Shall I go and join them—is it too late—will I be in time to see the ideal? Do I want to see the ideal? Or is it—tell me Bill—is it enough to have seen the real?" (275). Cather is surely Demarest grown older, who at the end of *Blue Voyage* realizes, one recalls, that he will have to save himself from an "art of life too fine-drawn by a bath of blood" (*CN*, 158).

Aiken finally employs the pig symbol for what resolution there is in the novel. In the final chapter, Andrew wakes from a night not as free of dreams as he had hoped, and it takes him a few minutes to remember that there is still Bertha and Tom, but that it is now past: "this blood which was now shed and lost. This wound which was now beginning to be a scar. The inevitable, and God-to-be-thanked for, cicatrix; the acceptance—but was it cowardly or was it merely wisdom—the acceptance of all of life as a scar. The pig, not crucified, perhaps, after all, but merely cicatrized" (285).

We come full circle. Andrew Cather's disillusionment, bitterness, and suffering, which had set him on a drunken, suicidal course, have been stemmed—at least momentarily. He will not be called upon to give up his life for his sins. His wound is not fatal; it will slowly cover with scar tissue, allowing him to enter the lists another day. He will be denied the waterfall at sunrise, but perhaps the waterfall is dishonest anyway; possibly the mud is more legitimate, as it is undoubtedly the seedbed for the new life of a heightened and ever-evolving consciousness.

In a spiral notebook, filled with fragmented pencil scribblings to be included in *Ushant*, Aiken has a significant note that speaks to this second novel: "Thus Great Circle ends virtually where it begins except that more items have been brought into view—if one adopts this view of art, the artist is a general, who merely receives reports from the different parts of the front, marks them down on his map—X has advanced, Y, withdrawn, Z stands still, A prepared to move. C's without support—the map once completed, all the information marked upon it, the general is ready to issue the order of the day but before he has issued it the work of—art is finished" (HHL MS. Aik 4187).

Chapter Six

THE "QUEER" BOOK
King Coffin

IN HIS DEDICATION of *King Coffin* to his uncle, Alfred Claghorn Potter, Aiken refers to his third novel as "this queer book."¹ In *Ushant*, where each of Aiken's other four novels is given an alternate title and then examined in some detail regarding the circumstances that prompted the writing of the book, its intention, and its reception, *King Coffin* is never mentioned. It is curious that this particular novel, whose strangeness most cries out for authorial comment, should be singularly omitted. When there were plans—eventually aborted—by English journalist and friend, John Davenport, to do an omnibus Aiken, *King Coffin* was the one novel he wanted to omit. Aiken tried making a special plea for the novel, suggesting it later be published alone and adding, "*That* book has had the sinister fate of becoming required reading in psychology at Harvard!"²

It is unfortunate that *King Coffin*, which explores the coldly logical and frightening ultimate extension of unmitigated, ego-dominated consciousness, should be praised or damned only as a study of a deranged mind, frequently without acknowledgment of the near-genius and utter lucidity of its hero, Jasper Ammen³—or of the fact that Aiken was working within a preconceived philosophical framework. Although Aiken himself called his hero a psychopath (in his preface to *Three Novels*), he would never agree with the *New Republic* critic who, in reviewing the *Collected Novels* in 1964, saw Ammen "in spite of the aristocratic hauteur of his mind . . . a moral monster."⁴ At the time of the original publication, the 1935 reviewer for the *New Republic* was closer to the mark when he saw the novel as "the criss-chart of a paranoid psychosis, complete with narcissism, megalomania, sexual symbols and a psychopathic inheritance, all conceived in strictly human terms and carried out on two levels with a superb, almost infallible art."⁵ The readings that dismiss

Ammen as a moral monster—and they are in the majority—fail to appreciate Aiken's own fervid sympathy with his hero and miss entirely Ammen's position in Aiken's overall exploration of the spectrum of consciousness. It is particularly for this reason that one must doubt Jay Martin's conclusion that in *King Coffin*, Aiken was playing "lightly with a serious psychological subject."[6]

It is, however, possible to draw this conclusion if one isolates *King Coffin* from Aiken's other novels and their metaphysical concerns. At the same time, if the novel must be read in conjunction with the first two novels to be fully appreciated in its widest philosophical implications, it is, perhaps, a flawed work. But it is reasonable to draw on the author's complete oeuvre to illustrate a part; there is nothing sacred about limiting one's perspective to the work at hand—assuming that at one level the work is aesthetically and organically satisfying.

King Coffin is a totally resolved novel in isolation. In many ways it is the only Aiken novel that conforms to a traditional structure. *King Coffin* has an immediately accessible plot: it is the only novel by Aiken with a table of contents listing chapter headings; significantly, it has thirteen chapters and midway—at the end of chapter 6—the hero/antihero (that is, the killer) has selected his candidate for the murder that is to be carried out by the conclusion. But beneath this conventional surface lurks the real novel. The intricacies and even quirkiness of Ammen's character are best understood within the context of Aiken's philosophical development. It is because he can be both "monster" and "angel," sometimes appearing ridiculous but often heroic, that the novel can tempt one into thinking of it as a parody of the psychological novel. But that is also why such a critical reduction seems simplistic and irresponsible, especially if one takes into consideration Aiken's relentless pursuit of the nature of consciousness. *King Coffin* illustrates a logical—but to be avoided—outgrowth of a particular extension of consciousness: the extreme development of the individual consciousness in isolation from all else.

The plot of the novel, although more dramatic than other Aiken novels, is still relatively simple: a young, particularly tall man, Jasper Ammen, is driven by a sense of superiority to assert himself through the gratuitous killing of a stranger, Karl Jones. In the end he is unable to commit the murder because, despite his firm resolution of detachment, he becomes hopelessly entangled in the life of his victim and realizes to his horror that he and the insignificant stranger are, ultimately, indistinguishable. He comes to understand that from the outset his aim had been self-destruction. By the time that Jones's wife gives birth to a stillborn infant (a metaphor for Ammen's abortive murder), Ammen has so identified with Jones that he no longer feels the necessity or the desire to kill him and instead prepares to kill himself.

Taking their cue from Ammen's soliloquies on his superior nature, the critics were quick to draw the similarities with Dostoyevsky's Raskolnikov. Jay Martin, for instance, notes the obvious parallels with *Crime and Punishment*, particularly the difference between the initial motives for the murders and the consequent actions: instead of simply killing Jones after a complete and impersonal study of him, Ammen's intent is blunted by his total immersion in the life of his victim. The comparison between Raskolnikov and Ammen is, however, one-dimensional. The formidable influences on *King Coffin* appear to be more Adler, Nietzsche, Karl Jaspers (to a lesser degree), and, as always, Aiken's own life than Dostoyevsky.

Aiken frequently acknowledged the contribution of the Viennese psychiatrist Alfred Adler to his thinking. In *Ushant*, for instance, while recalling the composition of "Punch," Aiken remarks that at the time he was writing the poem (the early 1920s), "he was . . . deep in Freud, Adler, Pfister, Ferenczi and Rank."[7] In his interview with R. H. Wilbur for the *Paris Review*, Aiken frankly admits, " 'Freud's influence—*and* along with his, that of Rank, Ferenczi, Adler, and (somewhat less) Jung was tremendous.' "[8] One of the only critics to remark on the Adlerian influence was Alfred Kreymborg, who, in *Our Singing Strength*, had high praise for Aiken despite what he saw as Aiken's ongoing disillusionment and his obsession with sex: "Kraft-Ebing, Freud, Jung, Adler, are set to music, music discovered and sung by the patient himself."[9] It is unfortunate, though, that writers such as Aiken who were interested early on in the whole revolution in psychology marking the beginning of the twentieth century were collectively labeled "Freudians" by the literary critics without any regard for the sharp and meaningful divisions, differences, quarrels, and allegiances within the psychological movement. Aiken, as we have seen, was almost always categorized as a "Freudian" in any discussion of his psychological persuasions; yet we have also seen how Aiken was sharply critical of Freudianism as a totally satisfying explanation for the nature of individual behavior. Understanding Aiken's commitment to the evolution of consciousness, one realizes that Aiken could never be reconciled with Freud's acceptance of so much of human action taking place beyond the conscious control of the individual. While critics are correct in ascribing the dominant psychological influence of Freud on *Blue Voyage* and to a lesser extent on *Great Circle*, they are at fault in not recognizing the far more important influence of Adler on *King Coffin*.

Aiken confided to his friend Houston Peterson that in 1911, when he returned to Harvard from a year abroad, he was reading all of the subversive doctrines of the psychiatrists.[10] This was a significant year in the burgeoning psychoanalytic movement, because it was then that Adler, who was developing theories at variance with those of Freud, was requested to present his findings before the Vienna Psychoanalytic Society, of which Adler was then president. His paper was met with such scorn by many members of the Society that Adler consequently resigned his office and severed his connection with Freudian psychoanalysis. The prevailing controversies among the practitioners would have been known to anyone with Aiken's interest in the movement. Further, Adler's most important works, *The Practice and Theory of Individual Psychology* (1927) and his contribution to *Psychologies of 1930*, were published just a few years before *King Coffin* (1935), at the height of Aiken's admitted enthusiasm for the new science. It is not surprising, then, to find many Adlerian premises at work in "this queer book."

First, unlike Freud who had maintained that man's behavior was primarily motivated by inborn instincts and conditioned by early influences, Adler posited that man was primarily motivated by certain social relationships. In Jasper Ammen, however, we have a protagonist who wants to deny any social relations at all, who starts from the premise that he is absolutely self-contained, who attempts—and significantly fails—to deny the necessity for any social contact whatsoever. Ammen holds all society in contempt, guaranteeing that people have only

remote, tangential connections with his life. He describes himself: "It was the Jasper who loved to keep secrets, and who
prevented his friends from becoming intimate: who had a kind
of genius for dividing up his daily life into separate depart-
ments, so that no one individual knew anything more of him
than the one department to which he had been assigned."[11]

A second Adlerian premise at work here is the insistence on
"the creative self" rather than on the self as a sum total of
primarily inborn instincts. Adler saw the self as a "highly
personalized, subjective system which interprets and makes
meaningful the experiences of the organism." Even more directly relevant to *King Coffin*, the Adlerian self "searches for
experiences which will aid in fulfilling the person's unique style
of life; if these experiences are not to be found in the world, the
self tries to create them."[12]

Related to this premise and important for an understanding
of *King Coffin* is a third Adlerian contention, the emphasis on
the uniqueness of the individual personality. Aiken, who had
long been a particular admirer of William James and the importance he placed on the individual, surely welcomed this direction in psychoanalytical thought. As early as *Blue Voyage* he had
been stressing the significance and uniqueness of the individual
consciousness. We also see in *Great Circle*, Cather/Aiken's annoyance with a Freudian predilection to label specific behaviors
rather than to see the whole individual ("Oh, damn you amateur analysts and all your pitiful dirty abstract jargon" [*CN*,
261]). Equally annoying is the drawing of facile, predictable
behavior links: "I say sweetheart to you, and you reply, brightly,
mother. I say drawers, and you say diapers. I say whisky, and
you say breast" (266).

Finally, Aiken applauded Adler's insistence on consciousness
as the center of personality, thus making him a forerunner in
the development of an ego-oriented psychology. Adler saw the
individual as ordinarily aware of the reasons for his behavior,
which placed him in opposition to Freud, who had made
consciousness subservient to the all-powerful unconscious.
Man's awareness of his uniqueness and of his apparent control
over his destiny is suggested often by Aiken through Ammen's
interior monologues. Ammen contemplates the pleasures of
personal alienation:

> He looked round him with a sharp sense of relief and detachment, he felt alone and tall and superior amongst the disorderly crowd of nocturnal pedestrians, and almost indeed as if he belonged to a different race or species; and as he stood still by the corner, observing first one face and then another . . . it occurred to him that a cat must feel something like this: a cat alone in a cellar, sitting . . . and watching the naive and unconscious antics of mice. (310)

At the same time, Adler's theories led him to deemphasize the role played by sex in the individual's behavior, further separating him from Freud. Jasper Ammen, unlike William Demarest and Andrew Cather, who are tormented by their vigorous sexual drives, barely has a sexual existence at all.[13] His is a nearly monastic, cerebral personality. Ammen stretches his credibility when he suggests to Gerta, the young woman with whom he has a relationship, that she find her sexual satisfaction in Sandbach, a mutual acquaintance whom Ammen holds in particular contempt. " 'The strong individual,' " Jasper tells Gerta, " 'makes his own laws, you make yours and I make mine, at this point we agree that you shall go to Sandbach so as to leave us free from this sex thing and free to co-operate in something new' " (CN, 318). Ammen concludes that this freedom will alleviate any personal pressure between them: "the relation could be calm, sexless, cerebral: the other aspect or possibility would be once and for all removed" (315–16).

Then, too, Adler insisted on what he called "fictional finalism." He argued that most individuals are highly goal-directed, that they are motivated by certain expectations of the future and live their daily lives in an awareness of these. In a central essay, "Individual Psychology," which he contributed to *Psychologies of 1930*, Adler made this point quite explicit:

> This was a further contribution of individual psychology to modern psychology in general—that it insisted absolutely on the indispensability of *finalism* for the understanding of all psychological phenomena. No longer could causes, powers, instincts, impulses and the like serve as explanatory principles, but the final goal alone. Experiences, traumata, sexual-development mechanisms could not yield us an explanation, but the perspective in which these had been regarded, the individual way of seeing them, which subordinates all life to the ultimate goal.[14]

All of *King Coffin* is a playing out of Jasper Ammen's "fictional finalism," the goal of murdering someone as an exhibition of pure superiority, of dynamic assertion of self—murder without the baser motives such as theft, jealousy, or anger. Those who miss this point, as many critics have, and read the novel with the same expectations that they bring to a conventional detective story are as sorely disappointed as those who read *Blue Voyage* anticipating a shipboard romance. Such a critic was the anonymous reviewer of *The Collected Novels* for *Time*, who concluded that in *King Coffin* "a paranoid ponders a murder for a hundred pages and then decides not to commit it."[15] Ammen's decision not to kill his victim comes as no great surprise to serious readers of the Aiken canon. The projected killing had always seemed more intellectual than visceral.

A final premise of Adlerian theory coloring Aiken's novel is the awareness that man's personality is characterized by feelings of superiority and/or inferiority. It is to Adler that we owe the terms *superiority* and *inferiority complexes*. The psychiatrist is convinced that the individual is driven by a desire to be superior:

> I began to see clearly in every psychological phenomenon the striving for superiority. It runs parallel to physical growth and is an intrinsic necessity of life itself. It lies at the root of all solutions of life's problems and is manifested in the way in which we meet these problems. All our functions follow its direction. They strive for conquest, security, increase, either in the right or in the wrong direction. The impetus from minus to plus never ends. The urge from below to above never ceases. Whatever premises all our philosophers and psychologists dream of—self-preservation, pleasure principle, equalization—all these are but vague representations, attempts to express the great upward drive.[16]

While the average person will strive to achieve superiority through generally acceptable means—basically socially acceptable means—the psychopath will not be bound by these parameters.

Ammen is adamant about his superiority. Frequently he removes himself from other people by thinking of them in animal metaphors, referring to them as mice, rats, and sometimes monkeys. Separated from his family—and with a bow to

Freud—Ammen hates his father, a Chicago capitalist authority figure who grudgingly provides him with an allowance out of a promise made to his dying mother. Ammen also dismisses the anarchist group to which he briefly belonged as lacking any individually superior people. He abhors their foolish groupiness: "Amateurs, you are all sickening little amateurs, not one of you has any guts, not one of you would have the guts to act alone, to take any risk by yourselves. . . . No brains, no pride. Just rats. You go round together like rats" (*CN*, 309).

One further recognizes in Ammen's metaphors a contempt for political systems that disregard the sacredness of the individual and that subordinate the one to the all. Ammen here shares a nineteenth-century vitalism with such literary figures as Lawrence and Melville—both of whom Aiken admired—but Ammen's specific political views are as reductive as is his need to isolate himself.[17] He sees his pure act of murder, in large part, as emanating from the necessity to extricate himself from a weak and inferior group: "He was going to *do* something, he must *do* something, there must be the final action by which he would have set the seal on his complete freedom. To escape the company of rats, to express the profundity of his contempt—to *kill* a rat——!" (*CN*, 309).

The most detailed metaphorical expression of Ammen's "fictional finalism" is the scene in which Ammen is standing still in the canyon of Beacon Street looking at a crowd of people—those contemptible fellow mortals loitering in front of the store windows—and mentally transforms his pipe stem into a machine gun and takes aim. Ammen has moved from an intellectual disdain for humanity to a shrill, vicious hatred. It is a devastatingly imaginative slaughter:

> The stupid backs were cut in two by death's mechanical rattle-snake chatter, the plate glass window was drilled shrilly from side to side, the falling glass made an irregular tinkling and chiming, and then everything was again silent. It was toward a group of dead men that he crossed the street, it was a group of corpses that he joined before the window, and looking over the heads he saw that the window had been turned into a little zoo, it was a cage of monkeys. A dozen little grey monkeys, with long ratlike tails, skipped, sat, or swung, stared sadly, peered out of kennels, or made rapid circuits of the interior, scarcely seeming to touch floor, wall, trapeze or platform in their soundless flight. Close to the window, in the foreground,

oblivious of the onlookers, one of them picked with fastidious little black fingers at the posterior of another, and tasted what he found: the crowd laughed obscenely, face turned grinning toward grinning face, their animal blood thickened and darkened. (314)

There is to Ammen's sphere of superiority, however, a natural concomitant that Adler has not addressed—loneliness. At first Ammen delights in his alienation, but he gradually edges toward paranoia. After Gerta leaves him one afternoon, "he suddenly ha[s] a strange feeling of loneliness" that moves rapidly toward panic and psychotic projection: "Yes, they all wanted to kill him, everyone really wanted to kill everyone else, to be immersed in a crowd was to be immersed in a world of enemies" (369). As the novel develops, Ammen becomes increasingly lonely and, as Aiken observes, "finds himself at the end, trapped in his own hate, and [realizes] too late that his hatred was really an inverted love."[18]

Aiken's exploration of Jasper Ammen's isolation strongly suggests the influence of Nietzsche, himself a profoundly lonely man. Just as Ammen finds that his superiority necessarily alienates him from the masses, so also Zarathustra found that his emphasis on individuality necessarily led to separateness—although it also made possible the evolution of a superman. Houston Peterson tells us that between 1911 and 1912, during his senior year at Harvard, Aiken read Nietzsche for the first time. Reading *Beyond Good and Evil*, *Thus Spake Zarathustra*, and *Ecce Homo*, he was "tremendously moved by the whole destructive attack."[19] Aiken's personal library, now part of the Huntington Library collection, includes the second and third editions of *Beyond Good and Evil*, as well as *The Case of Wagner*, *Nietzsche Contra Wagner*, *Selected Aphorisms*, *We Philologists*, *Human All-Too Human: A Book for Free Spirits*, and two editions of *Thus Spake Zarathustra*. Nietzsche, with his singular respect for the power of individual thought, would have understood Aiken's resistance to Freud's implication that the individual is primarily the sum total of his inborn instincts. Zarathustra's egoism, for example, comes from this life, this world, the individual "star" who can rise above the masses. Similarly, Ammen assures himself that "egoism is the essence of the noble soul, every star is a similar egoist, I revolve like Nietzsche proudly amongst my proud equals" (*CN*, 315).

Aiken is selective in drawing on Nietzsche to inform the character of Ammen. There is, first, the limitlessness of one's mind; that is, the thinkability of all things; second, the importance of pure evil; third, the necessity for taking action; and finally, speculation on the nature of time with particular reference to eternal recurrence. Ammen, acutely conscious of his own consciousness and thus of his superiority, gives full reign to his imagination, to the thinking of the wildest possible thoughts. Merely walking toward the subway amid the rush of the morning commuters, he can delight in his own mind: "conscious of his great height, and conscious of his consciousness," which was the "real and unspoiled secret: an immense sense of wealth, a multitude of treasure, into which one merely needed to thrust an exploring hand" (334). In his random thoughts, Ammen can think about so bizarre an idea as throwing a coffin party to celebrate his own suicide, complete to the invitations: "Mr. Jasper Ammen requests the pleasure of your company at a coffin party——!" In a section of *Zarathustra* entitled "On Self-Overcoming," Nietzsche had posited that possibly the only way that the superior man might make the world more acceptable was through thinking impossible thoughts: "A will to thinkability of all being: this *I* call your will. You want to *make* all being thinkable, for you doubt with well-founded suspicion that it is already thinkable. . . . You still want to create the world before which you can kneel."[20] The first step toward creating such a world is to think such a world. Ammen admits that one of the roles he enjoys playing in society is that of the "thinker," the part of the poet "detached, remote, inscrutable: the Zarathustrian prophet." On Ammen's living room wall there is a mask of Nietzsche.

Ammen shares with Nietzsche a belief in the value of evil, but, unlike Nietzsche, he erroneously makes evil and hate synonymous. When Zarathustra says, "For evil is man's best strength," he is praising the power and purity of real conviction—even the conviction of evil. He insists that great wickedness is preferable to weakness, because in evil's strength there is energy.

Whereas in the beginning Ammen expresses himself philosophically in terms echoing *Beyond Good and Evil* ("And in a world of unrealities, how could there be rights or wrongs or obligations? or injuries or thefts?" [*CN*, 306]), he ends, destroyed by the absence of human contact, by expressing a doctrine of hate. He assures Toppan, a fellow student, that the "essential thing in life is hate." But at the time he is telling Toppan this—early in the novel—the hate is still merely talk, a philosophical pose, an intellectual exercise. Gradually Ammen's hate moves to a personal hatred of particular individuals. He hates Sandbach, who heads the local anarchist group and who is in love with Gerta. Although Ammen, too, probably loves her, he can't separate Gerta from the rest of vermin humanity and thereby love her; but he is unhappy relegating her to the unthinking masses. Ammen, intellectually, would respond with Nietzsche: "Will free spirits live with women? In general, I believe that, as the true-thinking, truth-speaking men of the present, they must, like the prophetic birds of ancient times, prefer *to fly alone.*"[21] Consequently Ammen's idealistic hate here descends to fairly prosaic jealousy, although he assures Gerta to the contrary: " 'Incidentally, don't think any part of my hatred of S is jealousy. It's not. He's not the only one—I hate them all, the whole damned crowd. There isn't a soul in this city that I wouldn't willingly kill, they're all alike' " (*CN*, 319).

It is also on Nietzsche that Aiken appears to be drawing for Ammen's insistence on the singular importance of action. One must not be content with the thinkability, then, of all things—including the importance of pure evil—but one must act on one's speculations. His insistence on performance is one of the ways that Ammen originally separated himself from the anarchist group that sits around chatting about manifestos, propaganda, and founding and reviving such publications as *The Voice of the People*. Contrary to such idle, philosophical amusements, Ammen goes about choosing an actual victim and stalking him with the absolute intention of killing him.

Again one finds parallels to Nietzsche's meditations on time, on the importance of the present time over the past, and on recurrence. Ammen is clock-conscious even as he meditates on worlds out of time. Early on he assumes that his pure act of murder somehow exists out of the world of time and, further, that Karl Jones, by virtue of being murdered, will achieve immortality. The whole act, then, becomes, in a peculiar way, consecrated; religious idioms circle about it; it moves into the empyrean. Immediately after Ammen has decided on this method for demonstrating his superiority over the creatures about him—that is, by the conscious act of murdering one of them—he feels a great sense of relief that seems to promise him a strange exit from the world of time:

> And there was now, all of a sudden, plenty of time—for with the sense of relief had also come a curious alteration of his sense of hurry—as if the hurry need no longer be transacted eternally, but could become, and without pressure, *concentric*, an affair of his own, a mere matter of revolving within or around himself. . . . Between his own world and the world outside, a peculiar division had now arrived, and if time still existed importantly for himself, it had no longer any important existence elsewhere: in his own kingdom of thought, he could move as rapidly as he liked, stay as long as he liked, the outside world would meanwhile stand still, and he could rejoin it whenever he wished, and exactly at the point at which he had left it. (310)

But Ammen has no illusions about the necessity of the killing taking place in this time and in this place: "Once the weapon had been aimed, one could not delay indefinitely the pulling of the trigger; there must necessarily be a limit to the time during which one merely observed, from a distance, and for whatever satisfaction, one's quarry" (344). As the subtle identification of himself with his victim begins and killer and prey merge, Ammen, understandably, wants to slow time down: "It was as if abruptly he had stepped out of time into timelessness: what need could there be, any longer, for hurry? Jones was not only *there*, he was *here*: Jones had joined him, had joined his life: it was almost, in fact, as if Jones had become part of his own '*self*' " (362). As Ammen comes to realize more clearly that he himself is the real victim, the desire to kill Jones correspondingly abates. Ammen even tries to convince himself that the killing need not take place in the world of time at all, that "an action could have the purity of a work of art. It could be as abstract and absolute as a problem in algebra" (363). Yet he cannot fool himself into thinking that there was not originally the necessity for an actual—not an imagined—murder.

But Ammen continues to think of the murder as taking place out of finite time and out of real space because only in this way can it be distinguished from a mere vulgar homicide. Toward the evening of the first day, when Ammen has arbitrarily singled out Karl Jones—ascending from the subway—as his victim, he imagines the necessary culmination of his deed: "before nightfall a new and terrible circle would have been drawn. At the center of it, Jones was beginning to be immortal, beginning to be still" (349). The act is justified, almost sanctified, by its removal from the natural world and by its being in harmony with the cosmic order, existing at the still center.

Ammen anonymously sends Jones a complimentary ticket to the theater, goes to observe him close up, and begins to feel—as he increasingly will—the growing kinship with his ritualistic victim. But always hovering unpleasantly about this immortal act is the real world, with actual events measured in minutes and hours. For instance, when Ammen drives to the cemetery in the heavy rain to watch the interment of Jones's stillborn baby, he is intensely aware of every noise made by the car, the tires, the windshield wipers, the key ring clicking against the dashboard, and even the ticking of his wristwatch. In Aiken's attempt to make concrete the abstraction of time in motion, he makes effective use of film diction: "time made intensely audible, time made visible, time solidified in a concrete series of individual shapes—a slow-motion of time, almost in fact a 'still.' As if, at a given moment, one could take a cross-section of the universe, or slow down life itself to the point at which it was only once removed from death" (408).

Finally, *King Coffin* echoes Nietzsche's early speculations on the eternal recurrence of all things—that is, stated briefly, the doctrine that everything is ultimately recurring, and life is not forever new: "Everything goes, everything comes back."[22]

Recurrence works structurally as well as thematically in *King Coffin*. In the final chapter, prior to attending as voyeur the burial of Jones's child and preparing for his own suicide, Jasper Ammen, the totally self-sufficient individual, goes on an inexplicable impulse to St. Paul's Church. He arrives in time to hear the morning Angelus with its significant phrases, "blessed is the fruit of thy womb, Jesus" and "Holy Mary mother of God, pray for us now and at the hour of our death. Amen." On one level, Ammen's sensibilities are offended by the seeming carelessness of the service; on a deeper level, he is bothered by some disconcerting, haunting sensation. It is only on leaving the church that Ammen suddenly remembers that he had also gone to St. Paul's on the very morning that he had chosen Jones as his victim ("the thing shocked him"). Momentarily he thinks back over all that has happened:

> But more curious still was the fact that today, of all days, he should *again* have the impulse to go there. This was very peculiar, it had about it the air as of a compulsory completion of some obscure sort, like a forced move in chess. The idea had occurred to him casually, no doubt, but could he be sure that it had occurred without some deep reason? Its queer appropriateness—the appropriateness of the whole thing, the scene, the service, the words themselves—suggested a kind of *rootedness* in the pattern which it would be painful to investigate. (*CN*, 407)

Thematically, the doctrine of recurrence here touches on several ideas central to the novel. The Angelus commemorates the birth of Christ, but implied in the Annunciation is the Crucifixion. As with each of us, the ultimate death of Jones's baby occurred simultaneously with its birth. And Ammen, who opens the novel as the superior being, seeking a victim, becomes, by the end of the novel, one with his victim. He becomes one of the inferior beings "who wants to be killed." It is only fitting, then, that Ammen, the murderer, should be preparing to murder himself in the final pages of the novel. The passage between life and death, Aiken suggests, is cyclical, not terminal. Perhaps, too, in Jones's original emergence from the subway, he is symbolically coming from the dead, being born into yet another death.

· · ·

A scholar perceptive enough to appreciate Nietzsche early on as a serious philosopher was the Christian existentialist Karl Jaspers. In 1935, the year that *King Coffin* was published, when most other philosophers were still categorizing Nietzsche primarily as a poet or a prophet and not as a systematic thinker to be seriously regarded, Jaspers wrote a monumental study entitled *Nietzsche: An Introduction to the Understanding of His Philosophical Activity*. Considering his interest in Nietzsche, no doubt Aiken would have been familiar with the work of Jaspers. In addition, there was much in Jaspers's own Protestant existential philosophy that would have struck correspondent chords in Aiken. In 1931, appalled by the increasingly dehumanizing effects of the postindustrial world, Jaspers wrote a seminal study, *Man in the Modern Age*. This work, translated into English in 1933, just two years before *King Coffin* was published, defines a "true" hero in terms peculiarly applicable to Jasper Ammen:

> He rejects the lure of doing what all can do and what everyone will approve, and he is unperturbed by resistance and disapproval. With steady gait, he follows his chosen path. This path is a lonely one, for the dread of calumny and of arrogant disapproval compels most persons to do what will please the crowd. Few are equal to the task of following their own bent without obstinacy and without weakness, of turning a deaf ear to the illusions of the moment, of maintaining without fatigue or discouragement a resolution once formed. In view of the impossibility of self-content, the invisibility of one's own being can hope for an unverifiable affirmation only in its Transcendence.[23]

One must draw any parallels here between Jaspers and Aiken with large brush strokes, keeping ever in mind the essential differences between one's existential Christian hero and the other's potential murderer. But the motivation of discontent with modern society's dehumanization and the simultaneous hope for salvation through the strong individual prompts one to see comparisons. Ammen's intention, although the form it took for manifesting itself was extreme, is similarly prompted and essentially as noble. In *Man in the Modern Age*, Jaspers saw clearly how the "universalization of the life-order" was threatening to reduce the life of the "real man" in a "real world to a mere functioning in the void."[24] He saw the modern world as a process of reducing individuality to conformity. Aiken was equally appalled by the signs of the times that he saw about him, and his character Jasper Ammen is almost a hyperbolic alarm calling attention in the mid–1930s to the grave dangers of universal conformity.

Finally, Aiken's characters are usually given names that carry multiple meanings. We saw this with Aiken's two earlier heroes, Demarest and Cather, and there is no reason to suspect that this is not similarly true of Karl Jones and Jasper Ammen. The "Jones," of course, is common, as in Aiken's short story "Smith and Jones." Seeing it stenciled on the door, Ammen is excited that it is the name of the stranger he has tracked from the subway to his office. He thinks the name too good to be true:

"The anonymous one, the abstract one, the mere Speciman Man—it would be perfect" (*CN*, 341). I would posit, therefore, that Ammen's name was suggested by Karl Jaspers and that, further, Aiken then gave Jasper Ammen's victim Karl Jaspers's initials and first name, "Karl Jones," thereby subtly suggesting the ultimate oneness of murderer and victim (as the chapter heading intimates, "The Stranger Becomes Oneself").

. . .

While the psychological and philosophical speculations of Adler, Nietzsche, and Jaspers significantly inform the foreground of *King Coffin*, the autobiography of Aiken shadows the background. In part, *King Coffin* is Aiken's response to the contemporary insistence that artists speak to the political realities of the day—from the breadlines in the streets of America to the possibility of salvation through an international commune. While far less important to the novel than are the broader arguments over the philosophy of individualism and the individual hero, the political system is the narrative frame on which *King Coffin* is stretched. Sandbach, Toppan, Gerta, and Ammen are originally brought together because they are all Boston members of an anarchist party. Their group is the small, struggling type common throughout America in the 1930s: the few intense young writers, the wizened bookstore lady, the earnest students, the amateur psychoanalyst, "smelly young women and unwashed young men" (315). Ammen belonged to the organization for two years before he dramatically severed his connection and began treating the group mercilessly. The several pages that Aiken devotes to describing this ineffectual political cell are filled with such passionate denunciation that one suspects it is surely as much apolitical Aiken as Ammen lashing out against the uselessness of the group: "the lesbians and pansies, the endless pseudo-intellectual talk, the indiscriminate alcoholic amorousness" (315). Aiken's annoyance with the inaction of radical American political groups in the 1930s will appear again in his last novel, *Conversation*, in which the narrator explains another character's motives for stealing: "The stealing is only an idea, a protest—he's an anarchist and unlike most anarchists he practices what he preaches—doesn't believe in trade for profit or in property being used for profit by barter. And so he steals merely in order to redistribute goods which he thinks are unjustly divided" (*CN*, 484).

A corrective to this impatient view of the revolutionary movement in America in the 1930s is available in Malcolm Cowley's
fine article "A Remembrance of the Red Romance." In this
article Cowley writes sympathetically of these same small cell
meetings in which the artist was always a somewhat alien figure,
strongly motivated to support the poor and the weak by what
were often fairly ineffective methods.[25] Cowley writes in detail
of the formation of the League of Professional Groups in the fall
of 1932, an organization that subsequently drew up a statement
of support for the national candidacy of Communists William
Z. Foster and James W. Ford. The statement was signed by fifty-
three of the most important writers of the day, including Cowley, Theodore Dreiser, Sherwood Anderson, John Dos Passos,
and Edmund Wilson, among others. Conspicuously missing
was the signature of Conrad Aiken, who a few months earlier,
at the height of this political activity, had sailed for England for
the thirteenth time since his freshman year at Harvard in 1907.

Significantly, in the same year that Aiken published *King
Coffin*, he publicly justified his nonparticipation in all politics
(literary as well as national) in a long article, "A Plea for
Anonymity." He particularly abhorred the public's assault on
the writer's privacy and—what is even more relevant—he specifically saw the public's demand to *know* the artist related to
communistic and fascistic politics. The stridency of Aiken's
remarks in "A Plea for Anonymity" brings Ammen to mind:

> The public wants to find that [the writer] is just an ordinary fellow
> like themselves, has foibles and weaknesses and human traits,
> lectures badly, has a sense of humor, and in short *is not superior*.
> That is the important thing; in that, they tame him and feel that
> they can accept him, they paw him to receive him. In other words,
> the women's clubs and literary "gangs" who invite him to meetings
> are simply doing, in a more superficial way, precisely what the
> Communists or other political sects are trying to do: inviting, or
> compelling, the artist to undertake an *immediate* fulfillment of what
> they conceive to be his social contract, which means not his obliga-
> tion to the past and future of man, but his obligation to themselves
> at that exact moment.[26]

Behind their actions is their "unconscious and merciless" desire
to reduce him to their level.

Aiken passionately feared any individual falling prey to the
group; he himself strongly resisted joining anything his entire

life. His sympathies were with Nietzsche: "He who thinks much is not suited to be a party member: too soon he thinks himself through and beyond the party."[27] Aiken lamented, "The individual is being submerged, the clear notion of his value to society precisely *as* a non-conformist is being lost."[28] Thus, in part, *King Coffin* was a fictionalized personal protest against the political pressures of the 1930s. In *Ushant*, Aiken writes about the long and often angry political arguments he had had with Malcolm Lowry ("Hambo" in the autobiography), once again emphasizing his own political diffidence:

> Hambo had drifted pretty far, politically, toward something like communism: he had been through something like a social conversion, and clearly felt a need for some sort of fraternal joining and belonging: and D.'s and Lorelei's more abstract political views were not calculated to make him happy. It was true that D. had once voted for Debs, and that he had twice, too, voted for his great liberal cousin [Franklin Delano Roosevelt]; but he had never found it possible to take more than a casual and superficial interest in practical politics, viewing it, as he did, as inevitably a passing phase, and probably a pretty primitive one, and something, again, that the evolution of consciousness would in its own good season take care of. Revolutions were a waste both of time and human material;— you lost a hundred or more years only to find yourself just where you'd begun. (351)

Predictably, at a time when writers in general were never more politically active in America, Aiken—like Jasper Ammen—was listening to a different drummer.

But the futility of politics is not the only autobiographical dimension of this novel. Curiously, *King Coffin*—because of the profile of the protagonist—is usually and erroneously considered to be free of autobiography. For instance, in his *New York Times* review, Frederick Crews remarked that it was only in *King Coffin* that "Aiken for once gives us a protagonist who is not a slightly altered version of himself." In her dissertation, Mary Rountree insisted that "*King Coffin* alone among Conrad Aiken's five novels stands at a far remove from his personal experience. Except for details reflecting his student life at Harvard, Aiken's third novel cannot be considered in any way autobiographical."[29] Certainly Jasper Ammen, as he is introduced in the first chapter—tall, full head of dark hair—in "the prime assurance of his youth, in the fresh arrogance of his wisdom, and power in wisdom, with a sense of extreme handsomeness" is all that the young Aiken thought he was not. Though Demarest and Cather often looked long and hard into their reflections in the mirror, it was to plumb the mysteries of the face before them, never to admire it. But Ammen would stop at a hotel restroom primarily to admire himself in the mirror: "the fine forehead and the extraordinary eyes of the man who had now so clearly and calmly seen to the end of a human life: King Coffin" (*CN*, 342).

While clearly not as immediately apparent, this "queer book" is yet another chapter in the ongoing autobiography. Aiken, who had long harbored a fear of inherited insanity, introduces the character of Kay, Jasper's younger brother, who had gone progressively insane, to determine the fine line between the pure act and the insane act (in *Ushant*, one of Aiken's brothers is given the name "K"; Aiken had a sibling named Kempton). Aiken uses Kay to illustrate Jasper's (as well as his own) early insatiable mania to know everything by spying on people and recording his findings. As a boy, Jasper had kept photographs of Kay at different stages of his mental breakdown. He had read all the doctors', psychiatrists', and teachers' reports on him. He had observed Kay deteriorate from "the age of three, the sharp-eyed sharp-faced child who gazed with such burning intelligence over the back of the gilt-knobbed chair, ending with the fat and sleepy and stupid face of twenty-seven, from which all awareness of reality had suddenly faded" (307–8). Aiken also uses Kay as a foil to Jasper: Kay's madness, unlike Jasper's, is the medically identifiable type.

In an early discussion with Jasper about his grand plan, Gerta suggests that there is an element of insanity about it. Jasper sharply retorts: " 'You're thinking of Kay. But purity is not insanity' " (319). Yet the suggestion by Gerta that Jasper feels he must vehemently deny is obviously never very far from his own mind. When, for instance, his plan is nearing its conclusion and the murder is imminent, Jasper—after justifying it all once again to himself—looks in his bathroom mirror and is startled by his resemblance to Kay: "He repeated softly the word *shadow*, to watch the movement of his lips, drew the tip of a finger across an eyebrow, as if merely for contact with the bold image which seemed so haughtily to keep its distance, considered for a moment the resemblance of the forehead to Kay's"

(373). And, in his final letter to Gerta, written just before his planned suicide, he speculates on the possibility of a familial derangement: " 'Is it the shadow of Kay, and were you right after all?' " (412).

In his pamphlet, *Conrad Aiken*, Reuel Denny has pointed out that Aiken was aware of the presence of petit mal in his family background.[30] We know, too, that the marriage of Aiken's father and mother was a marriage of cousins.[31] Further, Aiken knew that the official explanation for his mother's murder and his father's suicide was his father's terrible fear of going insane and that, consequently, his wife would have him committed. As the *Savannah Morning News* sensationally headlined the story, "Consumed by the Mad Belief His Wife Wished to Have Him Forcibly Confined in an Asylum for the Insane, Frenzied by the Dread Nightmare of Dementia, Dr. Aiken Shot and Killed His Wife, Then Fired a Second Bullet Through His Brain—On a Single Subject He'd Been Insane a Year—Twice Attempted Suicide."[32] Finally, Elizabeth, Aiken's only sister, spent her long life in an insane asylum.

Everything in Aiken's life seemed to have to be written about, to be experienced again in order for him to move beyond it. He appears to have had a compulsion to put it all down on paper as accurately as fiction would tolerate. Aiken acknowledged in the interview with R. H. Wilbur for the *Paris Review* that "Silent Snow, Secret Snow" had been " 'a projection of my own inclination to insanity.' "[33] Surely Aiken's fear of madness urged a narrative exorcism in *King Coffin*.

A final biographical parallel in this novel is the specific manner in which Jasper Ammen attempts suicide:

> he went into the kitchenette, looked down at the gas-stove, returned to the sitting-room to make sure that the window was open, and to pick up the little green book from the table. Then he went back to the kitchenette, closed the door behind him, turned on all four taps of the stove, and sat down at the table with the book.
> The gas behind him made a steady *sh-h-h-h-h-h, sh-h-h-h-h-h*, soft and insistent, and opening the book he started reading—(all the while conscious of the little watch ticking on his wrist, the tiny hand creeping slowly towards eleven)—the page at which he had left off. (*CN*, 414)

We know that gas was one of the several methods by which Aiken's father had attempted suicide. The *Savannah Morning*

News reported that Dr. Aiken once made a serious attempt to kill himself with an overdose of drugs, and that later he "attempted to end his own life and that of his wife by turning on the gas in their room" (28 February 1901). Aiken's own aborted suicide had been by gas. The correspondence to Ammen's attempt is quite precise. Just as Ammen's impulse is to read while awaiting his death, so Aiken had chosen to read Wyndham Lewis's satirical attack on political journalism as he awaited the end: "And, therefore, Lorelei Two having gone off for the evening to the cinema so that she would be absent for more time than he would require for his purpose, and after a cheerful, but for once quite moderate, offering to the god, he had sat himself down to read Wyndham Lewis, under the electric light in the little subterranean kitchen, with the gas-rings and gas oven fizzing softly behind him" (*Ushant*, 226). It would seem, then, that *King Coffin* was no exception to Aiken's relentless exploration of his own life through his fiction, even though ostensibly Jasper Ammen stands far removed from Conrad Aiken.

· · ·

All these forces complement and expand the main theme of *King Coffin*, which is the single dominant theme of Aiken's entire canon: understanding the nature and dimensions of consciousness. *King Coffin*, although first giving the appearance of being a maverick novel—and being consistently considered as such by the critics—is clearly in the mainstream of the Aiken canon. One is forced to plumb the depths of one's own consciousness. Knowing, however, that one is actively pursuing a different and expanded level of consciousness often leads into terrible traps, one of the most dangerous being—as demonstrated in *King Coffin*—that this awareness of superiority, which is itself good, may tempt one into total egocentricity, which is itself evil. Aiken had already tentatively explored this particular aspect of consciousness, as was his pattern, in a number of short stories, including "Smith and Jones" and "No, No, Go Not to Lethe."[34] The parallels between *King Coffin* and the latter story are so obvious that Jay Martin has suggested that it was for this reason that Aiken omitted the story from his *Collected Short Stories*.[35] But it is substantially inaccurate to equate S. Pierce Babcock, the priggish English teacher and the protagonist of the short story, with Jasper Ammen. It is true that they share the desire to pry mercilessly into the lives of others, thereby gaining power over them, but for Babcock this is more an indulgent, idle curiosity than the necessary step in a philosophical process that it is for Ammen.[36] In addition, Babcock is such a one-dimensional character, merely a mouthpiece for an idea, that we feel no real sympathy with him when he—like Ammen—discovers too late that he is in love with his victim, Mary Anthony. She—like Gerta—had once been in love with Babcock but fled from him when she realized how she had been victimized. In writing the novel, Aiken wisely substituted a male victim, thereby avoiding any romantic confusion in his protagonist's psychological experiment or anything that might deprive the murder of its purity. There are, however, close parallels between Ammen's desire to know Karl Jones and Babcock's insatiable curiosity about Mary Anthony's every move:

> Gently, slowly, delicately, insidiously, he had wormed his way through her guard; his awareness had surrounded her completely; he saw himself as a kind of psychological octopus; a vampire; taking no *personal* interest in her, never for a moment allowing an atom of his own feelings to become involved, he had nevertheless attached himself to her with an exhausting completeness, and had, for her, assumed an exhausting importance. (*CSS*, 433)

Finally, though, Babcock's preoccupation is with his own power, his own ego as a luxurious end in itself.[37] While Ammen is aware of his own egocentricity and examines its inherent dangers throughout the novel, Babcock only comes to such a realization in a flash at the very end of the story.

In a less obviously relevant short story, "Smith and Jones," Aiken also grapples with the realization that an expanded consciousness has its liabilities—that is, in moving so far into the contemplation of consciousness, one risks becoming all cerebral, stripped of sensitivity to emotions, to humanity, to the attractions of the corporeal world. In the aptly titled "Smith and Jones," Aiken explores this particular aspect of Jasper Ammen, the two sides of the symbolic man that reflect the two dominant drives: the intellectual and the physical, or, expressed another way, the beautiful and the obscene. Early in this compelling short story, it becomes apparent that the two men, Smith and

Jones—who are walking in the countryside on a rainy evening—
are two sides of the same individual. Smith is the physical drive,
with the "morals of a snake," and Jones is the intellectual drive,
"all brains to the soles of [his] feet." It has been previously
agreed that cerebral Jones is to kill sensual Smith by the end of
the evening. But as they walk and talk, Smith has all the good
lines. He has observed that in life few things are simple or pure;
it is never simply a matter of the superiority of mind over body.
He explains:

> "We like and dislike at the same time. It's like an organism with a
> malignant fetid cancer growing in it. Cut out the cancer, which has
> interlaced its treacherous fibers throughout every part, and you
> extinguish life. What's to be done? In birth, love, and death, in all
> acts of violence, all abrupt beginnings and abrupt cessations, one
> can detect the very essence of the business—there one sees, in all
> its ambiguous nakedness, the beautiful obscene." (*CSS*, 199)

Jones begrudgingly allows that Smith has accidentally come
upon that observation but states that he is not intelligent
enough to do anything about it, to draw from it the appropriate
conclusions. Jones thereupon makes the observations:

> "What I mean is, that if you are right, and the beautiful obscene is
> the essence of the business, then obviously one should pursue that
> course of life which would give one the maximum number of—what
> shall I say?—perfumed baths of that description. . . . You say that
> this essence is most clearly to be detected in the simpler violences.
> In love, birth, death, all abrupt cessations and beginnings. Very
> good. Then if one is to live completely, to realize life in the last
> shred of one's consciousness, to become properly incandescent, or
> *identical* with life, one must put oneself in contact with the strongest
> currents. One should love savagely, kill frequently, eat the raw, and
> even, I suppose, be born as often as possible." (*CSS* 200–201)

Smith enthusiastically agrees with Jones's conclusion, but Jones
then introduces the essential academic question:

> "What's to be done about thought? . . . You see, this road of
> reflection is, after all, centripetal. It involves, inevitably a return to
> the center, an identification of one's self with the All, with the
> unconscious *primum mobile*. But thought, in its very nature, involves
> a separation of one's self from the—from the—"

"Unconscious?"

"From the unconscious. . . . We must be careful not to go astray
at this point. One shouldn't begin by trying to *be* unconscious—not
at all! One might as well be dead. What one should try to get rid of
is consciousness of *self*." (201)

Jones, however, convinced of Smith's accidental or intuitive
truth, instantly decides to burn a haystack, but Smith finds such
an action disappointing because it lacks real spontaneity. It is
an intellectual act of responsive frivolity, but one that then gives
Smith some insight into the limitations of "superior" Jones.
Consequently, Smith, who has characterized himself as one
who goes about fornicating, thieving, card-cheating, and murdering, in his "unreflective, low-grade sort of way," delivers
what he announces to be his deathbed scene (since Jones is to
kill him): " 'Well, Jones, you're the beautiful and I'm the obscene; you're the desirable and I'm the disgusting; and in some
rotten way we've gotten tangled up together. . . . You, being the
healthy organism, insist on having the cancer removed. But
remember: I warned you! If you do so, it's at your own peril' "
(205). And then—in what surely is an illustration of an essential
tenet of Aiken's philosophy—the sensual and passionate Smith
kills the purely cerebral Jones, who, because of his excessive,
narcissistic introspection, is alienated from his other self as well
as from humanity.

It is important to recognize (as early as this short story,
published ten years before the novel) this particular aspect of
Aiken's philosophy: the importance of the sensual to man's
totality, the related necessity for involvement with humanity,
and the concomitant caution against intellectual arrogance and
alienation. Such recognition challenges the contention consistently made that *King Coffin* marks a major philosophical shift
for Aiken in his giving notice of the dangers of ego-dominated
consciousness. In a discussion of the novel, Martin, for instance,
observes that beginning in the mid–1930s Aiken altered his
emphasis to "show how the ego, guided by love, inevitably
moves outward to humanity." As Martin stated, "self-extension
[is] the significant new element which *King Coffin* manifests in
Aiken's development."[38] But Smith had perceived a decade
earlier how sterile, how empty, and, finally, how dangerous
was the philosophy of egocentric Jones. It is for this reason that

when the corporeality of Smith is threatened by the intellectu-
ality of Jones seeking to establish its imperial position, Smith
almost mindlessly jettisons Jones, thus ridding himself of a
jaundiced consciousness unable to exist in harmony with the
total self.

King Coffin is, then, a continuation, not a disruption, of
Aiken's exploration into the nature of consciousness; but contained within it is a warning against the trap of the singularity
of the ego. Ammen makes the initial mistake of foolishly assuming the superiority of his ego and its independence from other
people. He is absolutely convinced that he needs no one: "especially people. With what person or persons, Jasper, do you
ever manage to establish even for the tiniest fraction of a second
anything like a reality of understanding? Good God, no. They
are nothing but shadows" (CN, 305). Significantly, Ammen
describes himself in terms of total egocentricity:

> The eyes were enigmatic and lynxlike, and with that profound and
> inscrutable impersonality which looks out of eyes which themselves
> see too clearly for any counteranalysis: all they offered was an
> anonymity of depth and light. They were pure vision. The controlled
> mouth, and the Greek serenity of the forehead, accentuated the
> effect of philosophic essentialness; the face, the body, the hands . . .
> were all one thing, they were a pure ego of unimaginable intensity.
> (322)

Another manifestation of Ammen's isolated consciousness
suggesting that he has extended the boundaries of consciousness too exclusively is his fanatical emphasis on purity. Early in
the novel when Ammen is thinking about the nature of human
relationships, of the little ways in which we hurt each other, he
concludes, "Good God, how dirty it all is. And how dirty I am.
But I'm damned if I'll be dirty. . . . I must be pure" (306).

It becomes increasingly evident that another important motive in Ammen's desire to kill is a need for a ritualistic purification: Jones becomes "the other chief performer in the rite, the
acquiescent one, the dedicated ram led garlanded to the pure
altar" (382). Ammen looks upon the murder as a necessary act
of cleansing: if the world were

> despicable, and if one was to sound one's contempt for it to the
> bottom, separate oneself from it, then the final and inevitable action

in the series would be simply an act of destruction: it would be the
only natural purification. It was not, in this sense, dictated so much
by hatred as by a need for purification. (363)

This constitutes, then, the need for the superior, clean, pure
being to separate himself from the inferior, dirty, impure beings, which amounts to the one who can kill separating himself
from "the one-who-wants-to-be-killed."

Ultimately, however, as Ammen's consciousness is expanded
by a growing involvement with the consciousness of the "inferior" Karl Jones, Ammen is shocked to find not the vast differences he had expected but—with horror—a growing awareness
of the salient similarities. This conclusion is reinforced by the
refrain that echoes throughout the novel: "If thou gazest into
the abyss, the abyss will also gaze into thee." The refrain
gathers incremental significance as the plot unfolds. What begins on Ammen's part as pure observation ends with a realization of communality or, even more shocking, a recognition of
mutuality.

Gradually Ammen begins to think of Jones in Jungian terms.
He imagines himself "To be alone with Jones—is that so difficult
or painful? Is it any deeper a corruption—or evil—than to be
alone with yourself? alone with your own shadow? It is merely
the sacrifice of a shadow" (373). Jones and Ammen are united
in this macabre dance of life or of death: "And if Jones was the
negative, he himself was the destructive positive, the anonymous lightning which was about to speak the creative Name. A
ritual, yes—it was in fact a sort of marriage" (382). But Ammen
continues to assume an intellectual control. He has arrived at
the destructive aspect of consciousness, believing that one can
enter into the abyss of consciousness while simultaneously
maintaining a strict subject/object dichotomy of sensibility—that
is, situating himself as observer. But the lines blur, and Ammen
becomes at once observer and part of the observation. Unable
to deal with the consequent painfulness of such awareness, he
begins to look to suicide for a release.

While suicide grows increasingly seductive, an alternative
salvation for Ammen is near at hand in the character of Gerta.[39]
She is the only one able to save Ammen from himself, but
Ammen is at first unconscious of this. Unlike Babcock in "No,
No, Go Not to Lethe," Ammen does, however, come gradually

to an awareness. When, for instance, he has invited his victim to the theater and has the revolver in his pocket, his thoughts turn to Gerta and intrude on the "purity" of the moment: "But exactly why in the midst of this action, had he wanted to deviate from it, to see Gerta?" (*CN*, 385). Despite protestations to the contrary, Ammen is not completely detached from others. He is quite prosaically jealous of Gerta's relationship with Sandbach, of whom he is contemptuous. When, for example, Ammen invites Gerta to watch his pistol practice, his whole pose, including his aiming of the gun and his shooting the heads off the dandelions, is as sexually charged as the performance of Sergeant Troy's swordplay for Bathsheba in *Far from the Madding Crowd*. At the end of this scene Ammen dismisses Gerta, assures her that he needs no one and that he is contemptuous of them all and of Sandbach in particular, and shouts, " 'I'll see you in hell.' " But as he walks back to his car he breaks off a birch branch and "whip[s] it, as he walk[s] against other birches, until it [is] stripped of its leaves, drop[s] it before him in the green path and [treads] upon it. This [is] Sandbach. For a few seconds he stop[s], [stands] still, close[s] his eyes—something ha[s] made him feel slightly sick, slightly giddy, the turmoil for a moment seem[s] unnatural" (371).

An understanding of what has made him "slightly sick" is the lesson that Ammen learns in the cemetery as he awaits the interment of Jones's baby and looks at the rows on rows of tombstones marking where the dead are collected, as if they were "rare stamps, or coins, or first editions"; it is an awareness of his place in the intricate fabric of humanity. He comes to realize the potential of each human being—and the vulnerability. He realizes that all the dead were once individual egos and that some of them perhaps thought themselves superior to the others. It is a sobering deduction for Jasper Ammen:

> And they were all alike, in the long view they were all alike, all they ever managed to say was a feeble and stammering "I." They said this with an air of extraordinary importance and bewilderment, made what they considered to be a unique gesture, and were gone. And then after them came the hordes, the shapeless hordes, the innumerable and nameless hordes, of the others, world without end, who would feel the same importance and make the same unique and imperious gesture. Each in turn would believe that in some extraordinary way he had really produced himself, wrought

his own intelligence and power, created his own individuality. . . .
Each would believe himself unique. . . . And after him would come,
until the dying world was inherited briefly by grasshoppers and
ants, the human swarm of others who would say and believe
identically the same thing. (409)

Ammen feels increasingly sick. His own mortality weighs heavily upon him, but what is even worse is that he realizes that the
entire plan, from its lofty conception to its aborted execution,
has not been pure. It couldn't be pure; it shouldn't be pure. The
elaborate scheme with all the lofty philosophizing is diminished
by watching this ritual, the undertaker carrying the coffin hardly
larger than a shoebox: "That it should all have come to this—!
This absurd little ritual in the rain" (411). As the funeral car
worms its way out of the cemetery, "a strange thing happen[s]
to him. He [feels] that he ha[s] died." The wife of Karl Jones has
given birth to a stillborn child, Jasper Ammen to a stillborn
scheme.

This bleak funeral procession prepares the way for Ammen's
final acceptance of the interdependence of human existence.
The essential insistence on extended consciousness is not denied, but the prohibition against egocentricity is clear. The
realization makes it particularly important that one read the end
of the novel very carefully and avoid simply assuming, as all
reviewers did, and all critics do, that Jasper Ammen methodically went on to commit suicide.[40]

In the final pages, as Ammen watches the funeral car bearing
Karl Jones turn the corner, he realizes that he will never kill
Jones ("Finished! . . . *Finis coronat opus*. King Coffin"), and his
thought is "to write to Gerta." He writes what is essentially a
love letter, a confession of human dependence, an acknowledgment that there must be a balance between blind participation
in the stupid fiction of the masses and total withdrawal to an
exclusive, isolated preoccupation with the individual and cosmic
consciousness:

"My dear Gerta—the master builder builds better than he knows.
. . . You were wise, anyway, you saw the queer shape of things more
clearly than I, and I can now salute your narrow vision with respect
if not with gratitude. . . . there must be a *half-way point which would
be good*,—too difficult, however, for me to try to analyze for you
now. No, it's all too despicable. . . . Ammen." (412)

It would appear that Ammen's recognition of the necessity for a "mid-point" plays an important part in his suicide preparations that occupy the last pages of the novel. Although, as mentioned, it is consistently assumed that Ammen does commit suicide, it seems that if he does, he does so with a desperate hope that he, like Aiken himself, will be interrupted before it is too late.

We recall that Aiken had confided to his friend George Wilbur, first in 1927, that he had considered suicide but didn't seem to have the nerve: "Evidently I don't want to die, much as I sometime think so."[41] Within five years Aiken had found the nerve. We have read in *Ushant* about the elaborate preparations for his death by gas and in his 1932 letter to Wilbur about his suicide attempt, but it is the particular details that are relevant here:

> Waited till Jerry had gone out to the theatre and gassed myself. And succeeded, too—or would have, if Jerry hadn't come back sooner than expected. Passed out very cheerfully and without a qualm, not a bloody qualm. The return to life wasn't so pleasant. The whole thing was an admirable experience, and has had a profound effect on me: difficult to define, but I feel myself permanently changed—hardened and detached. . . . To have made such a decision calmly and to have acted on it effectively—for to all intents I was dead—gives me an altered focus. Not least interesting however was the fact that Jerry found me lying against the door, where I had fallen or crawled: and as my last memory is of sitting at the table and reading an article by Wyndham Lewis I must have made this abortive attempt to save myself unconsciously: amusing to think of. Good old animal instinct, it takes a lot to beat it. (21 September 1932, *SL*, 191)

In *King Coffin* Aiken is precise about the timetable of Ammen's final actions. Ammen completes his telegram to Gerta, notices that the electric clock over the counter in the Western Union office says nineteen past nine, and he asks that the telegram be delivered to Gerta at exactly eleven o'clock: " 'This is important, do you understand? It might be a matter of life and death. I want this note delivered to this address at *precisely* eleven—not a moment before, and not a moment after' " (*CN*, 413). If Ammen were not planning, or at least not hoping, that Gerta would interrupt his final act—as Aiken's wife had interrupted his—it would not matter in the least how many moments past eleven o'clock the telegram were delivered. Ammen's speculations are also important: "It was Gerta's day at home, she wouldn't be going to the Museum, and the chances were, of course, that she wouldn't have gone out before eleven. If she had——?" (413). As Ammen makes his suicide preparations, he makes certain that the sitting-room window is open before turning on the gas jets in the kitchenette and sitting down to read ("all the while conscious of the little watch ticking on his wrist, the tiny hand creeping slowly toward eleven" [414]). As he gets drowsy, he thinks, "And Gerta—would she be there? would she come?" (414).

It is unimportant whether Gerta gets there in time or not. Aiken's protagonist has had his moment of truth; he has ended his reign as King Coffin. Realizing his superiority to the absurdity of conventional reality, he has totally divorced himself from it and from all the people who believe in the fiction; he has asserted his separation by plotting a gratuitous murder, which it becomes unnecessary to commit; he has entered wholly into the abyss of the self, looked into the gaping mouth of Gehenna, the chaos of the entirely interior self. Aiken never denies the attraction of uncharted consciousness and the superiority of the individual who attempts to extend himself in the direction of becoming an *Ubermensch*, but he warns that in making such an attempt one must not deny one's humanity—the rest of consciousness.

Chapter Seven

THE FICTIONAL END
A Heart for the Gods of Mexico and Conversation

IN MANY WAYS Aiken's final two novels, *A Heart for the Gods of Mexico* and *Conversation or Pilgrims' Progress*, act as fictional postscripts and, as such, should be considered together. They both deal significantly less than the other novels with the exploration of individual consciousness; their themes complement each other; they are shorter and slighter novels; and they were published within a year of each other. While both novels have some merit, most readers will share Aiken's own estimate of them alternately as "lighter, both in depth and intention" (preface to *Three Novels*) and "pot-boilers."[1] They continue the autobiography insofar as Aiken also made a somewhat frantic trip to Mexico in 1937, accompanied by his artist-friend Ed Burra and Mary Augusta Hoover, whom Aiken was to marry after getting a Mexican divorce from Clarissa Lorenz. And certainly Aiken—with three wives—was no stranger to the sorts of marital disputes that dominate *Conversation*.

For a quarter of a century, since his first publication, *Earth Triumphant*, in 1914, it was as though Aiken had been writing his *Holy Living*, and in his penultimate novel, *A Heart for the Gods of Mexico* (1939), he tries to piece together his *Rule and Exercises of Holy Dying*. Haunted until the very end of his life by the suspicion that "there are no final solutions, that things may have no meaning,"[2] Aiken realized early on that it was necessary to live as consciously as possible. But he also realized that the natural eventuality of living was dying ("She was living her own death"[3]). He had frequently touched on the relevant philosophical doctrine of eternal recurrence. As early as 1925, in "The Room," he had posited that out of chaos comes order and, in turn, out of order comes chaos, to be followed by order in an eternally recurring pattern; as late as 1969, he reiterated, "Every-thing is in a sense reversible."[4] So it is only fitting that in mid-life—*Nel mezzo del cammin di nostra vita*—he would examine the actual physical process of dying. Aware, however, of the sub-ject's inherent sentimentality, Aiken chose to write the novel as a short prose lyric.[5] His stylistic decisions for *A Heart for the Gods* (which he calls a "fugue") make it different from any of the other four novels and in some ways closer to the consistently lyrical passages of *Ushant*.

The faults of the novel are easily assessed; the subtle strengths are more elusive but lie primarily in the perfect wed-ding of thesis and form. As a critic, Aiken had always insisted that the two were indivisible; he had frowned on the emphasis—beginning in the 1930s—on form to the exclusion of feeling. In "Back to Poetry" he maintained that the contemporary insis-tence on not saying anything but saying it aesthetically was responsible for the withering away of poetry. Much the same could be said of prose:

> These earnest theoreticians of poetry—these scholiasts—subtle eyebrow-combers of style, calligraphic text-combers—have worked just as zealously to bring about a "poetry of exclusion." . . . The poem, it would seem, must be conceived of as a detached aesthetic object, hung in the void, which has been shaped quite without feeling, exists by itself, and makes no statement: no statement, that is, but an aesthetic one. But just how it is supposed to work, this epistemological miracle, this process of poetic "being" without "meaning," and just how it is that the most supremely articulate statement of which man is capable (and that is what poetry is) can exist without meaning, are nowhere made clear. (*ABC*, 100)

The subject that Aiken lends meaning to is, quite simply, how someone prepares for death and how someone accompa-nies another on this voyage toward death. Aiken's narrative is extremely slight and melodramatic: Noni, a fairly young and attractive woman, learns that she has a heart condition from which she will shortly die. Since childhood she has been good friends with Gil, "an idealist, a real dyed-in-the-wool Puritan, self-sacrificing, honest, everything" (*CN*, 418) who had wanted to marry her years ago; instead she had married Giddings, "a first-class A-number-one bastard" (419) who early on fled for-ever with a sizable share of her money. Gil, too, had made an unhappy marriage, to a woman who soon after their wedding emotionally deserted him. Gil enlisted in the service hoping to get honorably killed, but just before he went overseas his wife repented and promised that if he returned they would have a baby. He returned; she had the baby, but neither mother nor child survived the birth. Gil almost died of despair but was saved by the faithful solicitations of Noni. Now, years later, Noni, on learning of her own impending death, wants to make a frantic trip to Mexico to obtain a quick divorce from Giddings so that she can marry Gil. She wants "to *give* him something—in fact the best thing she had: herself" (424). Blomberg, a mutual friend, Noni's confidant, a book reviewer (like Aiken), and the narrator of the tale, is sworn to secrecy: Gil must not know that Noni is ill and has, at the most, one year to live, and probably a good deal less than that.

Aiken has taken some big risks in trying to put together a convincing narrative in which he can make some philosophical assertions, and he knows it. Therefore he provides the novel with its own devil's advocate in the person of Key, the character to whom Blomberg must relate the circumstances surrounding the trip in order to borrow money to help finance it. Key's comment is surely that of the doubtful reader: " 'I see; she'll marry him and then drop dead on the wedding night! That's my idea of a swell treat for Mister Gil' " (424–25). Key asks the question that reflects the confusion in the minds of readers—that is, why Blomberg is accompanying the couple: " 'What I don't see . . . is why *you've* got to go. Or what the hell Gil thinks you're going for, if he doesn't know the situation. Kind of a fifth wheel, aren't you?' " (425).

Blomberg's reason for going is presumably to expedite matters, but he also allows that he loves Noni. Once again Aiken touches briefly on the possibility of a higher, purer love between a man and a woman, one that is elevated beyond the sexual (" 'it was too good and too deep for that—don't smile, such things do happen. . . . I suppose sex must play a part in it, but if so it's so deep and anonymous as to become in effect spiritual' " [428]). Of course, structural considerations dictated, to some extent, Blomberg's being the narrator (for the first time, Aiken's protagonist does not tell her own tale). The choice was undoubtedly made to avoid sentimentality and for the obvious, practical narrative reason that Noni dies on arriving in Mexico.

The idea of a confidant was a master stroke: we get insights into the character journeying into death and at the same time insights into the effect of that journey on someone who accompanies her.

Aiken draws certain philosophical conclusions from Noni's voyage into death: in dying, just as in living, one should be as conscious as possible; in dying well, one illustrates the immense dignity of the individual, which lends hope to those who have despaired of humanity; finally, death is, in fact, a natural stage in the cycle of recurrence from order to chaos to order. In short, the trip to Mexico is a metaphor for the journey into death. Gradually it becomes apparent that Noni is going to be sacrificed on the altar of the sun-God, that she is going to marry Death, not Gil: Noni is "on the great circle to Mexico, taking her heart as an offering to the bloodstained altar of the plumed serpent . . . her face, closed like a flower, but ready to open as soon as the sun shone—and this, too, she knew and waited for, the sun that was already pursuing them westward around the dark rondure of the turning world" (435).[6]

Aiken emphasizes Noni's capacity for consciousness by recording her acute sensuous responses. Blomberg, for instance, characterizes her as the "*nakedest*" soul he has ever met. By way of illustration, he explains that although she plays the piano rather badly, she does so with such intensity that she plays more movingly than anyone he has ever heard: " 'some people have that astonishing integrity of living or loving, or seeing and feeling—*really* love and feel—while the rest of us poor guys have to wait and be *told* when to love' " (*CN*, 427). It is with this compelling intensity that Noni faces her death and for this reason that Noni's death, which at first seems so meaningless, unfairly random, takes on the dimensions of an artistic masterpiece ("it's the creation of a work of art, a piece of superb music" [429]).

Noni's beautiful dying, then, grows out of her beautiful living—her love of living, her love of others. Aiken subtly suggests this second philosophical aspect of Noni's death—that is, the paeans to the dignity of the individual—by setting her in subtle opposition to people whom the three encounter on their trip, people with their "withered faces and scrawny necks, their dead eyes and dead souls" (448). For instance, the Indians who get on the train as it moves into Mexico are sharp counterpoints to Noni: "Derisive and demoniacal laughter, full of fierce and abandoned hatred, the pride of pridelessness, the arrogance of the self-condemned; and the often-turning reptile-lidded eyes, which slowly and malevolently scrutinized the three strange Americans" (455). There is always running beneath these implied comparisons the ironic and incongruous fact that all of this grossness and bestiality will live and Noni will die. But as one of the few supportive critics of the novel pointed out in her *Times Literary Supplement* review, "In his only really good novel, *A Heart for the Gods of Mexico*, a woman, beautiful, kind, subtle, vital, is presented against the background of her imminent death: and the anguish that a perfection can be destroyed is balanced against the miracle that it can exist at all."[7] This is the conclusion that Aiken draws when Blomberg contemplates the dead body of Noni in the closing pages of the novel: "that a life should have been so beautiful, and so devoted to good and beautiful things, in the face of the uncompromising principles of impermanence and violence, came to him as a fierce renewal of his faith in the essential magnificence of man's everlasting defeat" (*CN*, 470).

Surely Aiken remained haunted from childhood by the absurdity of life, which could so quickly, prematurely, and dramatically cease. Thus through Noni's pending death, Aiken can once again explore the complexities of being within the intricacies of time. Early in the trip it becomes apparent to Blomberg that the only immediately recognizable reality is the train that is carrying them to Mexico; everything else appears to be dissolving into time and sound, "a fragment of ether-dream, a little picture seen in a picture book, brightly colored but unreal. . . . but the train, hollowing a gold and evanescent tunnel through the darkness, fleeting and impermanent as a falling star, denied all things but itself" (433).

Just as the train exists on the level of perceptible reality, it also exists in the superficial world of time: the train would take three-and-a-half days to get to Mexico, but how long to eternity? Aiken, as always, is concerned with timeless time, time beyond time, or, as he phrases it in a refrain threaded throughout the novel, "Time with a hundred hands, time with a thousand mouths." Such is time without end, or circular time; in such a time dimension Noni is not making a trip from Boston to Mexico but is on "the great circle to Mexico." The reference is first made in the opening pages when Blomberg thinks aloud about Noni, "solitary as a bird, on the great circle to Mexico" (428). The refrain suggests, then, that death in Mexico is not an end but only a part of the cosmic great circle.

Aiken reiterates the thesis that Noni's death reflects the dialectical movement from order into chaos by repeatedly speaking of the trip to Mexico as a moving away from civilized Boston toward the violent and primitive inferno: "The wheels, the bells, the whistles, the sliding and whirling land, the centripetal and tumultuous descent into the Inferno, the descent into Mexico—Oh God, how were they ever going to endure it?" (433). Again, reading a guide book about some native festivals, Blomberg concludes, "My God, what a people; the whole land bathed in blood——!" (455).

The reader gradually realizes that it is a kind of blood wedding—rather than the professed civil wedding—toward which they are moving in order for Noni's death to fulfill Aiken's metaphor. Reminiscent again of Lawrence's *The Plumed Serpent*, there is a tone of relentless hysteria associated with exotic Mexico. Blomberg, for instance, becomes aware of and horrified by the frank sensuality of the Indians who board the train as they get closer to their destination: "these lynx-eyed cut-throats, looking at Noni like that, with that look that stripped a woman down to sex and nothing else, exactly as you'd flay a fox! Jesus! . . . what an astonishing thing that as if by a sort of instinct Noni should have projected herself—with her consciousness of death, death as immediate as a hand at the throat—into a scene of such basic fertility and filth and cruel vitality!" (458).

Once in Mexico, Aiken's pilgrims are assaulted by a seething, poisonous, primitive, violently disordered country. Even the animals and insects suggest a hostile and destructive nature. Mammoth birds howl and scream in larger-than-life trees. There are *ninos*, little cricketlike insects so deadly poisonous that there are no known antidotes for their bite—"Your throat swelled up until you died of suffocation" (466)—and lizards with pouches under their throats, "beautiful little things; you would see them sitting on the rosetrees—deadly poison too" (467). Blomberg lashes out at this ghoulish, surrealistic country, "My God, *everything* here seems poisonous!" (467).

The nightmarish quality of the country is heightened by their arrival during the San Manuel fiesta. The town rings with loud marimba bands, and the narrow streets are filled with reeling drunks. And the final descent into chaos is reflected in the scenario of the probable knife murder of "his woman" by Pablo, the servant in Hambo's house, where the three travelers are staying. This elemental, sensual, and vital scene serves as the backdrop for the climax of the novel.

Pablo is so drunk that he cannot remember if he actually knifed the woman or not, but he has staggered back to the house for his wages in order to flee. Hambo pays him his pesos and is in the process of explaining to the other three that Pablo was so full of *pulque* that he probably imagined the whole thing when Pablo, cursing and falling up the tile steps, returns—to the utter consternation of the group—because he wants to examine his blood-covered knife. Hambo explains too loudly and too consciously symbolically: "It was life in the tropics, life in the jungle, nature red in tooth and claw! Of course. It was the heart torn from the victim's breast, the head spitted on the *tzompantli*, the dark underworld current of destructive and creative blood" (469).

At this juncture, Noni, leaning against the door jamb, crumbles to the floor; her heart has ceased to beat; it has been sacrificed to the primitive gods. The night is ushered in by a violent thunder and lightning storm, and the novel ends with Blomberg appropriately desiring to "laugh out of pure misery" and with his meaningful summation, "Christ, but I'm a long way from home!" (472).

· · ·

A reader of the Aiken canon would immediately be aware of the limited number of themes in *A Heart for the Gods* as compared to the other novels. One would further notice the relatively direct plot narration. But the power of this novel lies precisely in its singleness, in its relentless and contracted pursuance of the principal theme of the passage from life to death. To limit himself in this way to a theme with such a potential liability for melodrama and cloying sentimentality, Aiken substantially altered his prose style from that of his previous novels. He writes what is surely a prose poem or an intensely lyrical novel. This is not to suggest that there was little lyricism in his earlier works, but rather to insist that in *A Heart for the Gods* the emphasis shifted to the lyricism.

However, this posed fewer technical problems for Aiken than it might for another author for whom there were sharp distinctions between poetry and prose. In a 1925 *Dial* review of J. Romains's *Lucienne*, Aiken was emphatic: "There are no canons for the novels. The novelist, so long as he remains interesting, can do what he likes." Even more to the point, Aiken states, "Whatever mode he chooses he will impregnate deeply, if he is successful, with his own character. The novel is the novelist's inordinate and copious lyric: he explores himself, and sings while he explores, like the gravedigger" (*ABC*, 347). Aiken certainly did not choose the simile casually.

In *A Heart for the Gods of Mexico*, Aiken made certain technical, poetic choices. First, in order to sustain the intensity of the experience, the novel had to be short, and in *The Collected Novels* it runs only fifty-five pages. Further, Aiken broke the short novel into five chapters: the first three are long chapters detailing the slow, rambling train trip across the country to Mexico City; the last two—about the inferno and the death itself—run only six and three pages respectively.

Second, Aiken limited himself to two archetypal symbols—excluding the obvious heart—to carry his thesis: the train trip and water. Undoubtedly in both cases Aiken was influenced by Freud, who had unequivocally declared that departing on a journey was one of the most common, frequently authenticated symbols of death. The train that carries them relentlessly to Mexico is often personified: "the train had increased its speed once more; it was on the last stretch, it was hurrying home" (*CN*, 462). And in the end of the novel, with definite symbolic referents, it frantically plunges them into the heart of Mexico:

And in fact the train had now become positively suicidal. It was at last rushing downhill, hurling itself precipitately down the mountainsides, down gorges, down tunnels and valleys, lurching in breakback fashion around screaming bends, falling and then checking momentarily in the pitch darkness, only to resume its headlong disastrous plunge to Mexico City. (462–63)

The chapter ends with the dismissal of, or sloughing off of, the cocoonlike train ("And this familiar world, this train, would be lost forever" [463]).

The second important symbol in the novel is water—as it suggests both the baptismal rite and eternity in all its chaotic manifestations. It is only by understanding the larger dimensions of the novel, and thus of the trip, as Gil cannot, that Noni's insistence on putting her hands in the Mississippi River—though the walk taken during a change of trains will exhaust her—makes sense. It constitutes her baptism or initiation into the world of violence, her return to the chaos from which she came. Freud had insisted in *Beyond the Pleasure Principle* that the goal of all life was death, positing our strong death instincts on the conviction that the inanimate preceded the animate. Noni says whimsically, " 'Ah, . . . the Mississippi—the father of waters—now we can go home!' " The observation is incomprehensible to literal-minded Gil, who asks, " 'Go home?' " (446).

It is at this particular point in the journey when Blomberg notices that Noni is beginning to have an astonishing sense of peace and that she is beginning "to *let* go." After bathing her hands in the river, she announces, " 'Now I've got Indian blood' " (448), suggesting that she is baptized into the violence and chaos earlier associated with the Indians and the country itself.

The poetic device of significant word repetition is clearly evident in Aiken's many uses of "heart." Key, who puts up a hundred dollars for the trip, is said to have a "heart of gold" (418). Blomberg notices a juke box, a "coffin full of records," and listens to the "gross throbbing of the music—like a bad heart" (420); Noni's house is said to have a heart ("It's alive. It glows. It's got a heart" [427]). Repetition of phrases such as "Bless his heart" and "Cross my heart" too often makes us mindful that Noni is taking her heart to Mexico.

Finally, *A Heart for the Gods* is the most imagistic of Aiken's novels. In *Ushant*, Aiken chastises himself for much of the "fine writing" in the novel.[8] While undoubtedly portions of it are overwritten, many of the descriptions of nature are worthy of the poet who wrote them. For instance, the morning after Noni's death—the morning after a nightmarish storm—Blomberg awakes to a new world:

> When he emerged on to the verandah, it was to face a world which overnight had been brilliantly re-created: everything flashed and sparkled: in the dazzling east, once more visible, the great volcano sunned its shoulders of ice. . . . The morning was still—the wind

had dropped—the banana leaves hung limp and unstirring. He noticed that the lower leaves, the older ones, were ragged, split in parallel fringes, or fingers—they had a longer knowledge of the wind; the upper and younger leaves were still smooth and in one piece. And that scarlet dragonfly—it had a favorite observation post, it returned always to one rose-tree tip, and sat there always facing exactly the same way. (CN, 470–71)

In writing an unabashedly poetic novel, Aiken was practicing exactly what as a critic he was concomitantly preaching. In short, as mentioned earlier, Aiken faulted the poetry in his own day as lacking in ideas, of being "detached authentic objects" concerned exclusively with form. But, also as noted earlier, a second fault that Aiken found with contemporary poetry was a lack of passion, an embarrassment over feeling. He suspected that the demise of poetry, beginning in the 1930s, could be traced, ironically, to the fear or reluctance of poets to be poetic. In the central essay, "Back to Poetry," Aiken observed:

> almost everywhere in the poetry of this group, from early Auden and Spender and Macneice and Day Lewis down to the least and valetudinarian note, the seemingly off-hand but careful flatness of the language—the voices are the voices of weary and excessively refined young men, anxious to avoid any overstatement, whether overt or implied; and anxious above all to avoid the "poetic," if only because to be poetic was somehow to be bourgeois. (ABC, 95)

He went on to call for precisely the kind of writing that we have in A Heart for the Gods:

> But for goodness' sake let us have back as well a few blistering sunrises and peculiar sunsets, a few fierce loves and melodramatic despairs—our private loves and terrors, like the grass blade, the sun, and the unexploded atom, will still be in fashion when the social cleavages and surfaces of our day, with all their ephemeral lumber, will have been forgotten. Let us be reckless, lavish, generous, afraid of no extremes and no simplicities. . . . The cult of carefulness has gone far enough. . . . We need more . . . affirmation, a blood-filled affirmation. (ABC, 102)[9]

The spectacular poetic passages in the novel explain, in part, poet Hayden Carruth's enthusiasm for the novel in his review of it for the Nation: "Aiken's prose is fiercer and keener in this book than in the others, and yet gentleness, even humor, pervades, with the result that an immensely complicated synthesis of moods and meanings is sustained without a single recourse to direct statement. Everything is transmuted into visual terms. I could not help thinking, as I reread it, that it would make a perfect script for a film, in the hands of the right director."[10] Carruth's praise, however, is distinctly a minority evaluation. Jay Martin rightly observed that most critics seemed unaware of the novel's existence. Martin himself finds it to be Aiken's "least successful novel" and dismisses much of the writing as "mere local color."[11] Mary Rountree similarly dismisses it as a novel filled with "melodramatics and an almost hysterically inflated rhetoric."[12] One's appreciation of the prose here depends on one's propensity for being simultaneously enthusiastic about Emily Dickinson and Walt Whitman. The language is the novel's strength; its main weakness is its central character, Noni.

Noni is one of Aiken's ethereal, Poe-like women: slender, fair, with Nordic blue eyes like the fringed gentian.[13] The particular faults with her portrayal may once again have stemmed from Aiken's falsification of the biographical persona on whom Noni is modeled. He intended, according to *Ushant*, to write about the tragic death of Louisa, an actual young girl he knew well in Boston, who was probably in love with him and whom he did not visit when she was dying. He acknowledged that he had not written honestly about the whole relationship, and, for Aiken, such deception was deadly: it stains the fiber of the whole work. While it is true that Aiken frequently altered the precise biographical *facts* when turning them into fiction—for instance, changing his parents' murder-suicide by gunshots into his uncle-mother's death by drowning in *Great Circle*—without diminishing the novel, it is the alteration of the essential *truth* of a biographical situation that is fatal. In *Ushant* he treats his dishonesty harshly: "For, of course, the falsification of Louisa had inevitably falsified the whole thing. After that grievous initial error, there was never a chance that it could be anything but what it was—a piece of work of which not even surface, the writing, could achieve any excellence, because the theme itself was entirely spurious: it was a fraud" (347).[14] He sees her as silly and insipid, an unworthy symbol of the potential for the perfection of which all life was capable; and he sees her also as an unworthy symbol of the potential for despair, the possibility that at any irrational moment life can cease. (Noni's name appropriately suggests the Spanish word, "nona," or none, the last of the canonical hours.)

A further autobiographical falsification in the novel—and considering the intimacy of the Aiken-Malcolm Lowry relationship, a more grievous one—is that of Hambo. The round, red-faced affable man walking with the forked stick to meet the train from Boston is Lowry. But, according to Lowry's biographer, Douglas Day, Lowry was at this juncture in a particularly bad way, a far cry from the jovial, pipe-smoking host of Cuernavaca pictured in the novel. In a letter to Aiken from Lowry, written from Mexico just prior to Aiken's trip there, one hears a true note of desperation, despite Lowry's usual, comic overtone:

Dear old bird:
　　Have now reached condition of amnesia, breakdown, heartbreak, consumption, cholera, alcoholic poisoning, and God will not like to know what else, if he has to, which is damned doubtful.
　　All change here, all change here, for Oakshot, Cockshot, Poxshot and fuck the whole bloody lot!
　　My only friend here is a tertiary who pins a medal of the virgin of Guadalupe on my coat; follows me in the street (when I am not in prison, and he followed me there too several times); and who thinks I am Jesus Christ, which as you know, I am not yet, though I may be progressing towards thinking I am myself.
　　I have been imprisoned as a spy in a dungeon compared with which the Chateau d'If—in the film—is a little cottage in the country overlooking the sea.
　　I spent Christmas—New Year's—Wedding Day there. All my mail is late. When it does arrive it is all contradictions and yours is cut up into little holes.
　　Don't think I can go on. Where I am it is dark. Lost.
　　　　　　　　　　　　　　　　Happy New Year
　　　　　　　　　　　　　　　　Malcolm[15]

Aiken, ever the first to identify his own lapses, admits in *Ushant* that he had "over-simplified and romanticised" Lowry in the novel: "Of the marital and alcoholic misery and despair into which he daily sank deeper—while he grappled stubbornly and unremittingly with his unappeasable vision, in that nest of old rags and blankets in which for the most part he lived . . . of all this, not a trace" (348).

A final critical qualification of *A Heart for the Gods* is that it unsuccessfully attempts to suggest one's transcendence, to suggest that in death one is ennobled. But, by limiting the novel's intentions to this vague idealism, the reviewers do the work an injustice. Frederick Crews, in assessing *The Collected Novels* for the *New York Times*, is one such critic: "In the two final novels Aiken tries and fails to convince us that self-transcendence is a real possibility for him."[16] Rountree similarly places the emphasis here and talks in terms of "self-sacrifice" and "courage" as "ennobling" spectacles.[17] Martin, too, insists that Aiken had progressed from the "divine to the human pilgrimage. It is the way [Noni] lives her life, not what she discovers about her self, that is important. She lives her life lovingly. With an acceptance beyond mere understanding she incarnates *caritas*."[18] When, however, Martin and the others see this novel signaling a turning away from the pursuit of consciousness, or the "divine pilgrimage," and toward an examination of living life within more traditionally circumscribed horizons, they are failing to see the larger implications of the journey as perceived by Blomberg, the narrating consciousness.

All this criticism that emphasizes Noni as heroine leads to a plastic-saint piety that is antithetical to Aiken's intent. While Noni is the raison d'etre of the voyage, she is not the consciousness of the novel. It is true, of course, that Blomberg talks about a faith in man, but it must not be overlooked that it is a faith in his defeat: "that a life should have been so beautiful, and so devoted to good and beautiful things, in the face of the uncompromising principles of impermanence and violence, came to him as a fierce renewal of his faith in the essential magnificence of man's everlasting defeat" (*CN*, 470). It is essential to reiterate that the emphasis in the novel is not on Noni's discovering herself or on Noni's self-transcendence but unequivocally on Blomberg's observations. Transcendence, then, is not Aiken's primary interest; his is a horizontal philosophy, not a vertical one. It was always the great circle that commanded his respect, not Jacob's ladder. The paradigm for *A Heart for the Gods* appears to be "Mr. Arcularis," the short story in which the protagonist approaches death through a journey back to genesis, to the moment of creation out of chaos, and, like Noni, almost reaches out for death as the final creative experience. It is this vision into the abyss of chaos—with its potential for order—that makes the novel the qualified success that it is. The return from death—that is, the philosophical doctrine of rebirth—although implied in the doctrine of recurrence and suggested in *A Heart for the Gods of Mexico*, must wait to be explored thematically in Aiken's last novel, *Conversation*, which, to this extent, is a companion piece.

. . .

Although four years passed between the publication of *King Coffin* and *A Heart for the Gods of Mexico*, only six months elapsed until the appearance of Aiken's next and final novel, *Conversation or Pilgrims' Progress* (1940). Each of Aiken's first three novels had been preceded by a volume of short stories, but this was not true of the last two, and perhaps this contributed to the weaknesses of both. Aiken acknowledges in *Ushant* the difficulty of getting back into writing after "those interregnums in one's ability to write" and suggests that "the tools are dulled with disuse, the hand has lost something of its cunning, the imagination its agility" (342). But, in its way, *A Heart for the Gods* had primed the pump: "Six months later, for example, and no doubt as a result of this very piece of desperate unsuccess, he had found himself, for *The Quarrel*, in a complete state of readiness" (*Ushant*, 342).[19] *A Heart for the Gods* had put Aiken back into writing fiction in general, but the rapidity with which his last novel followed its predecessor probably reflects the thematic relationship between the two books. The first took us from the order of life to the disorder of dying, with the dialectic of recurrence implied. But speculations on anything beyond the physical act of dying would make risky narrative fare. So instead, in Aiken's final novel, he deals with the return from disorder into order—that is, with rebirth—but he wisely chooses to deal with the metaphysical problem metaphorically.

Conversation is clearly Aiken's weakest novel, and one wonders whether Aiken, with his uncompromising and trained critical mind, realized this also and whether it influenced his decision to stop writing fiction (his final volume of short stories had been *Among the Lost People*, published in 1934). This novel is the first in which there is a real departure from the dominating theme of consciousness—the very word itself is absent from the text. However, the principal external problems explored in *Conversation*—the artist plagued by doubts and the husband and wife trapped in marital quagmires—are those that in the past lent themselves to vintage Aiken. But in *Conversation* Aiken chooses to write a far more traditional narrative, one that involves many minor characters in ongoing dialogues rather than one that revolves around the usual relentlessly centered introspection of the protagonist. The novel gets bogged down, however, as the narrator touches on a host of topics close to the heart of the author but not convincingly of concern to the novel's personae. It gets further stymied by Aiken's overlay of the death-into-rebirth theme. Consequently the novel is fragmented, successful neither as a traditional, realistic novel of domestic strife nor as an interior monologue of a sensitive consciousness. Its power is vitiated further by the inclusion of a potpourri of minor matters touched upon while in pursuit of the central theme. Typically, Aiken's own estimate of the novel alternated between enthusiasm and misgivings: "I have a feeling that it's terribly alive, people, background everything—that's when I have a moment of confidence. But I also have a dread that it may be very dull" (letter to Robert Linscott, 20 May 1939, WUL MS.).

In *Conversation*, Aiken once again experimented with his prose form, choosing this time what he calls a "4-movement symphonic structure" that corresponds to his chapter divisions.[20] In turn, each chapter, to greater and lesser degrees, contributes to the central theme of death and rebirth: the death of a marital relationship; the artist's career; cultures, English and American; and the cycles of the natural world.

The plot is structured on the arrival of Jim Connor, a professional fur thief and friend of the narrator, Timothy Kane, on Cape Cod for a visit. Connor shows up accompanied by an assortment of his Greenwich Village friends—thus posing a threat to the civil security of the resort as well as to the already precarious domestic harmony of the Kane family.[21] Enid Kane, puffed up with social pretensions and smoldering with general dissatisfaction over her artist-husband's faltering career, demands for her sake and for the sake of Buzzer, their only child, that Tip have nothing to do with Connor or his equally unacceptable hangers-on. The marital quarrel is intensified by the concentration of the novel into a twenty-four hour period—that is, from the time Enid closes her bedroom door to Tip on one evening to the time they retire together the next.

Such a conclusion rounds out the broader philosophical require-
ments of the novel, but, unfortunately, at the narrative level, it is
unconvincing. We are to assume that domestic bliss has been
restored and, by implication or extension, that Kane's artistic career
will also be revitalized, but Enid, on whom much of this rebirth
depends, is not developed fully enough to allow us to expect any
real generosity or maturation in her attitude. And the extent to
which Tip's affair—now mutually concluded—with Nora, a Boston
acquaintance, acts as an aphrodisiac to reconciliation is problematic. After all, it is Enid who has made the seemingly unreasonable
demands on their relationship: the nagging about the money, the
housework, the education of the child; the insistence that Tip not
see his friends. Further, her final, rude, inhospitable gesture toward Jim Connor when he gallantly comes to the Kane house—
when he apologizes for the trouble he has caused, promises to
leave, and brings a birthday present for the child—does not augur
well for our acceptance of Enid in a quasiredemptory role. It is,
however, Tip who makes the initial motion toward reconciliation,
and Aiken provides little explanation—other than a smoldering
sexual appetite—for his move. We are also expected to believe that
Tip has come to accept the necessary routine of marriage, since
Nora has "instinctively restored to him his belief in the illusion, his
belief in the illusion as the only reality. Or more simply, taught him
that the real world was illusion enough!" (*CN*, 520). Further, the
dialogue of reconciliation in the last pages of the novel is unconvincing; the heavy-handed purple prose is the language of the soap
opera. One is tempted to read it as pure parody, except that the
rest of the novel does not support such a reading:

> "Darling, will you forgive me—"
> "Of course, Tip, dear, if you'll forgive me, too—"
> "No, I'm afraid *I* was the naughty one—but *oh*, what a relief—!"
> "Isn't it *heavenly*—!"
> "Just to be *together* again, after all these days and days—"
> "I've been very hard and mean and selfish, Tip, I'm so dreadfully
> ashamed, but I'll do better."
> "No, darling, no. It's only that things have been difficult for
> us—" (572)

Aiken is here stressing that through the "death" of their marriage comes, almost miraculously and spontaneously, a rebirth.

That the marriage had reached a fatal point is clear by the end of the second chapter when Enid asks Tip to get away from her: "It was as if a gulf had opened between them, and as if she had become a stranger."

To reinforce the underlying marital angst in this novel, that familiarity breeds contempt, Aiken suggests that not even art objects are exempt from indifference spawned by familiarity. As Tip sits alone in his half-darkened living room after Enid has pouted off to bed, his eyes rest on a Japanese print, *Famous Place to See Moon*, which he and Enid had bought a number of years before, and he recalls how magical it had then appeared and how he has not "seen" it again for a long time.[22] He suspects that the aesthetic object has not diminished but that the eye of the perceiver has. The print coaxes Tip into the formulation of a theory of aesthetics that has close parallels to his assessment of human relationships. He accepts that the ecstasy of the perceiver must necessarily dim, but "the *thing itself* was as beautiful as ever: the leaf, the Japanese print, or the woman one loved: it was only oneself that failed. The eye became fatigued, ceased to see—ceased to look—and instead of love, by god, marriage settled down to being just the terrible bed of habit" (*CN*, 558). Yet Aiken posits that there is an absolute use to which the death of Kane's marriage can be put: it is the seed bed for the vital rebirth of their relationship.

In reference to both *Blue Voyage* and *Heart for the Gods*, we saw that Aiken had confessed in *Ushant* to falsification of the auto-biographical artifacts and that such falsification necessarily diminished the artistic success of the works. While such an uncompromising need for unabashed honesty might not be endemic to writers, it remained a truism for Aiken throughout his life. He understood the need for the mask but insisted that it be a completely genuine mask. Perhaps, then, the weakness of *Conversation*, too, grows out of biographical fraud and out of Aiken's trying to pay his debt to the "other woman," to Marian of *Ushant*, who is the model for Nora and the pivotal female character in several short stories, including "The Night Before Prohibition," "Bring! Bring!" and "The Last Visit." In *Ushant*, Aiken devotes five pages to his extended affair with Marian, "the golden core" of those war years in Boston and Cambridge. The precise plot of "The Night Before Prohibition" is sketched in *Ushant*—how D. maneuvered to see Marian again, taking advantage of Lorelei One's trip to Montreal with the two children, and how he ended the evening disgusted with himself, shamelessly sending Marian home on the last trolley car from Harvard Square, the owl-car filled with singing drunks and no other women. Jay Martin, in writing about this story, perceptively concludes that this tale, like so many of Aiken's works, is an attempt for him to remember, by recording it, the pain he caused both others and himself. In his consciousness of his failures, he seeks forgiveness and then more than forgiveness: the understanding that will allow him to transcend them, in life as in art.[23] In *Ushant*, Aiken acknowledges that it was no wonder that Marian refused to see him again after that evening. More than a year later, and after she had married, he accidentally met her in North Station, but she refused to go to dinner with him. In words directly transferred to *Conversation*, she assured him that "she was very happy, and hoped *he* was, and they had had a good time together, hadn't they?" (*Ushant*, 210). When they parted, Aiken says he realized that she had truly loved him and he had loved her, but as so many times before he had missed the realization until too late.

It does seem, however, that while Aiken's personal debt to Nora might have warranted in his own mind giving her such a priestly role—the gentle intercessor in *Conversation*—she is, nonetheless, not entirely believable within the novel. Perhaps, again, this resulted partially from Aiken's falsification of her essential character. Her participation in the novel, for example, is in the form of a letter, which Aiken admits she would never have written:

> In *The Quarrel*, for instance, amongst so much else that was so obviously transposed directly from the life at South Yarmouth, with Lorelei One . . . it was Marian alone who was absent; or present only in the form of a letter which in fact she had never written, and never *could* have written; and nevertheless it was Marian who had been the germinating force for the entire action, just as, in delicious recollection, and with recollected love, she had so generously given him the love with which to write it. (*Ushant*, 316)

Nora's midwifery role in the marital rebirth is complete at the end of the novel when, the affair over, Tip suggests to Enid that they have a son. Since one grievance in Enid's catalogue of offenses was Tip's denying her more children, the regeneration thesis is manifest in potential childbirth.

The artistic career of Tip Kane likewise goes through a death/ rebirth cycle. In the opening pages of the novel, we find Tip restless and unhappy about his work. Though the family has moved to the Cape to better afford him the opportunity to paint, he has virtually not painted. While he argues with Enid that she burdens him with chores, he knows that the real reason is within himself. He looks at an unfinished work on the easel and laments that it is his own impotence—"the hand powerless to shape the actual, the vision powerless to purify" (*CN*, 478)—that is the trouble.

Both Tip's child, Buzzer, and his friend, Jim Connor, act as important ancillaries to Tip's artistic and spiritual rebirth. Neither Buzzer nor Jim is worn down by pedestrian realities. Buzzer believes in and trusts implicitly the natural world around her. Aiken's characterization of the father-daughter relationship is particularly sensitively drawn and no doubt reflects his own closeness to his "inestimably precious children, the nuggets, the rubies of his heart" (*Ushant*, 141). Tip wants to be near Buzzer because of her enthusiasm about life, her child's acceptance of the "mystery, mystery, mystery" of the world, the ease with which her imagination can, for example, transform an ordinary walk home from the post office into a suspenseful stalking of an Indian settlement. Jay Martin makes the cogent suggestion that Jim Connor functions as an adult version of the child's romanticism, and it is for this reason that Tip is attracted to him.[24] Jim steals furs in Robin Hood style in order to get cash to support struggling artists, most of whom seem neither grateful nor talented, but Jim's idealism will not be blunted. His totally selfless, outgoing personality contrasts dramatically with the introverted selfishness of the people around him. There is, though, another reason for Tip's attraction to Connor; again, it lies in Aiken's biography: Connor, in his personal pursuit of a redistribution of wealth, is Aiken's answer to his personal impatience with the small revolutionary groups of the 1930s, the do-nothing anarchists of *King Coffin*. The initials of the long-suffering and selfless Jim appear significant, especially in light of his being regularly referred to as the Messiah by one of the artists he is treating to a New England vacation.[25]

Nonetheless, in *Conversation* Aiken has overstated his case. It is true that the artist must retain a sense of idealism and must not be overwhelmed by the daily drudgeries of bourgeois living, but Connor is so extreme that in comparison Enid is a termagant. Her preoccupation with practical affairs and social pretension is compulsive to the point that it becomes difficult to accept her apologies and promises in the final pages of the novel. The extremes illustrate thematically the artistic problem facing Tip, the coming to terms with which makes possible for him a return to his painting. When he says in the last few pages, " 'It's Boston for me, in the morning!' " (CN, 574), Enid does not bemoan her being left on the Cape with the dirty dishes but rather agrees, " 'Oh, of course,' " and one is supposed to assume that she will no longer be an impediment to his art but, in their paradise regained, a helpmate. Unfortunately, in its saccharine patness, it is almost comic.

A third and final manifestation of the death/rebirth theme in *Conversation* is reflected in the subtitle, *Pilgrims' Progress*, and in the chapter epigrams taken from *Mourt's Relation*, all speaking to the ending of the old order and the start of the new—the landing of the Pilgrims on Cape Cod.[26] Throughout Aiken's early adult years, he was attracted alternately by the two cultures—English and American—shuttling between Cambridge, Massachusetts, and Rye, Sussex. He saw each of these trips motivated to a greater extent by subtle psychological factors than by immediate practical considerations. The tension that resulted was apparently the only major psychological problem that Aiken had not yet sufficiently written out in his fiction. He had touched on the dilemma in *Blue Voyage* by pitting the old-world snobbery of Cynthia against the new-world uncouthness of Demarest, but he had not developed the theme. He was to write about it in a number of major poems after *Conversation*, especially in "The Kid," but the issue is given its fullest prose attention in this last novel.

Aiken made his first trip to England in his senior year at Harvard and writes of that experience fully and euphorically in *Ushant*. England was, for the young Aiken, an escape into his past, both familial and literary. He bicycled through the Lake Country, Wordsworth in hand, dined in London pubs, and talked long into the night with young Englishmen. He first looked on the country with a sophomoric ebullience, describing it in rhapsodic terms, but with each successive trip Aiken became more and more permanently and seriously attached to

England—picking up the accent, buying a house, enrolling his three children in English schools.[27] Yet Aiken had always felt a haunting sense of desertion when he was living in England:

> The preoccupation with that England, that London, that Lake Country . . . —all this was attacked as snobbish and inimical, if not indeed plain treason. What? There was not enough cultural background, or humus, or milieu, or history, or mulch, in which the new native roots could thrust and thrive? What about Hawthorne, and Poe, and Whitman? What about Dickinson? Thoreau? If Poe and Whitman could stay in New York, why not oneself? (*Ushant*, 136)

Aiken saw this tension in psychological terms as well. He came to believe that England represented his mother and America represented his father. Further, the house itself—Jeake's House—which he bought in Rye and managed to keep during all kinds of financial crises, and to which he carried all three of his wives, was of immense, even symbolic, importance to him:[28] "And if Ariel's Island was his mother, whom he must cross the sea to rediscover," he asks early in *Ushant*, "would the ingenious Jacob [pseudonym for his psychiatrist friend, George Wilbur] say that the House was the veritable womb?" (22). Later in the autobiography, Aiken goes so far as to suggest that this psychological attachment to England was to a large extent even responsible for his restless sexual and marital ambience:

> I'm the unhappy man who fell in love with an island, when he was too young to know better. Incurably, hopelessly, and fatuously, in love. . . . And how neatly it explains everything. Exonerates all. . . . All those "love-messes" . . . all the infidelities: the pattern of instability, restlessness, dissatisfaction: the remarkable inability to remain faithful to any of the beautiful Loreleis, or the minor Loreliebchens in between—for what chance did *they* have, poor darlings?—yes, it explains all. For if your own true love is an island, your mother, your alma, your soul, what's left with which you can attach yourself to a mere beautiful woman? Tenuous and feeble at best. Off you go again, if only to see if the precious image is still there, and still what you thought it was; and sure enough, it is; and then you resent it, for that involves an infidelity to—the father, perhaps? So back you go once more, agonized, to measure the shoreline of Long Island, or the wooden houses of Staten Island, or the skyscrapers of New York, against the pale sunshot headlands of Eastbourne. (60)

But gradually—as his friend Eliot was becoming more Anglicized—Aiken was realizing that his roots were truly in America. He wrote to John Davenport, an English journalist and old friend, about his final acceptance of the new world where one has an extraordinary "feeling of FREEDOM" where

> you suddenly feel that you can breathe, walk, run, shout, commit murder or fornication, sign cheques, say what you think, stand on your head, laugh immoderately, and think with amusement even of the Bank of England. Indescribable——Yes it is better than Rye, it is better than London, better than England: I no longer have any doubt of that. Much to dislike, and hate, even, much that stinks, in people, daily press, the vulgar little sprawling towns, Hyannis, for instance, and many of the *mores* offensive, but add it all up and its got the necessary, it's alive!——I shall *go* back, I hope soon and often, but as from *here*.[29]

In a small notebook, a log filled with phrases, sentences, random thoughts, Aiken had toyed with this subject: "The return to England in *anticipation* of disillusionment. The inevitable retreat to America? The problem solved? Ariel's Island (1) changed (2) no longer needed (3) Savannah-New Bedford triumphant?" (HHL MS. Aik 4179). In *Ushant* he makes explicit the further choice, that between the North and the South:

> For in the end, there could be little question that of the two places New Bedford was by far, for his own purposes, the richer and more sustaining, and not merely because it was his inheritance, or because, when the Quakers "thee'd" and "thou'd" him, he was made to feel that he belonged, but because it was semantically his, his own language. Savannah, after a few years in the north, began to seem, if still magically beautiful, and of an incredible and cruel fertility, an alien place, another country. (89–90)

Aiken took great pride in his family's contribution to early America—from the importance of his Grandfather Potter and the founding of the Free Religious Association to his Great-uncle George, who had built the "Constitution" and at its launching in Boston shook the hand of Talleyrand (this, in turn, rendered him "so hopelessly conceited that he had never done another stroke of work in his life" [*Ushant*, 92]).

A democratic strain in Tip rubs abrasively against Enid's old-world, class-conscious snobbery that identifies Jim Connor as "nothing but a jailbird" and perceives those "very nondescript young women he's brought with him" are also bad and should be avoided. Tip sensibly responds that Enid is unable to separate herself from County Street, New Bedford, or Beacon Street, Boston, and sarcastically sneers that he, too, would have been " 'a lot more refined in my tastes if I'd been sent to the Friends' Academy in New Bedford, or Miss Nonesuch's Nunnery for Beacon Street's Best' " (*CN*, 511). Tip admits to a real " 'hatred of these damned little snob-schools, where they turn out scatterbrained little one-design nincompoops, with social registers for brains and cash-registers for hearts' " (511). Again the biographical parallel is direct:

> Well, to be sure, there had been the problem of [the children's] education: it was thought, by Lorelei as much as by himself, that the Cape Cod or Cambridge public schools were not good enough: little D. I had begun coming back from the South Yarmouth grammar school with an accent that lacked a good deal of the lapidary perfection of County or Hawthorn Streets, and with words unknown to Brattle Street, too. (*Ushant*, 138)

The strain of American egalitarianism is also sounded in Tip's explanation to Buzzer of why the headstones in the Quaker burial ground, which the two pass on their walk home from the post office, are all exactly the same size and exactly alike—to remind people not to be too proud, to be humble, not boastful:

> "You see, the Quakers thought to put up a huge great pompous marble tombstone was like a boast, was like saying, 'Ho, look at me, how grand I am! Ho, look at me, don't pay any attention to that little *Smith* fellow down there, with that measly little stone of his, like a school slate. Why, you've only to look at his stone to see how unimportant he is!' " (*CN*, 515)

Ultimately Aiken came to realize that his long romance with England was as essential to his coming to terms with America as was the acceptance of his mother in order to bring about a union with his father. He came to see the contributory role that England played in his career as a writer. He saw that the constant departures from America and the restlessness in England kept his creative senses finely honed. It was good to feel unsettled. But Aiken realized that he would always feel alien in

England. He recalls in *Ushant* an occasion when he was walking with some American friends on the Salts near Rye and one of them asked him if he really felt at home there, "and he still remembered with what a shock of surprise and recognition he had received the question, and the conscious duplicity with which he had answered it. He had answered, to be sure, in the affirmative; but the sudden question had revealed the truth to him: he did not—in the sense that the question implied—truly feel at home there, and he never would" (334).

Aiken pays tribute to his native New England in *Conversation* through the headnotes to each chapter taken from the *Journal of the Pilgrims*.[30] There is a narrative progression in the notes beginning with chapter 1, in which the grateful pilgrims land on Cape Cod in November; the epigram in chapter 2 deals with the exploration of the interior of the Cape and the fortunate discovery of water; the epigram in chapter 3 tells of the approach to an abandoned Indian settlement; and the fourth and final headnote declares: "This day some garden seeds were sown." Just as the previous headnotes had obliquely reflected the progress of the Tip-Enid quarrel, significantly it is in this last chapter that the reconciliation takes place and with it the promise of the birth of another child.

The flowering of America out of the seeds of the old world, along with the more general theme of death and rebirth, is also reflected in the number of seasonal metaphors scattered throughout the novel, which takes place in the fall. But the rebirth is best metaphorically expressed through Tip's planting of a hundred new lilac bushes. They arrive in three boxes that "lay like great coffins on the grass" (*CN*, 481). Since Terrence, the helper, had warned of pending frost, he and Tip plant the hundred lilacs that evening in the moonlight, mixing the cold roots with the cold soil and cold sand. The lilacs placed in the wintry ground carry with them the promise of spring, of massive blossoms, of turning the place into "The House of a Hundred Lilacs." For Aiken, no doubt, lilacs carried the same kind of fertility symbolism that the pointed, phallic, odorous flowers with heart-shaped leaves did for Whitman. That Whitman was in Aiken's mind is suggested by one of Tip's passing references to his lawn looking like "the uncut hair of graves" (531). We learn from *Ushant* that the lilac planting had its specific origin in the author's life, and that the soil of the two countries reflected the tension between England and America that often worried Aiken:

> How revelatory it was to remember the revulsion he had experi-
> enced, first at Inglesee . . . [to] his very own garden . . . the singular
> repugnance he had felt about touching that dark, rich, and let us
> admit it, that alien earth! He had literally been unable to bring
> himself to touch it with his hands: even to use a trowel or spade in
> it had been offensive to him: the digging and planting he had had
> to leave to others. At the time, he had been able to dismiss this as a
> mere neurotic wantonness—a whim, a distaste for those gigantic
> English earthworms. . . . But the real truth was that to touch that
> earth was treason. And the hands which had dug the sandy holes
> for the lilacs at South Yarmouth, on that night of frost and moon-
> light-hurrying, too, with Clarence, to get them safely bedded in
> before the frost should strike the naked roots—could not bring
> themselves ever again to dig any other. (333–34)[31]

The death and rebirth, sowing and reaping theme is finally echoed in a refrain: *"Cut all things or gather, the moon in the wane; but sow in increasing, or give it his bane."* Tip recalls the lines as he is putting Buzzer to bed the first night of the quarrel, and he repeats them to Enid on the following night, the night of restored harmony.

The novel alternates between the practical world of domestic strife and the metaphorical world charged with Aiken's meta-physics. Some of the weaknesses of *Conversation* are in these alternations. Aiken himself said at one point that the novel was comic (preface to *Three Novels*); certainly Tip sometimes feels that way about his life, and the prose is often humorous. For instance, the prose of the quarrel is as real as that of the reconciliation is unreal. At one point Tip has tired of Enid's sulking: "And if she could keep it up, so could he. Two could play at *that* game. And if she wanted to sulk, and go into a silence . . . by god he'd show her what a real A-number-one brass bound steel-riveted silence could be. A silence with velvet knobs on it!" (*CN*, 524). When Tip is looking at one of his paintings with particular disgust, he sees his very existence as a "vast joke" or "gigantic hoax." The novel, too, contains a number of truly comic characters, especially the handymen Binny Ratio and Terrence, with their dry Yankee wit, and Will Pepoon, who cleans outhouses. Finally, Aiken ends the tale lightly. Enid, who has made it monotonously clear how she wants to increase the family, begins to hesitate, wondering if everything has been considered, and Tip replies, " 'And to hell with considering anyway! I want a *son*, see? Even if he's born, like me, with a cleft palette in his hand!' "

But Aiken did not see *Conversation* as a joke. Sorely disappointed when Scribner's, his American publisher, refused the novel, he wrote a passionate letter to Maxwell Perkins, assuming a posture markedly different from his usual one of diffidence and modesty:

> I knew that Great Circle and King Coffin were not only good books—better than anything else you were publishing—but were perhaps by way of being classics: I feel pretty damned sure now that The Conversation is another: and it has amazed and saddened me that you should be so blind, so addicted to other and it seems to me shallower ideals, that you were not only unable to see this but actually convinced that the books were really inferior. . . . I must admit that I'm rather relieved at the prospect of at least hoping for a publisher who will see The Conversation as it *is*, a classic domestic symphony, and do it justice as such, instead of dismissing it because it's short or because it's "about a small domestic situation!" Good heavens, of course it is! That is its precise virtue—that the small domestic situation is turned into a symphonic poem on married life, which, in small compass, nevertheless says so much, reaches so far. It *is* made into a poem, that is the point: it *does* achieve beauty: it *is* significant, profoundly so. (6 July 1939, *SL*, 231)

After the novel was finally published by Duell, Sloan and Pearce, it was poorly received, as Aiken complained to Malcolm Lowry: "The novel is being peed on, crapped on, spat on, sneezed on, coughed on, ejaculated on, died and rotted on, by all the critics from the Nation up. And bang—I fear—go our hopes" (1 April 1940, HHL MS. Aik 2553). Aiken sounds uncharacteristically shrill in both letters. Undoubtedly personal circumstances at the time—specifically a dire need for money— motivated, in part, his literary assessment, since, as noted earlier, he was later to call *Conversation* a "pot-boiler" in *Ushant*. But just as the letters are uncharacteristic, so also is the novel: missing is the psychological probing of the mind of the protagonist and the beautiful lyric poetry of his best prose.

Aiken came very close to capturing the "final ecstatic 'Ahhhh!' of creative death" (*CN*, 502) in *A Heart for the Gods of*

Mexico, but the regenerative phoenix eluded him in *Conversation*. Aiken had, perhaps, suspected this and had therefore tried working the idea out in several different ways—the reconstruction of a marriage, the revitalization of the creative imagination, the rejuvenation of western civilization, the rebirth of nature— but instead of capturing the intensity that he strove for, the result was a vitiation of his thesis and an artistic failure.

Chapter Eight

THE CONSISTENT VIEW
Ushant

ALTHOUGH CONRAD AIKEN continued to write for another thirty years after the publication of *Conversation*, he never again published a piece of prose fiction. Since he offered no explanation for this, one can only speculate. If one accepts Jay Martin's observation that Aiken wrote his fiction out of his private life (with his poetry less personally precipitated) and in order to atone for it, one might suspect that he had simply confessed all that cried out for confession. Martin maintains that as early as the *House of Dust* (1920) Aiken had, for the most part, accumulated his experiences and that from then on he would enrich his awareness of himself and perfect his talent for articulating the "gold-mine of consciousness," as he defines it in *Ushant*.

In the novels, Aiken had transcribed his personal myth with a vague progression—moving from the exploration of the individual's consciousness in *Blue Voyage* (primarily a bachelor's monologue) to *Great Circle*, in which the protagonist continues to explore primarily his own consciousness, but also as it touches on that of his wife and friend. In *King Coffin* the hero contemptuously posits the superiority of his own consciousness and its independence from the rest of humanity, but with disastrous consequences. In *A Heart for the Gods of Mexico* Aiken shifts his emphasis primarily to an elaboration of his theory of recurrence; he does move his protagonist outside of herself. It is important to keep in mind that in *A Heart for the Gods* Aiken is hedging: Noni is facing certain death in the immediate future, and, consequently, her heroic self-sacrifice and inordinate concern for others is undoubtedly influenced by this awareness. Finally, in *Conversation*, through the elaboration of the death and rebirth theme, the artist realizes the necessity for and responsibility of the individual's involvement with humanity. Undeniably there is this progressive, ever-widening circle of exploration of the theme of consciousness—individual and societal—in Aiken's fiction. This is not to suggest that each novel reflects a progression in artistic realization; on the contrary, the last two novels are decidedly the weakest.

Once Aiken had seemingly exhausted the theme of consciousness in his fiction, he returned to pursue it yet again in his autobiography, *Ushant*. It might reasonably be suspected that Aiken came to feel restrained by the fictional genres and was looking about for an even more truthful vehicle to carry the theme. *Ushant* appears as the culmination of Aiken's metaphor of the mirror, which he had used extensively in his fiction and in his poetry. In the first few pages of *Blue Voyage*, Demarest had looked long and hard into his stateroom mirror trying to determine exactly what he saw reflected there; his attempt at an analysis constituted the novel. In a similar way, *Ushant* acts as a mirror for Aiken as it reflects most of what has gone on in his creative art. It is as though for almost every sign, Aiken must give a countersign in *Ushant*—a reflective commentary, a critical elaboration. It is as if Aiken sensed that a work of art could never be totally finished, absolutely complete. As autobiography, *Ushant* is ostensibly a nonfiction piece (technically not one of his novels), but "fiction" and "nonfiction" are no more useful terms when talking about Aiken's art than are "prose" and "poetry." *Ushant* is simply another port of call on the journey into eternal chaos begun so tentatively with *Blue Voyage*.

. . .

Aiken once allowed that his first novel was prompted by the idea that it would be valuable at midpoint in his career to expose the man who had been "writing and thinking these things: to make an accounting and to give away the sources." He intended to offer an explanation of himself, the writer, to his public. In *Ushant*, approaching the end of his career, Aiken tried to explain himself, the man, first to himself by amassing selected experiences and filtering them through the consistent view that understanding is only possible through the expansion of one's consciousness. To that end he tried to perfect the art of translation (he called it "conation"); that is, he tried to find metaphors to express the seemingly unexpressible and finally to shape himself—his consciousness—into a symbolic entity that held meaning simultaneously for the writer and the reader. Aiken

saw *Ushant*, then, as a commentary and apologia, the continuation of the myth of himself. In his preface to *Three Novels*, he
candidly places *Ushant* in his autobiographical and literary saga:

> And I think it should be added that *Ushant: An Essay*, a kind of
> autobiography, narrated in the third person, and of which the hero,
> D., is really the Demarest of *Blue Voyage*, but now more at sea than
> ever, should be read along with all of these: it is the complement of
> *Blue Voyage*, the statement of the writer at the end of his career, and,
> if anything, a deeper probing into the problem, or predicament, or
> *obligation*, of the artist in society, than any of the others. . . . It also
> contains an analysis of my aims, whether in verse or prose, towards,
> on the one hand, a contribution to an increase of consciousness—
> the evolution of consciousness—and, on the other, toward the
> perfecting of the statement, or artifact, in which it is made. I do not
> pretend to have succeeded in this. I only hope that I have indicated
> what I think is a direction.[1]

The principal challenge in writing what is essentially an
autobiography is obvious: how to prevent the process of recollection from turning into a self-serving, narcissistic exercise
rather than a work of art. This is not to suggest that the work is
limited to "Conrad Aiken's Life Story," a "self-hagiography,"
as Edward Butscher denounces it in his biography. Aiken always
saw himself as a "coordinate of the personalities . . . of the
literary and philosophic and psychological personalities who
have impinged upon him" (HHL MS. Aik 3593). He was acutely
aware of the built-in liabilities in pedestrian autobiographies. In
several spiral-ringed notebooks in which he kept notes for
Ushant over the years of its composition—often philosophical
musings—he acknowledged: "The egotism, admitted, and
viewed as 'material,' but as confessedly a social menage, if also
as the adverse of the insecurity & petit mal: this is what I am
and have, what *they* and I, between us, have made, and it should
be put at the disposal of mankind, if necessary on the chopping
block or the dissecting table: therefore, the 'narrating' D. must
be wholly neutral to the 'subject' D.——" (HHL MS. Aik 3593).
The magnitude of the difficulties inherent in the genre is attested to by the lamentably few enduring autobiographies.
There are unquestionably great ones: Augustine's and Rousseau's *Confessions* and Proust's *Remembrances* come immediately
to mind. But when, for instance, one examines the genre in

American literature, only *The Education of Henry Adams* and Franklin's *Autobiography* are monumental—though one might include Garland's *Middle Border* series and *The Autobiography of Lincoln Steffens*. But none of these appears to be an antecedent to *Ushant*; there is a closer affinity in such fictional autobiographies as *Moby Dick* or Poe's *Narrative of Arthur Gordon Pym*.

The scope of Aiken's autobiography was novel, and, as he explained to an interviewer for the New Bedford *Sunday Standard-Times*, it called for a "new form of prose," one that was near to the poetic, in which he could "range over the whole field and could embrace the poetic without falling into verse."[2] The whole book, Aiken insisted, was no less than a "commentary on life as a conation, an attempt to reach that which is impossible of attainment." Impossibility is itself echoed in Aiken's title, "Ushant," which functions both literally and symbolically. The word, pronounced "You shan't" in English and spelled "Ouessant" in French, is the name of a stormy, rockbound, barren spot off the tip of Brittany. As the last point of solid land one sees before setting forth onto the unfathomable ocean and the first point one sees on returning from across the sea, it functions both as a point of departure and of reentry between the conscious and the unconscious world. Yet the prohibition implied in the name symbolically suggests that Ushant, in all its barren remoteness, is the unattainable state of full consciousness—which one nonetheless strives for through perilous self-awareness.[3]

Throughout his long career Aiken had pursued this theme in every genre—poetry, prose, and even drama, but after publishing *Conversation* in 1940 Aiken must have realized that the total immersion into consciousness must be autobiographical and must at one time subscribe to the directness of prose and allow the metaphorical possibilities of poetry. That same year Aiken wrote the first eight pages of *Ushant*, but then dropped it until 1950; he completed the work during the next two years while he was Poetry Consultant at the Library of Congress. Although always keenly critical of his own works, Aiken was unequivocally pleased with *Ushant*. In 1969, he confided to an interviewer that "forgetting for a moment the poetry, which is such a mass of stuff that it sinks or swims by itself . . . probably the autobiography, *Ushant*, is my favorite child. It sums it all up. It illuminates the poetry and is illuminated by the poetry. I am very much pleased that there are signs it may be published again."[4]

. . .

Conrad Aiken was essentially a private man both by nature—as witnessed by the shyness that plagued him throughout his school days and that many years later made him hesitate to accept membership in the Learned Council of Arts if it required attendance at an installation ceremony—and by design—he was ever fearful of the pernicious effect of public acclaim on the integrity of the artist. Yet, somewhat ironically, in *Ushant* Aiken relentlessly exposes the inner man with all his weaknesses, laying bare the meanest, most petty details of his life. For instance, he recalls with a young man's shame how he had once given a woman whom he loved an inscribed copy of one of his books and later had misgivings that she might one day take advantage of him and use the autographed gift against him; so one evening, when she was momentarily out of the room, he ripped out the incriminating page from the book: "And had never known—to add to his misery—whether she had ever noticed or guessed."[5] In another instance, he remembers his embarrassment over the "infinitely humbler" home of his father in Watertown ("even by comparison poverty-stricken") to that of his aristocratic mother, "so that to begin with at Harvard he had been really ashamed to take his friends there" (102). In *Ushant* D. is scrupulously examined as a child, as a young man, and in middle age through the critical eyes of the sensitively observant writer, Conrad Aiken, who, nonetheless, maintains the posture of, what he calls in his notes, "the anonymous transmitter" or "the nameless link."

There is no attempt, however, on Aiken's part to be methodically all-inclusive, to marshal all the autobiographical details. Rather, large segments of D.'s life are completely omitted. For instance, there is not a single date given for an incident; there is virtually nothing about his elementary or secondary education; the autobiography is, in one sense, totally timeless. Aiken remarked that only one out of every hundred people he had known came into the book. Consequently, the reader does not come away with a comprehensive, year-by-year account of the life of Conrad Aiken. Despite this, or perhaps because of it, one is left with a sense not of knowing *about* Aiken but of having touched the very consciousness of the man. Merrill Moore, psychiatrist and poet, was one of those overwhelmed by Aiken's Herculean efforts to clean the Augean stables of the subconscious, "not to mention the infra Id," and was astonished at the candor of *Ushant*: "as near a revelation of the naked self as it is possible to get—and how useless to write an autobiography if this isn't its object!—your book stands head and shoulders over any that I have read" (HHL MS. Aik 1255).

. . .

While *Ushant* is not technically divisible into three sections, it does, nonetheless, concentrate on three distinct phases of D.'s development. First in importance is D. as a child and his relationship to key locations—Savannah and New Bedford—and to key people—his parents, grandparents, and assorted aunts and uncles. Next is D. as a young man at Harvard, in England, in Italy, and in France and the people and events important to the maturation process: his sexual partners and his friends; his first marriage, divorce, and subsequent loss of his three children. Finally there is D. as a writer, his theories of art, the details of the composition of his individual works, and his relationship to the literary world.

The biographical details from D.'s childhood are fairly evenly divided between those in Savannah and those in New Bedford and are primarily seen in relation to the respective houses. For instance, the large, comfortable home in Savannah with its curved staircase ("that house and the vivid life in it—father and mother, and the tremendous parties downstairs, which D. could watch through the banister of the curved staircase" [*Ushant*, 300]) appears several times in *Ushant*. D. peeks through the railings and sees his father sitting on his mother's knee, chastising her for a too-active social life: " 'Yes, if you don't stop this insensate round of party-going, with the inevitable neglect of your children, then there's just one way to put an end to it: I'll have another child——' " (302). This specific scene—as most of the others in *Ushant*—had previously been transcribed by Aiken. The incident was related almost verbatim in the short story "Strange Moonlight," published in *Dial* more than twenty-five years earlier. Here the young boy, peering over the banister, observes "with horror" that his mother is sitting on his father's knee, and he overhears a disconcerting conversation:

"It's two parties *every* week, and sometimes three or four, that's excessive. You know it is."

"Darling, I *must* have *some* recreation. . . ."

"Recreation's all right," he said, "but you're neglecting your family. If it goes on, I'll have another child—that's all."[6]

Similarly, the stoop of the Savannah house is assigned important autobiographical significance. Initially, Aiken tells us, it functioned in the fantasy life of D. as a ship; as he descended its brown steps, he moved ever closer to the imaginary ocean, which D. assures us was so "incomparably more real and fascinating than any mere Atlantic, or Bay of Biscay, was ever to be" (*Ushant*, 41). D. speculates on how much of his lifelong preoccupation with the sea—real and metaphorical—began here.

The imaginary voyages launched from the stoop are replaced by the real waterfront of New Bedford and Fair Haven and by the real voyage down Buzzards Bay on a whaling ship. While young D.'s parents had been primarily projected against the Savannah house, the portrayals of his Grandfather (William James Potter), Aunt Jean (Jane Delano Kempton), the Beloved Uncle (Alfred Claghorn Potter), and the Frightened Uncle (William Hopkins Tillinghast) are sketched against their New Bedford houses. D. was adopted by the Frightened Uncle, who had himself been orphaned when he was eight and subsequently adopted by his guardian, D.'s grandfather (such recurrence had important meaning for Aiken).

In addition to the writer's concern with people projected against their "places" (that is, characters and settings), Aiken is keenly interested in D.'s earliest memories of "scenes," particularly of "continuous scenes" (that is, narratives). *Ushant* includes D.'s first recollection of a cursory scene: dropping his younger brother's milk bottle over the dark banister of the stair railing. The mature D. suspects that he remembers this because it unmistakably included an "element of calculation . . . a *suppressed* beforeness" in it. He likewise remembers the earliest "plot": his mother coming out on the stoop and announcing to him that his Grandfather Potter in New Bedford had died and then his being specifically dressed to walk with his mother to the telegraph office.

The young manhood section of *Ushant* covers Aiken's resignation from Harvard, purportedly over his anger about being dropped from the dean's list, and his probation for missing two weeks of classes while he was working on a verse translation of Gautier's *Morte Amoureuse*. But he hints elsewhere in *Ushant* that the real reason for his leaving the college was his fearful reluctance to fill the position of class poet to which he had been elected and that would have required a public reading. The autobiography only glancingly touches on D.'s flight to Italy and to France but deals extensively with his various sojourns in England, firmly establishing the philosophical and psychological grounds for the tension that the maturing Aiken felt between England and America. The young manhood years particularly illuminate D.'s preoccupation with sex and tangentially with the relationship between sex and art that he explored so exhaustively in *Blue Voyage* and continued in *Great Circle* and, to a lesser degree, in *Conversation*.

Two of the most detailed sexual "experiences" related in *Ushant* are those with Alice and with Irene, the former merely a fantasy and the latter D.'s first real sexual encounter. The descriptive language with which Aiken chooses to relate both incidents is marked by idealistic, specifically religious diction, frequent use of the indefinite pronoun, and a reliance on passive constructions—casting D. in the role of a neophyte preparing for initiation into a sacred mystery. It is also diction that, unfortunately, borders on bathos, thereby blunting the impact on the reader of what was obviously a powerful emotion in the writer. The language of guilt that surrounds the first incident is missing from the second, and the reason seems to be—strange as it may sound—a conversation the young D. has with a Franciscan monk that appears to absolve the tortured young man and to usher in his mature sexual life.

The relationship with Alice occurs during D.'s trip to England the summer that he is nineteen. He recalls that his first "definite desire" was for the slightly older daughter of the couple who ran the cottage where he was staying. He nurtured the romantic hope that Alice would magically appear in his room one night and that he would be "deliciously seduced." His memories of Alice are expressed with appropriately sophomoric rhetoric: he hoped that she would approach him in some "fantastic" way, and he confessed that his "fantasies about her were endless"; he "ardently" hoped that she would help rid him of his "troublesome virginity"; he ached to be introduced to the "sacred mystery." D.'s sexual imagination at this time is further inflamed by a scene he accidentally witnesses one day while biking on the far side of Lake Windermere. He comes suddenly on a couple copulating under a tree. D.'s language here discloses his sexual fears: the incident, he says, filled him with "the shock of discovery," with "dismay," with "excitement, even . . . horror." D.'s diffidence in describing the event is suggested by his awkward reliance on the vague, impersonal pronoun: "He now knew, quite appallingly, quite deliriously, what *it* looked like. *It* would be—if she did come to his room at midnight—like *that*, with Alice" (65; italics mine).

D.'s dream of his bedroom seduction is not realized that summer or the next. Alice does, however, appear in his room, but not to seduce him. His sexually aroused imagination conjures up a picture of Alice cleaning his room and finding the green tube of clap ointment—albeit unopened—that a traveling salesman from Detroit has given him. This frightfully embarrassing possibility accompanied by the ever-present guilt is recorded in *Ushant*: "the shame of it all, which was to keep its redness and soreness for years!" (65).

Two years later, twenty-one years old and in France, D.'s determination to shed his "troublesome virginity" still preoccupies him. He now sets off on a determined quest: "on that journey which, he was now explicitly aware, was aimed at carnal knowledge: he must somehow, by hook or by crook, god help him, get himself seduced" (161). Despite the seriousness of the adventure, Aiken can see the humor in his own inability to lose his virginity, but he is still a passive questor ("get himself seduced"). D.'s blond, innocent look attracts the attention of a Franciscan monk strolling through the Borghese Gardens. The monk enters into a flirtatious, bantering conversation with D. on innocence and experience, culminating with the question, asked incredulously, " 'Tu es virgo?' " The guilt-ridden D., fearful of vague religious prohibition, is delighted to think (and to believe) after this extended conversation on sexual mores that his own first sexual experience is to be sanctioned by the hand of God—in this case, his clerical representative: "It was as if destiny . . . with the sure ethical and aesthetic hand of the artist, had chosen for him this form of annunciation, in order that not only the sense of guilt might be exorcised, but that it should be even accompanied by the blessing of the Catholic church" (162).

The seriousness with which Aiken views the centrality of sex to all else is illuminated by the religious diction he calls on to relate D.'s encounter with Irene Barnes, a Tottenham Court prostitute, who finally presents him with the "gift so princely." The situation moves beyond D.: "How miraculously one knew what one was doing without any conscious formulation whatever" (189). D. walks with Irene on a June evening toward the "blessed hotel" for an assignation that he later terms a "transfiguration":

> after that, in a way that he could not possibly have foreseen, everything was to be changed—chemically, somatically, psychologically, spiritually: in effect, it amounted to a revolution of the soul. . . . He had put on a new body and a new mind. . . . He had come to life's very center, and stood there with a feeling of precarious and impossible security, and as happy as a blossoming tree anchored in wind and light. (189)

In retrospect, D. remembers "how radiant" had been the influence of that evening; the whole summer had been "illuminated" by it. From then on, D. insists, the grand tour became a pure fugue with two themes, "two voices, pursuing and overtaking and overlapping each other, the twin and ambivalent themes or voices of sex and art" (164). In his *Ushant* notebook, Aiken had directed himself:

> analyze the sexual behavior and the loves as something neither to be approved or disapproved but as the co-efficient of the necessary love, energy,—vanity?—for work. AND, often (give instances) the material for it. And can't this too be related to the consistent view, the evolution of consciousness. How to love, live, indulge, and just the same do one's *ultimate* duty by one's notion of the only good! (HHL MS. Aik 3593)

At this juncture, D. cloaks all sexual references with a linguistic mantle of naïveté and idealism; the language continues to be inflated. Numerous "instances" are detailed in *Ushant*, each selected for an experience not suggested by another. Here, for example, D. gives an account of his introduction to homosexuality. He and his friend Heinrich (Harry B. Wehle, a Harvard friend and classmate) accidentally meet Hawkins—a young, cultured Englishman—amid the Roman statuary in the British Museum. After dinner the three retire to the Americans' room for a night of lively conversation in which the exquisitely mannered Englishman gives them eye-opening reports of all the varieties of the "ambidextrous" sexual encounters he has enjoyed. But it is only after he makes several attempts at embracing them and after it becomes evident he intends sharing Heinrich's bed with him that "the first horrifying revelation of the existence of homosexuality" (*Ushant*, 126) dawned on D. In the days that follow, D. works through an initial revulsion of Hawkins's homosexuality to a general alteration in his attitude toward what he considers sexual deviation. He goes through what he calls a "process of transvaluation of values"—in short, an expansion of consciousness:

> If people like Hawkins existed, and made a kind of brilliance of their existence: if the sickness . . . could be by a process of secretion and sublimation made over into a nacreous "culture," or even cultural pearl—and certainly by any standards, Hawkins had achieved a refinement of taste, and a logical system of behavior, which made the liberalisms of Harvard and Boston look pale indeed: then, surely, one must widen one's categories of acceptance and tolerance. (127)

Finally, the three women whom D. married are included in *Ushant* under the pseudonyms of Lorelei One, Two, and Three but—curiously—are scarcely discussed. One can only guess at the reasons for Aiken's reticence here. That the women were alive and easily identifiable at the time of publication must certainly have been a consideration. Whatever guilt Aiken felt over the two divorces is partially explained away by his suggestion that sex and art, though frequently intricately intertwined, are in competition with each other; and when they are, art must take precedence.[7] One cannot help but wonder to what extent this was theory and to what extent this was rationalization for the divorces and desertions:

> Sex and art, yes, for those two twin divinities—unless indeed they were one and the same, a Janus god, who turned first one radiant

but imperious face and then the other—his whole life was to be a perpetual series of forced marches, forced moves. But was art, in the end, to have rather the better of it? Yes, there could be little doubt of it. That virus, in the imagination, was a doom, a dedicated and delicious doom, in itself. (*Ushant*, 185)

Aiken does, however, give fairly extensive treatment to the loss of his three children, which the divorce from his first wife necessitated. He admits that perhaps he understood his real feeling for the children only when he was about to lose them. (He speculates on whether this might not perhaps be true of everything, that it was only in the "profoundest experience of annihilation, and of the dissolution of all hope and pride and identity, in the great glare of cosmic consciousness, that one could regain one's power *to value*?" [223]).

The sense of desertion threads its way through *Ushant*—whether it be D.'s desertion by his parents or D.'s desertion of women he loved or married or of friends or children. Yet D. finds consolation in his insistence that all experience contributes to the evolution of consciousness, out of which—through the intercession of the imagination—comes art:

Art and sex, or art and love—that was the primary order, for if one could sacrifice love for art, or one love for another, one could never—could one?—sacrifice art for love—or only momentarily, and with an eye over the shoulder, the unsleeping knowledge that this, like all experience, but more than most, was the indispensable raw material of art; for everything, and finally one's heart itself, went into that alchemist's alembic. (185–86)

The third distinct biographical phase in the life of Aiken recounted in *Ushant* is his career as a writer. The specific circumstances surrounding the composition of each of his novels, except for *King Coffin*, and many of his major poems, as well as incisive, relentless criticism of them, are here detailed. Further, under the protective guise of fairly transparent pseudonyms, Aiken makes incisive comments on several major literary figures of the twentieth century and on the general literary scene. There are some devastatingly frank accounts of the literary jockeying of the 1920s. For instance, he includes his early and persistent reservations about the Imagists and his arguments over free verse with John Gould Fletcher ("Farouche

John"). He reflects on the rise of the "little" magazines: " 'Others,' and all the others, for they sprouted on all sides, quarreled, debated, made their own little private and esoteric splashes and died" (218). *Ushant* provides amusing, gossipy insights to a number of Aiken's literary acquaintances all demurely veiled in this roman à clef: Harold Monro ("Arnault"), John Freeman ("Gentle John"), Ezra Pound ("Rabbi Ben Ezra"), among others. But of the literary figures, it is Malcolm Lowry ("Hambo") and T. S. Eliot ("Tsetse") who dominate *Ushant*.[8] Further, it was, as D. remarks, "An era of legend and myth-making, of cutthroat jealousies and vendettas, of gossip and wild parties, of murderous exclusions, and, of course, of the all-too-eager joinings and belongings as well. An era of the picturesque, and picaresque, too, when the improbable was the order of the day" (*Ushant*, 218). Aiken's own peculiar perspective on the writers and the literary movements lends an honesty, a sharpness, and a sensitivity to *Ushant* that rivals Cowley's clearly etched *Exile's Return*.

. . .

The strictly biographical details in *Ushant*, however compelling in their own right, are nonetheless subordinated to the single theme of consciousness, which, as we have seen, dominated Aiken's art his entire life. "That great consciousness, wouldn't it have found something to bless in D.'s 'consistent view,' the notion that consciousness was itself the chief of blessings?" (245). *Ushant* becomes the means for Aiken to explore the genesis of his created world, his fiction, his poetry, his criticism in an attempt to know himself as well as to know the sources for the strengths and weaknesses of his art. He begins with the knowledge that once the mind is fully aware of itself and of the universe, the inevitable process to know more and more is endless—that is to say, organic as opposed to static. For instance, while *Ushant* reflects on all Aiken's important works that preceded it, he confided to Lewis Nichols at the time of its publication that maybe at some future time he would write a commentary on the work itself: "There are a lot of suspended themes there. In 'Ushant' I tear some of my earlier books apart, suggesting the falsehoods, saying how they could have been better. I can do another and tear this apart, saying how it could be better."[9] Such an idea was jocularly considered by an interviewer, who commented on the expressed curiosity about particular unidentifiable people in *Ushant* and concluded, "The result has been talk—not to be taken seriously—of writing ' "Ushant," a Glossary,' or 'Recant, an Annotation' to accompany the book."[10] The 1971 second edition included just such a glossary.

The exploration of *Ushant's* central motif of consciousness is posited on this all-consuming desire of the protagonist to know: that is, the pursuit of greater self-knowledge and, by extension, the establishment of a reality. He wants to *know*, and he wants to know *how* he knows, by what process. Although all his conclusions are tentative, D. broadly assumes that the individual shapes himself through expanding his consciousness—that is, primarily through greater self-knowledge and through love, both sexual and sympathetic, or what he calls "caritas"; the individual shapes his world and his reality through seeing life as a *process* and through becoming an onomasticon, a namer—that is, reality comes into being through language. This philosophical position is pursued in detail and with a welcome clarity of expression.

Such a distillation of *Ushant's* basic theme must be set against the important, constantly reinforced axiom that nothing is final. For instance, D., in calling to mind his early meeting with Lorelei One on an October walk through the drift of leaves, concludes: "it was the beginning, in fact of things that would *never* be finished, poems, loves, lives, books—it had seemed from very early, perhaps always, to be in the very principle of things, or at any rate in himself, that nothing should ever be truly completed" (*Ushant*, 57). Over and over again, D. insists on the importance of being ever sensitive to the presence of flux, to the process of becoming. It is through the various processes that one gradually takes on an ever-changing identity. D. recalls at length his arduous, infatuous love of the pristine, inaccessible, stained-glass Cynthia (of *Blue Voyage*) and how, in part, she was replaced by the seductive Faubion with her "earthen vitality," thus adding another dimension to D.'s awareness. He concludes that this is true of each new encounter with every new individual:

In each new meeting was the instinct for the love-dance, and out of each, no matter how fleeting or slight, one hoped for the blossoming of that moment of semantic discovery, which at its best must be reciprocal—: the new bead of light and meaning to be added to one's ever-lengthening chain, each one an increase in the vocabulary of self. "What is there in thee Man that can be known?" Only this, this process of collection, this mysterious process by which the psychic mirror stored away its reflections of the ever-changing colors and shapes of other psyches, other things, and fashioned thus the luminous Joseph's Coat, ever more variegated and prismatic, through which it gave back to the world the brief light of the soul. Mimicry, mimicry, mimicry—one's whole life was spent in mimicry. And in the end, one's personality was nothing whatever but an anthology of these mimicries and adaptations, one was oneself simply the compiler. The onomastic. (48–49)

This process, if sensitively observed, would reveal certain patterns only dimly and gradually discernible to the individual: the process is a spiral one, not one of revelations in ascending order. The patterns that *Ushant* brings to light are far too many to enumerate, but one, for purposes of illustration, is D.'s realization that he flees to England at moments of personal— often sexual—crisis and that there exists real tension for him between England and America similar to the tension between Savannah and New Bedford, between a Southern and a Northern ambience; it shares something with the tension emanating from his alternate allegiances to his mother and to his father. In another instance, D. sees his abandonment of his own three children when he divorced Lorelei One as part of the betrayal pattern begun by his own parents' abandonment of him through their death: "And the abandonment—hadn't that too been a compulsory repetition of the family pattern? . . . If *he* had been thus abandoned, flung overboard, should not they?" (222).

Sometimes even more frightening autobiographical patterns surface. For instance, D. sees his own suicide attempt, described in *Ushant*, as a reenactment of his father's suicide, an act almost summoned by his father's death. It was, he says, "predestined, yes: for had he not always admitted, almost as a kind of necessity, if he were to achieve identification with the father, the need of emulating him even in self-destruction?" (222). The psychiatrist G. B. Wilbur, Aiken's close friend, responded to Mary Aiken's message about her husband's death: "Your news tonight comes as a sort of relief. As you understand Conrad struggled all his life to avoid sharing in the fate of his father. I feared he was losing the battle for reasons I knew nothing about nor could help. So that is over" (17 August 1973, HHL MS. Aik 4166).

Yet the whole process—the accretion of experience, the recognition of patterns, the examination of the past for the relatively immediate sources for the present, and the voyages into
the unconscious for the primal material—remains of limited
value to D. as an individual until it is transmuted into a reality
by language; and it remains of limited use, in general, until it is
transformed into art. As Howard Nemerov said in his praise of
Aiken's autobiography: "All authors try to write the world, but
only a very few succeed in teaching us how to read it."[11] Just as
power was acquired over the created world and over particular
individuals in the Old Testament through the process of naming, so also in *Ushant* D. exercises a control over the inchoate
world through language and art. It appears that the created
artifact provides a semblance of resolution to the dichotomous
view of reality that is Aiken's: on the one hand, he insists that
chaos prevails, that all is flux; and on the other, he posits that
there is a preordained order to life that will emerge through the
artist's recognition of the subtle patterns and through his making them known in a work of art, complex and multileveled
enough to do them justice. Yet in *Ushant* D. readily admits: "that
unfathomable, and yet to-be-fathomed, pluralism, the plural
mind in the plural universe, must forever partly escape the
flung net of symbol. That eternal problem of language, language
extending consciousness and then consciousness extending language, in circular or spiral ascent" (*Ushant*, 167). Aiken had
early been interested in the evolution of language and its relation to thought. In a 1942 book review for the *Atlantic Monthly*,
he developed a detailed commentary on the growth of language
in which he concluded:

> In this trial-and-error evolution of consciousness, a new word
> meant, to all intents, a new feeling: a new cluster of words meant a
> new complex of feelings; and in each item it could perhaps properly
> be said that this new perception or feeling represented a splitting
> and refinement of the coarser and simpler perceptions which had
> preceded it. . . . And in this evolution of language, which is also the
> evolution of literature and consciousness, it must be borne in mind
> that the process has always been a strictly individual and minority
> affair.[12]

So for D. there was always the realization that one came to
know oneself through language. Two of his earliest memories

were of himself as a maker through words. First, the epigraph to *Tom Brown's School Days*, the book given to him as a boy, became his talisman for life. In the early pages of *Ushant*, D. proclaims, "I'm the poet of White Horse Vale, sir, with Liberal notions under my cap" (52). And in the closing pages, he queries:

> Hadn't he, ever since, every time he set sail for England, actually been setting sail for that carpeted floor, on which the copy of *Tom Brown's School Days* still lay open at the luminous fragment of verse? Hadn't time stood still, ever since, at that echo of a moment, that phrase of incantation? And hadn't his entire life been simply a *locus* bending again and again, after no matter how many interruptions and diversions . . . to this limit, this perhaps unattainable limit, this imperative and imperishable Ushant? (300)

A second, related reminiscence was young D.'s first poem, put together in school from the spelling lesson words scrolled on the blackboard: "The lions had waited all the day, lying concealed in the grass, for their prey—." D. recalls the wondrous experience of creating that line of verse:

> This extraordinary thing had come from himself, he knew that— and yet it had also come from somewhere else. It was a new existence, an addition to all that had existed before, it was here on the paper, both his and not his, so that one hardly knew whether to take pride in it or not. If from somewhere else, from where? How had it happened? All very well to understand, years later, the logical sequence of the steps that had led to it, but the fact remained that at the moment of conceiving, and then of writing, it had been a sort of apocalypse, a seizure, the self becoming merely the invisible and nameless lightning-rod for an alien and unfamiliar lightning. (109)

From that time on, D. was certain that his tools of consciousness were to be words. He would only come to understand his nature through language: "This nature, it appeared, must learn to shape itself in words; words, and the rhythms of words, were the medium in which it seemed most likely, or at any rate most happily and magically, to find the equivalents of being, the equivalents of the still shadowy self. Here was the clearest process, and evidence, of growth; these were the tree's leaves" (92). (Throughout *Ushant* Aiken employs this nature metaphor of buds expanding and of trees burgeoning into foliage as one of the ways to suggest the expansion of awareness through words.)

Early in life D. had assured himself that it was *translation* that would make possible the discovery of the underlying order, and it was that on which he expended his life's energies. Although he knew that the translation would never be perfect or complete, it nonetheless remained the "consistent view" to which D. consecrated his life. It was for this reason that Aiken viewed the writer with such reverence. In a letter to John Gould Fletcher, he took serious exception to Karl Shapiro's dismissal of the function of the poet (in his book, *Essay on Rime*) as being unimportant or at best harmless and amusing. Instead Aiken insisted that the writer had the priestly charge of advancing the "consciousness and conscience and genius of mankind." He sees him as a forerunner, a firebringer, an orderer, and a releaser; "the one who by finding the word for life makes life possible and coherent, and puts it within the reach of all." He juxtaposes the writer against the scientist, philosopher, and mathematician, who make only partial statements about life because they leave out the feelings; the writer, however, transmutes his knowledge "*through* the feelings, makes, at each stage of man's development, the *whole* statement; he always has the last word, because it is always the first—the poet was and is the one who invents language. Which is tantamount to inventing experience, or awareness."[13] But having formulated and verified this godlike role for the writer and the artifact, Aiken characteristically begins to have his doubts. He asks himself in his notebook,

> would the logical end of civilization be, not in the artifact—which was an objectified synthesis of private cum-social conflicts and aspiration, but, at last the LIVING itself such an artifact, synthesis? *and*, therefore the necessity for breaking down the process of artifaction into its own dynamics (of human psychology) progressively to the point at which one could at last say that the work of art was unnecessary, one could imagine it and be it, oneself, with one's *own life*. (HHL MS. Aik 3593)

In Howard Nemerov's high praise for *Ushant*, he perceptively cites Wordsworth's *Prelude* as its poetic counterpart, noting that both works illustrate "the art to see through art." *Ushant*, continues Nemerov, is "art becoming conscious of itself, and with that, though often heroically, doubtful of itself."[14] We have, on the one hand, disclosures of the most important autobiographical details in the life of the writer and, on the other, a highly critical study of the art of art; the relationship between the two is seen through the artistic creations of Conrad Aiken.[15] There was, however, no traditional paradigm for precisely what Aiken wanted to do. While Nemerov noted the thematic similarities between *Ushant* and the *Prelude*, he might have mentioned the structural ones as well. *Ushant* is, in many ways, a long poem, lyrical, epical—a spiritual autobiography. Like Wordsworth, Aiken discovers the source of art and reality—the imagination—by writing it out of himself. Surely Aiken must have toyed with the idea of casting his autobiography in the form of a long poem—certainly extended verse marked his style—before he chose an ostensibly prose form. But, rather, for his artistic and spiritual chronicle, Aiken created a new form, subtitling the work "An Essay" and explaining, "It is an essay both in the sense of literary composition and as an attempt at a new form of writing."[16] In 1947, a decade after he had tentatively begun *Ushant* and a decade before its completion, Aiken had promised his publisher, John Davenport, that he would give him the "new novel" when it was done; but he cautioned him that it would be some years in the doing: "I don't want to rush it, I allow five years in fact if necessary, and I don't minimize to myself the very real possibility that it may not come off at all: it's at best a most precarious and rarefied piece of scaffolding, pinnacled *very* dim in the intense inane, or immense immane, and I might quite likely get thoroughly lost up there and never find my way down again!——" (HHL MS. Aik 3817). He told Robert Linscott that he was working on a "new Chinese-puzzle-box of a novel" (10 March 1947).[17]

Aiken described this new form as "spiral," one that would allow him "to keep in what was worthwhile and leave out what was trivial . . . and to keep the reader interested."[18] The spiral form accounts for the simultaneity in *Ushant*, giving one the sense that D.'s entire life is present at all times. Unidentified characters, for instance, move in and out of the early pages of the book, and their importance only gradually becomes evident later through the elaboration of a particular incident or through the subtle accretion of small details. Similarly, the shadow of the death of D.'s parents dominates the whole of *Ushant*—as it dominated the whole of Aiken's life and art—from its earliest pages, where oblique references to it abound; but the account of the tragedy does not appear until the last chapter, just sixty-three pages before the end of the autobiography.

The architectonic form of *Ushant* suggests the extent to which Aiken was part of the stream-of-consciousness experimentation marking the first half of twentieth-century literature. As a student, Aiken had been an admirer of Whitman's technique of free association. He admitted to R. H. Wilbur in the *Paris Interview* that Whitman had had a "profound influence" on him: "That was during my sophomore year when I came down with a bad attack of Whitmanitis. But he did me a lot of good, and I think the influence is discoverable. . . . He was useful to me in the perfection of form, as a sort of compromise between the strict and the free."[19] But Aiken was sensitive to the dangers inherent in both the techniques of stream of consciousness and free association, and in *Ushant* he admits to an essentially conservative bias in matters of form, an insistence that form must be form:

> that intentions of form must keep a basis in order and tradition, that a mere surrender to the pleasure (which was undoubtedly to be had) of chain-making in the bright colors of the colloquial and the colloquial cadence was not enough, not a substitute for the dark and difficult and, yes, painful process of cryptopoiesis, and that this, in turn, must, like a compass, have its true North in the shape of a conscious and articulated *Weltanschauung*, a consistent view. (219)

Aiken's "true North" here was the attempt at achieving the impossible task suggested by the title: reaching the rocky coast of Ushant, although threatened by the ever-present possibility of shipwreck and accompanied by the realization of the impossibility of reaching it. Such a thesis partially explains the complexity of the structure of this autobiography, which is totally unlike any other.

On the surface, *Ushant* is simply the relating of the shipboard experiences of a man who left America for England immediately after World War II on a recently converted troop ship. The reader comes to know D. as a fifty-year-old writer enjoying the company of his fellow passengers: the Mad Swiss, returning to

England after years of painting houses in Canada; Blimp, with his big cigars; Hardie, dying of diabetes and making the trip in order to turn his boys over to the care of his sister; and seasick Blunden, among others. On another level, we microscopically examine the entire lifetime of D. through the interior monologues of his waking reminiscences and through his tortured dream world. On yet another level, we enter into the world of the novel that D. is planning to write—a novel based on a vague "ambiguous, ambivalent and shimmering" dream he had once had about four translators: Hans (Malcolm Lowry), Elspeth (Jan Gabriel Lowry), the Teacher from the West (William James Potter, his grandfather), and himself.[20] Gradually D. realizes that the novel he intends to write already exists: it is the very work on which the translators are engaged. It is, in fact, *Ushant*—which is being written before the writer's and readers' eyes.

Aiken begins *Ushant* with a dash, followed by a variation on *Genesis*: "beginning without beginning, water without a seam, or sleep without a dream, or dream coterminous with sleep and the sleeper; flux and reflux, coil and moil." He ends 365 pages later (all editions are set to end on page 365) with the same dash preceded by "as it had no beginning can have no end," thereby suggesting both the spiral form of *Ushant* and the fact that the whole book has been a dream. The emphasis on the dream world is consistent with Aiken's sustaining belief in the connections drawn by Freud and Jung between the dream world and the unconscious and Aiken's extension of the relationships among the dream world, the unconscious, and the evolution of consciousness. Aiken had insisted in "A Basis for Criticism" that dreams were not simply escapes *from* ourselves but also incursions *into* ourselves, ultimately existing to free us or "to find ourselves": "But what part of ourselves is it that we find? Is it not exactly that part of us which has been wounded and would be made whole: that part of us which desires wings and has none, longs for immortality and knows that it must die, craves unlimited power and has instead 'common sense' and the small bitter 'actual': that part of us, in short, which is imprisoned and would escape?" (*ABC*, 62). Aiken uses the dream as an essential structural device of the novel, and at the same time he pulls together the subtle, thematic relationship between the process of dreaming and the process of creating, as he had previously done in other works, especially in *Great Circle*.

In addition to recurring dreams and recurring biographical incidents that contribute to the spiral structure of *Ushant*, Aiken repeats particular words and phrases reflective of his philosophical attitudes: "pattern," "process," "evolving consciousness," and "consistent view"; as well as italicized refrains, including *"Rooms, Streets, and Houses"* and *"Your ghost will walk, you lover of trees"*; and the paragraphs echo with references to bells. Some writers on *Ushant*, such as Vance Mizelle and Gertrude Maurer, are tempted by the recurrences to identify the form of *Ushant* as musical, specifically symphonic, and write in terms of the principles of "counterpoint," "repetition," "variation," and "contrast." Aiken's own description of his structure as "spiral" is more accurate, or, to employ another Aiken metaphor, its form is, again, a variation on the "great circle." He begins without beginning, circles back to his childhood, touches often on the one most dreadful memory, is driven back further than birth, glances at the maturing years—goes backward in order to move forward, goes deep in order to ascend. In his spiral copybook of notes for *Ushant*, Aiken sketches his thoughts on the form he is working toward:

> everything presented as on one time level—the image of focussing a whole series, a battery of telescopes, each on a star at a different distance, so as to have at a given moment in a given place a simultaneous view of all possible distances and places—the past, the present and the future all given at once—the important and the unimportant—Senlin is this, Festus is this, Great Circle is this, Blue Voyage—there is no progress in this sense, as in the usual—it is a sort of static-dynamic—everything back is given (hypothecated) everything future is implied—in this kind of stillness is all motion the humming centre—is this form of classic? is this what classic is? action has preceded this, action will follow—but the moment is comprehension. (HHL MS. Aik 4187)

This all-inclusiveness and universality of intention within *Ushant* is reflected by Aiken's early notes, in which he lists "the 7 days of creation," "infancy through senescence," "the various shipboard watches," and Shakespeare's "7 ages of man."

Within the total spiral configuration of *Ushant*, there is, in conjunction with the dream structure, a further elaborate symbolic structure commencing with the conventional voyage itself, which quickly moves away from the actual trip—toward Liverpool to reclaim the house at Saltinge vacated during the war— to the pursuit of self-knowledge and cosmic enlightenment. The voyage over the sea functions throughout Aiken's works as a traditional symbol for the chaos from which one is created. The waves suggest D.'s alternations between memories of the past and images from the present, which in his mind play against each other as he lies half-asleep in his stateroom on the last night of the trip.

To illustrate the totality of the symbolic structure, one could move from the archetypal voyage, sea, and waves to the complexity of the ship symbol. The Grey Empress has its symbolic genesis in the boat that D.'s father once promised to build in the Savannah backyard but never completed. It is also related to the ship on which D. met Cynthia on two different trips to England. D. allows that perhaps even now—in *Ushant*—he was himself still occupied in building and launching and sailing that adventurous little Argonaut:

> that unbuilt boat was the Grey Empress, at this moment, and all the countless other ships he had sailed in, forever pointing a hopeful bow in a new direction: towards Liverpool tonight, as on the first of all occasions from Quebec, with the Scotch carpenter . . . towards foaming Ushant and moaning Cherbourg . . . all these, and all the others, of course they were the unbuilt boat in the backyard, he had been building it ever since. (*Ushant*, 47)

Ushant is laced with symbols drawn from D.'s waking and sleeping world—houses in England and America, circles, dances, and on and on—giving the book a dense, symbolic richness. Yet *Ushant* is, finally, not a fragmented piece: its basic spiral configuration, its dream and symbolic substructures, its cast of characters, and its singleness of theme and tone all contribute to an intrinsic organic unity. Aiken himself provided the most perceptive analysis of his form in a BBC broadcast, in which he identified it as a

> spiral form of layer on layer of memory—going in and out of the memory and to analysis, and back and forth; and without any sort

of particular point of entry to begin it with, or any particular point of departure on which to end. But treating experience as a sort of spiral flux which is enterable at any point and departable from at any point. So that the book itself has an annular form if you like. You can start in the middle if you want and read from there; or you could read backwards and come to the same sort of thing. It's like the self-swallowing snake. (HHL MS. Aik 3593)

Consistent with the pattern set by Aiken's other works, *Ushant* was enthusiastically reviewed in the serious publications and subsequently unread. Edward Dahlberg's diffident, even inhibited review for *Poetry* was the exception. He railed that *Ushant* was an "archive of piddling obscenities and . . . a loose-anecdotal recollection of puerile eroticisms" and that its author was "placeless . . . as ungraspable as Proteus. . . . He is loose water, and all the glyphs, mementoes, and reminiscences are written on the unstable surfaces of the sea."[21] Such a review misinterpreted the essential, integrated strengths of the book as accidental weaknesses. The necessary looseness of style, however, posed no problems for most reviewers. W. T. Scott in the *Saturday Review* observed that *Ushant* "is an autobiography whose intention, like that of a poem, is to be no mere record but, rather, a created, living thing; the mutability of life shuttling through a racing, tumultuous language, adverbial as a brook."[22]

Several reviewers placed Aiken's autobiography on the same scale with those of Augustine and Rousseau, and Malcolm Cowley perceptively acknowledged that even if *Ushant* were not of the same magnitude as Proust's *Remembrance of Things Past*, it would at least be in the same great line. Cowley recognized the complexity of the book and prefaced his *New Republic* review by stating, "A second reading confirms my first impression that *Ushant* is one of the great American autobiographies."[23] And Mark Schorer agreed, "It is difficult even after three readings, to be merely descriptive."[24] But the finest compliment to *Ushant* was a personal letter (reprinted on the book jacket of the 1972 second edition) to Aiken from Lewis Mumford, once again holding out the promise that Aiken's day was about to dawn:

This is a letter, dear Aiken, that I have been on the point of writing to you all winter: or at least from the time that my delight in your novels led me to re-read USHANT. As you perhaps remember, that marvelous account of your life and loves entranced me when I first read it: but it gave me even greater pleasure when I read it for the second time. As a biography [it is] as near a revelation of the naked self as it is possible to get—and how useless to write an autobiography if this isn't its object! Rousseau, no less than Augustine, is too full of cant to be put alongside you. And your prose!— No one else has written such incomparable prose, at least in English, this last half-century: it's on a par with your very finest poetry— and higher praise I can't give. . . . There's no one around now to touch you: and those who claimed the limelight in our time will not hold a candle to you, once a later generation sits in judgment on your work.

The tribunal of a reading public for *Ushant*—as well as for most of Aiken's work—has yet to assemble. It is fortunate that writing itself served a vital, personal function for Aiken—the means for framing the consistent view that had "shaped itself slowly and intermittently out of the incredibly rich pour of new discoveries, new ideas, the miraculously rapid expansion of man's knowledge, inward and outward, whether into the ever farther-reaching astro-physics of the heavens, or of man's mind" (*Ushant*, 219). The autobiography has never been extended further. *Ushant* remains a compelling, artistic, poetic testimony to Aiken's conviction that through the exploration and expansion of the individual mind the world itself moves toward a "brilliance of consciousness." The joy that the reader experiences in joining this pilgrimage, in reaching a total consciousness, is blunted only by the awareness that—finally—USHANT.

Chapter Nine

THE CIRCLE COMPLETED

MARK SCHORER'S OBSERVATION that about Conrad Aiken there appeared to be "a conspiracy of silence" and critic Henry Popkin's oft-repeated estimate that he was "famous for not being famous enough" point to the realities of the writer's acceptance as a literary figure of the twentieth century.[1] Aiken expressed his neglect even more graphically: "At any given moment in the Pegasus Sweepstakes, in whatever Selling Plate or for whatever year, this dubious horse has always been the last in the list of the also-ran,—he never even placed, much less won, nor, I regret to report, have the offers to put him out to stud been either remunerative or very attractive."[2] Although Aiken was none too happy to have Louis Untermeyer title an article in a popular journal "Conrad Aiken: Our Best Known Unread Poet," the title unhappily reflects the truth about the readership of his fiction even more than it does his poetry.[3] Malcolm Cowley lamented that Aiken had been more neglected than any other major writer since Melville and Dickinson.[4]

On the one hand, it is possible, though difficult, to understand Aiken's being entirely omitted from broad surveys of American literature, such as Leon Howard's *Literature and the American Tradition* or George Snell's *The Shapers of American Fiction, 1789–1947*. But, on the other hand, it is inconceivable how the author of *Blue Voyage, Great Circle,* or *King Coffin* could be omitted from specialized studies such as Simon Lesser's *Fiction and the Unconscious* or Irving Malin's *Psychoanalysis and American Fiction*. Any historical study of the continuity of psychological prose in America must see William Demarest and other Aiken protagonists as direct descendants of Samuel Sewell and other introspective Puritan diarists and must accept Aiken's kinship with Jonathan Edwards, Charles Brockden Brown, Poe, Hawthorne, Melville, Emerson, and Whitman. *Ushant* has fared no better in the arena of autobiography: "Ironically enough, recent studies in autobiography contain no hint that the innovative design of *Ushant* takes the genre to a further stage of fictive detachment, lyrical affirmation, and self-understanding."[5]

Aiken—as person and writer—always stood outside the establishment; he was neither a member of a literary circle nor a writer in a particular "school."[6] This posed difficulties for critics in placing his work when they reviewed him. But a more formidable stumbling block was the inability or reluctance of critics to understand or to take seriously his essential theory of consciousness, now commonplace in postexistential criticism. Aiken's exasperation over critical misreadings can be heard in his appreciative letter to Malcolm Lowry several months after the publication of *The Soldier: A Poem*: "I was grateful for your letter about my tin soldier. He had a poor press, on the whole, and a stupid one, I thought—so few saw that the real theme was the evolution of consciousness, with the soldier as incidental to it, and the socratic gnothi seauton as its core. Does one have to print an explanatory note with every book?" (14 September 1945).[7] Aiken's philosophy was called everything from "extreme nihilism" to "healthy skepticism" and "creative hopefulness." James Dickey, in reviewing Aiken's "The Morning Song of Lord Zero," explains the general neglect of Aiken as stemming in part from his being evaluated by "standards which are inimical to his temperament and the character of his verse." This is equally true of his fiction. Dickey appreciatively and poetically observes that the aim of Aiken's

> life-long reverie is not to send one back into one's external world, where the thorn draws blood and the sun shines differently from moment to moment, but into the endlessly ramifying labyrinth of one's own memory, and it is no small compliment to Aiken to say that, once one enters there with the total commitment Aiken's example encourages, one is struck by its likeness to Aiken's: to that vast, ectoplasmic, ultimately inexplicable—though one tries to explain—and often dimly beautiful universe whose only voice he is.[8]

There are, of course, a number of other explanations for Aiken's modest public. As a critic, for instance, he frequently made enemies in high places. A good illustration of this is the predictable result of Aiken's damnation of Amy Lowell's verse. As the titular head of the Imagists and as an editor with financial resources, Lowell's influence throughout the first quarter of the twentieth century was not to be denied. This in no way deterred Aiken, when reviewing her *Con Grande's Castle* for *Dial*, from bluntly observing, "Viewed simply as a piece of verbal crafts-manship it is a sort of Roget's Thesaurus of color. Viewed as a piece of historical reconstruction it is a remarkable feat of docu-mentation. . . . Viewed as poetry, or prose, or polyphonic prose—or let us say, for caution's sake, as literature—well, that is another question."[9] It is not surprising, then, that Lowell wasted no love on Aiken. There is, by way of illustration, a relevant, unpublished letter in the Berg Collection at the New York Public Library from Lowell to a Mrs. Becker of Brookline, Massachusetts, who was to give a lecture on the value of various contemporary writers and who had apparently asked the poet's opinion. Lowell particularly warned the woman in her reply: "Conrad Aiken's *Scepticisms* I should consider taboo. Aiken would be a brilliant critic if it were not for the perpetual chip on his shoulder. . . . I find his book is a most biased and unreliable guide and will do more to confuse and disillusion a reader than it will do anything else" (7 July 1923). Aiken's harsh but honest criticism of Lowell was in no way atypical of him, nor probably were Lowell's retaliations atypical of her.[10] His criticisms, how-ever, derived from candor, not malice. For instance, he once admitted that "it was important to fight Louis Untermeyer, you see. I mean it was a duty, because his taste was so bad and his influence so enormous."[11] Nor did Aiken mellow as he aged. During an interview on the occasion of his eightieth birthday, he surveyed the condition of American letters and was not sanguine. He declared that neither Nabokov nor Bellow was "first-rate" and although Updike had started out strong, he was showing "signs of petering out." Untermeyer he dismissed as "a rather simple soul" and Edmund Wilson as a wonderful example of a critic "with no style or taste."[12] Aiken did not reserve his acerbic pen for fellow writers. He did not hesitate to attack the Royal Academy in one of his "London Letters," a column that he wrote for the *New Yorker* from 1935 to 1936. Of the 168th Academy show, he assured his readers, "Not that there is anything in it to set the world on fire, that would be altogether too much to expect of the Academy. But the percent-age of the really dreadful is notably smaller than last year."[13]

From the start, however, Aiken was acutely aware of the penalties he was going to pay for being what Marianne Moore once called "the perfect reviewer, Diogenes' one honest man."[14]

Unable to find a publisher in England for his *Preludes, Osiris Jones,* a volume of short stories, or *Great Circle,* he wrote to Robert Linscott: "Must I at last give up my vow of not playing the Literary-Social Game, go back to America, frequent Teas, and Meet People, and Butter Editors? Is that the answer? For god's sake say no" (9 November 1932, WUL MS.). A decade later the problem was the same. In 1941, for instance, he wrote to thank Malcolm Cowley for answering an attack on his poetry by Randall Jarrell. Aiken ended his letter by observing that in Jarrell's attack there must be a lesson to be learned, "something like Play the Game, you dumb cluck, or take the consequences. Well, let's take the consequences—" (23 February 1941, *SL,* 253).[15] The cost of Aiken's unpolitic manner remained high enough for Cowley to comment on it in his tribute to Aiken, read before the American Academy of Arts and Letters at the time of the writer's death:

> He refused to cultivate the literary powers, if such persons exist; instead he went out of his way to offend them. Always for the best of reasons, he bickered with editors, jeered at anthologists, rejected his own disciples one after another, and made cruelly true remarks about fellow poets who soon would take their revenge by reviewing his books. He must have expected those reviews, familiar as he was with literary folkways.[16]

He did expect them. As he confessed to an interviewer, " 'If you don't go along with the gang, and stay by yourself, you make it much harder, and of course, I've never read or spoken. I can't do it——The average poet nowadays is a combination of travelling salesman and poet.'"[17] Malcolm Lowry, dismayed by Aiken's critical abuse, wrote to him:

> It seems to me that these oaves of reviewers must have some grudge agin you. As though you had wounded some of these little men on their amour propres in bygone years. Else why is it you so often get stupid reviews, but what has been unfavorably reviewed never fails to get mentioned in the same paper a couple of years later by someone younger as a masterpiece? which it proves to be. Anyhow, I think you're one of the five living greatest writers and most other people do too, to whom literature is not merchandise. (9 April 1940, HHL MS. Aik 2510)

In *Ushant*, Aiken twice mentions being reproached by Ezra Pound for "insubordination." Pound, in an angry letter to Aiken (then in England) opening with " 'Jesus Gord, D., you poor blithering ass,' " chastised him for not attending the *Blast* dinner "as he had been instructed to do, with Amy Lowell and Wyndham Lewis and the rest" (206). But Aiken had already written to assure Cowley, "There are literally *no* english literary folk whom I have the very smallest desire to meet. (However, that's equally true of my beloved compatriots)" (26 March 1923, *SL*, 75). Aiken recalls again in *Ushant* another rebuke by Pound for his:

> having been somewhat remiss, or unfortunate, or misguided, in his choice of friends. "I hear that you have not been altogether wise in your choice of friends, in London." Yes, there it was again, the party line; one mustn't on any account stray from the chosen circles; *a* and *b* and *c* were all right, or even *de rigueur*, but if one showed the least signs of dallying with other groups, or persisted in the attempt to remain independent of all groups, choosing one's literary friends simply where one found them, or liked them, and regardless of political sides or currents, one was at once suspect.[18]

Surely Aiken's candor, his bluntness, and his refusal to cultivate or even to participate in the literary scene (which he once identified as "the whole gossipy personal tea party kind of maggot broth" [letter to Robert Linscott, 12 November 1930, WUL MS.]) contributed to his low book sales. In a letter to Cowley, Aiken reported that his *Great Circle* had "a sale of 26 copies in its second half year," and that *Preludes for Memnon*, which he thought of as his "best book" had sold "about 700 copies in three years."[19] The actual sales figures for the first three novels, all of which were published in America by Scribner's, are bleak by any standard: *Blue Voyage*, 6,854; *Great Circle*, 2,287; and *King Coffin*, 1,425.[20] About a half year after the publication of *Blue Voyage*, Aiken wrote apologetically to his editor, Maxwell Perkins: "I'm sorry, for your sakes, the sale of Blue Voyage hasn't been larger,—but for my part I regard 5000 as quite enormous. In England, the book sold 337."[21] Aiken, moreover, never fooled himself about his literary stature. When, in 1952, the editors of *Wake* planned to devote a special issue of the journal to him, Aiken responded, "Don't do it! It's suicidal. I've never been fashionable or in the public eye."[22]

Another way that Aiken failed to "puff" his own literary reputation was never taking advantage of his critical discoveries or breakthroughs. If he had exploited these, they might well have brought his own work more consistently into the public ken. For instance, as early as 1924, Aiken wrote a long and enthusiastic essay for *Dial* on Emily Dickinson, which he then reprinted as a preface to an edition of her poetry that he had published in London (*Selected Poems of Emily Dickinson*). But one of Aiken's notes for *Ushant* recalls that "his view of E.D. had not been validated by Tsetse—Pound—as in other matters he stood alone?" (HHL MS. Aik 3593). A curious sidelight to Aiken's enthusiasm for Dickinson is that Eliot and Pound both fought with him, trying to dissuade him from bringing out the collection. As Aiken recalled, they were " 'very much annoyed with me for bringing out Dickinson. They did their damndest to stop me from doing it. I think they thought this was really cutting the ground from under their feet—I mean, to have a great poet looking over their shoulders suddenly; a little embarrassing. So they pooh-poohed it and said no, no [she's] just a little blue-stocking; a little country blue-stocking.' "²³ Objections from such influential persons may have contributed to the fact that it wasn't until fourteen years later that Dickinson was "discovered," and the credit went to Yvor Winters's *Maule's Curse*. Again, Aiken recognized the genius of William Faulkner beneath the faults of *Mosquitoes*, which he reviewed for the *New York Post* in 1927: "These defects being admitted, the critic must also admit, and without a shadow of reluctance, that the book is a delightful one. And one adds Mr. Faulkner's name to the small list of those from whom one might reasonably expect, in the course of a few years, a really first-rate piece of fiction."²⁴ But Cowley's introduction to the *Portable Faulkner* (1946) is consistently heralded as the first serious appraisal of Faulkner's literary talent.

In 1929 Aiken, in his *American Poetry 1671–1928*, included large selections from relatively unacclaimed poets and was damned by reviewers for his strange choices. In his preface to the anthology, Aiken had anticipated such criticism, acknowledging that there would be objections to his minimizing Longfellow, Holmes, Whittier, Lowell, and Lanier and to his having given generous space to Poe, Whitman, Dickinson, and poets of the last twenty years:

To such an objection he can only reply that in his opinion the poetry which begins roughly, with Emily Dickinson, has been the richest which America has produced; and that our so-called classics have been very seriously overestimated. If he can disturb prevailing notions about these things, and set in motion a revaluation of American poetry, which will find perhaps a higher place for comparatively unknown poets like Anne Bradstreet or Thomas Chivers or Trumbull Stickney than for Longfellow or Lowell or Bryant,—not, be it understood, in point of range, but in point of sheer excellence or intensity,—he will consider that he has been of some small service to American criticism.[25]

Aiken then went on to make several unusual choices, considering the date of his anthology: only one short poem by Carl Sandberg but twelve pages of poems by Wallace Stevens, including "Peter Quince at the Clavier," "Sunday Morning," and "Le Monocle de Mon Oncle." He selected what might be considered at this early date a disproportionate amount of Eliot, including "The Love Song of J. Alfred Prufrock," "Sweeney Among the Nightingales," "Gerontion," and "The Hollow Men."

Aiken's perceptiveness in recognizing literary genius was paralleled by his unique contribution to literary criticism in general. Stanley Edgar Hyman, in *The Armed Vision*, pointed out that in his publication of *Scepticisms* in 1919, Aiken had preceded I. A. Richards in opening up the whole study of poetry by formulating the basic assumption that poetry "is a natural, organic product, with discoverable functions, clearly open to analysis." But Hyman also made the all-too-true observation that Aiken lacked the literary influence to redirect modern criticism, which I. A. Richards did in 1924 with *Principles of Literary Criticism*. He acknowledged, too, that Aiken was one of the first men in the country to give Richards a sympathetic reading and—sadly—one who "with a comparable audience, influence, and documentation, would undoubtedly himself have begun the modern critical movement."[26]

Aiken's circumscribed literary popularity also resulted from his always being out of step with what most writers were doing at any particular time. For instance, in America in the 1920s, experimentation was absolutely de rigueur, but primarily in the area of poetry; Aiken was then experimenting with prose. As Maxwell Bodenheim noted in his *Saturday Review* article surveying the state of the novel in 1927, critics in America "are moderately responsive to experimentation in poetry and implacably opposed to the slightest innovation in the medium of prose fiction." Ironically, Bodenheim went on to call for a novel that was very much like *Blue Voyage*, which was published the same year. He suspected that fiction would only be revitalized when

> American novels desert their cut-and-dried, often tediously elaborate "plots"; when they become more concerned with inward investigations and less immersed in outward, colloquial, and visual fidelities; . . . when they regard reality as a lure and not as a definite end whose attainment can be clearly established . . . and when they regard individuality as an inevitable foundation, and not as the spectre that must be subdued.[27]

In short, he sounded a clarion call for precisely the kind of fiction that Aiken was then writing and would write for the rest of his career.

In the 1930s it was thought that Aiken was out of sync because he did not appear to have an involved social conscience and because he was unconcerned with the masses in the way that Auden, Steinbeck, and Dos Passos, for instance, were. Those were roughly the sentiments of Harold Strauss, who reviewed *King Coffin* for the *New York Times*; he was certain that the novel would not be popular because, among other things, "Aiken is not attuned to present material conditions of society. . . . He is a product of the period which discovered the literary possibilities of psychoanalysis and those ailments which are essentially prerequisites of the leisure class-psychoses."[28] Yet Aiken, long before it was fashionable, wrote in defense of what subsequently came to be called "popular art." It was a defense that would incur the wrath of the establishment writers, such as I. A. Richards. Aiken warned the critics that they could neither ignore nor dismiss with a sneer the tastes of the common people, because those tastes clearly reflected the common denominator of art—that is, wish-fulfillment, without which there would be no art. Cheap novels, melodrama, farce, musical comedies, comic strips, and movies must not be categorized as inferior art. "They *are* the art of the people for whom they were created; they give these people illusion, escape from themselves—and that is beauty" (*ABC*, 64). So while Aiken was not involved in social progress in the political sphere, he was engaged with it in a way that might have appalled elitist writers actively sympathetic to the political causes of the day.

The irony of Aiken's being ignored in his own time is compounded by the realization that his work so accurately reflected the temper of the times, especially the theological or metaphysical crisis of the modern age. Houston Peterson had early sensed the writer's ache of quiet despair: "He is an incorrigible victim of modernity. . . . He traffics with the unconscious, bows before 'the great God Flux,' exploits personal experiences directly and shamelessly, cultivates the blur, and tries to convert poetry into a kind of absolute music."[29] Decades later, critic Donald Davidson similarly noted Aiken's sensitivity to the modern temper: "Disaster and a sort of sweet despair are his fundamental tone— the disaster and despair of the modern who has looked, Actaeon-like, upon a knowledge forbidden." Yet, ironically, Aiken's specific portrayal of the state of discontinuity and the fragmentation of the twentieth-century sensibility no doubt contributed to his unpopularity. In speaking of *Blue Voyage*, Davidson, for instance, remarked that the novel was a success but "at the same time it makes somewhat the same impression on you as a suicide, well-planned that comes off perfectly."[30]

Finally, Malcolm Cowley, in his American Academy tribute, offered a convincing explanation for Aiken's limited reputation: it was in part the result of a conscious or unconscious choice by the writer himself. Cowley pointed out that, despite the host of literary awards won, Aiken had confided to him that two years after receiving the National Medal for Literature in 1969 his *Collected Poems: Second Edition*, "containing the work of a lifetime, had a sale of 430 copies in its first half year." Cowley was convinced that in part this neglect must be attributed to "policies more or less deliberately adopted by the author. In his heart he didn't want to become a celebrity."[31] Cowley recounted Aiken's various quarrels with editors and fellow writers that had frequently resulted in bad reviews for him, which Cowley allowed made him angry, "but did they also give him a somehow comfortable assurance that he would continue to live offstage, obscurely, and would follow his own bent?"[32] Cowley further speculated as to whether this desire to be out of the public eye could be traced back to the time he resigned from his senior year at Harvard rather than write and read the class poem. Once again *Ushant* provides a commentary on the conflict, an authorial analysis. Aiken frankly admits that the prospect of being the class poet had filled him with horror: "Had he been more honest, or more courageous, he would have refused the nomination, for he half knew, in advance, that if elected he would run away rather than go through with it. But no, he wanted his cake both ways, he would indulge his vanity in allowing himself to be elected, then to resign, in order that P. who had so desperately craved it, should take over" (*Ushant*, 148). Foreshadowing Cowley's suggestion, Aiken goes so far as to suggest in *Ushant* that his decision to live offstage was more or less necessary in order for him to deal with a personal physiological and psychological malady, an inherited tendency to petit mal (*Ushant*, 165–66). A letter from Aiken declining an invitation to do a reading in 1940 at Colby College reflects a perfectly consistent pattern:

> Many thanks for your very kind invitation. Unhappily, I'm one of those people who find public appearances quite definitely a nightmare: my attempts at reading are few and far between, and usually a dismal memory for all concerned. My voice doesn't carry far—my knees knock together—and my existence for a month before the occasion and weeks after is that of a man condemned to death, executed, and then somehow inadequately revived.[33]

It had been almost thirty years since Aiken resigned as Harvard's class poet, but the private man had not become a bit more the public performer. As Aiken explained in a letter to Harvard President Nathan Pusey when he turned down Harvard's offer of an honorary degree, "Privately, might I add that a *part* of my reason (not all) is a life-long horror of public appearances. It cyant be did. Bad enough when I was young— it prevented me from staying at Harvard, the year after we met, because I was asked to give a lecture course, and knew I couldn't lecture—it's far worse now. An affliction, and I know I should be ashamed (24 January 1961, *SL*, 307–8).

With the publication of each new volume of poetry, a collection of short stories, a novel, a book of criticism, and both editions of the autobiography, certain reviewers invariably hailed the book at hand as the one that would finally precipitate an Aiken breakthrough. But it never happened. Consequently, Mark Schorer, in reviewing the reissue of *Ushant* in 1972, reluctantly admitted:

> Almost twenty years ago, Malcolm Cowley wrote: "The discovery—one can hardly call it rediscovery—of Conrad Aiken is coming soon." This hope (as it proved to be) was expressed just a few months before the publication of *Ushant: An Essay* (1952), a work so extraordinary in American literature that its admirers (including this reviewer, then as now) thought that it must bring about that discovery. But nothing happened except in the consciousness—I use the word advisedly—of a handful of readers who, as a small underground audience, have kept the book alive over the years. A few months ago the book was handsomely republished, with photographs and a key to its characters, and the faithful said to themselves that now, surely it *must* happen. But nothing has.[34]

A few years ago Cowley reluctantly admitted that the "discovery" of Aiken is no nearer now than it was over thirty-five years ago when he had so anxiously anticipated it. To a suggestion that he edit a Portable Aiken, along the lines of his fine *Portable Faulkner*, Cowley replied:

> There's no book that I should more enjoy editing than a Portable Conrad Aiken. But I would have to persuade the Viking editorial board that the book would pay for itself. They would say to me, "We've been looking at Aiken's sales record and it isn't promising." I would say, "I'd try to present the book in such a way as to reach a new audience." And they would say, "On the record, we don't think the time has come for an Aiken Portable." Practically, they have said that already. Isn't it a frustrating situation? Here are these extraordinary books, and almost all of them are hard to find on sale.[35]

The expectation of Aiken's recognition from the republication of his works has been raised so often with such disappointing results that one can barely believe in its possibility any longer. Instead one must look about for another leaven that might give rise to the long overdue acknowledgment of the writer as a force in American literature; and perhaps it is to be found in his influence on other novelists.[36] Certainly the major novelist influenced by Aiken was Malcolm Lowry, whose stature is rapidly rising in literary circles. Douglas Day, in his biography of

Lowry, relates how the young Englishman came upon *Blue Voyage* by accident: "And his future lay clear before him: he would absorb all of Aiken's work, then go to Aiken and sit at his feet until he had absorbed all of the American's genius as well."[37] Aiken, nearly destitute in the summer of 1930, took on the in loco parentis role for Lowry for twenty guineas per month. This relationship continued for two years and was the beginning of a life-long friendship between the two writers.[38]

However the discovery of Aiken does come about, there is no doubt that once it does Aiken will be celebrated not only for his imaginatively and consistently developed thesis of consciousness but also for his essential originality as a writer of fiction, his unique contribution to the psychological novel, the lyrical novel, and to the novel/autobiography. His artistic innovations in *Ushant* carried that genre into a realm of imaginative artistry previously unknown in American literature.

Aiken incorporated the emerging findings of Freud and others into his psychological novels, always, however, insisting that the theories undergo a metamorphosis to create aesthetically satisfying works of art, not thinly disguised case studies. Aiken had always been able to use his sources rather than to be used by them. Elaborating—for the *Wake* issue—on Aiken's use of Freud, the psychiatrist Henry A. Murray commented colorfully: "He allowed the Freudian dragon to swallow him, and then, after a sufficient sojourn in its maw, cut his way out to a new freedom."[39]

Finally Aiken contributed significantly to the development of the lyrical novel in America. His are short novels characterized by a form that moves radically away from the traditional, linear narrative structure, frequently beyond a time-centered reality. There is, in his novels, little attempt to examine the traditionally perceived world; rather, the action is primarily interior, and the reflections are the poet's images of the world. Aiken's interest is in examining perception, and for him the basic paradox of perception is that of immanence and transcendence, to use Merleau-Ponty's terms. Aiken knew that objects and experiences contained more than what was simply given; they had transcendence. So Aiken, in all his fiction, deals with protagonists who are, finally, aspects of Aiken's own consciousness in search of transcendence. His pattern was to dispense quickly with the objective reality about his characters—that is, the reality that they were middle-aged, middle-class, educated writers, artists, and so forth in certain situations. One would, for instance, never suspect that during the fifteen years spanning the publication of Aiken's novels there was a worldwide boom, a depression, and an international war. Rather, Aiken's world was a near-timeless one, and he quickly emptied his characters of their factual, objective selves and approached them with what Husserl calls "transcendental subjectivity." And herein Aiken lost many of his readers.

Further, Aiken wrote his lyrical novels in a prose always bordering on poetry. He makes particularly effective use of the stream-of-consciousness method to present a series of images that filter through the character's evolving consciousness. His are truly poets' novels. Hayden Carruth, while praising *A Heart for the Gods of Mexico* in a *Nation* review, generalized about the lyrical fiber of all Aiken's novels, which, he said,

> sustain themselves in our anti-eloquent age by their unspoken insistence that the intelligence and creativeness of rhetoric are enduring virtues. Aiken's rhetorical spirit links him to a deeprunning current in American letters. . . . Aiken takes his place in the succession of Hawthorne, Melville, Henry Adams and Santayana, but for the time being at least, his contribution seems more urgent than theirs. (172)[40]

While Carruth's praise would appear to be no more than what Aiken's novels deserve, unhappily, his art was perhaps too analytically subtle, too finely honed for the reading public. In a foreword to Thomas Hardy's *Two Wessex Tales*, Aiken could have been speaking of the relationship between himself and his readers: "Hardy is a novelist, in consequence, who supremely demands that his reader shall have courage. He offers no bright panaceas, no subtle consolations. He is a merciless determinist, a passionate ironist. He sees the life of man as a harsh glare of prearranged tragedy, and he takes pleasure in standing helpless but resolute, in the full dreadfulness of this glare."[41] There is no denying that Aiken makes real demands on his readers, and these demands have limited the size of his readership. It would, however, have been antithetical to Aiken's critical theories if he had been truly "popular." *Blue Voyage* is not *Dead-eye Dick*; *King Coffin*, in spite of its title, is not a "shilling shocker"—nor were they meant to be. Rather, the fiction of Conrad Aiken makes its appeal primarily to the intellect. It encourages one to contemplate the macabre abyss of the chaos that is oneself and that is existence itself. He holds out the possibility that through evolving consciousness one will perceive—though imperfectly and erratically—an order that may at least temporarily lend meaning to existence. Aiken's five novels and his autobiography stand as literary logs of his own journeys into consciousness, and, as such, they are souvenirs of the hazardous terrain, appropriately reflective of the sensitive pilgrim who traveled them.

Notes

CHAPTER 1: Introduction

1. Conrad Aiken, "William Faulkner: The Novel as Form," *Harvard Advocate* 135 (1951): 13.

2. Ironically, Faulkner, as an undergraduate at the University of Mississippi in 1921, wrote a review of an early Aiken work, *Turns and Movies*, holding out the possibility of a delayed recognition of Aiken's genius: "It is interesting to watch, for—say in fifteen years—when the tide of aesthetic sterility which is engulfing us has withdrawn, our first great poet will be left. Perhaps he is the man." Carvel Collins, ed., *William Faulkner: Early Prose and Poetry* (Boston: Little, Brown and Co., 1962), 75–76.

3. See Edward Butscher, *Conrad Aiken: Poet of White Horse Vale* (Athens: University of Georgia Press, 1988), the first of a projected two-volume biography.

4. Conrad Aiken, "Personal Anthology," produced by P. H. Newby, BBC, 1 April 1954. Manuscript in the Conrad Potter Aiken Collection at the Henry E. Huntington Library and Art Gallery, San Marino, California, Aik 3766 (hereafter cited as HHL MS.).

5. Robert Lovett, "Melody of Chaos," *New Republic* 79 (May 1934): 81.

6. Conrad Aiken, *The Collected Novels of Conrad Aiken* (New York: Holt, Rinehart and Winston, 1964), 141 (hereafter cited as *CN*).

7. Malcolm Cowley, "The Orange Moth," *Dial* 79 (December 1925): 508.

8. E. P. Bollier, "From Scepticism to Poetry: A Note on Conrad Aiken and T. S. Eliot," *Tulane Studies in English* (1963): 102.

9. Reprinted in Conrad Aiken, *A Reviewer's ABC* (Connecticut: Meridian Books, Inc., 1958), 26 (hereafter cited as *ABC*).

10. Conrad Aiken, "What I Believe," *Nation* 135 (July 1932): 79 (hereafter cited in the text).

11. Edmund Wilson, "What I Believe," *Nation* 134 (January 1932): 98.

12. Bill Winn, "America Going to Dogs? Poet Aiken Says No," *Atlanta Journal*, 21 January 1968, 6A.

13. Conrad Aiken, *Collected Poems*, 2d ed. (New York: Oxford University Press, 1970) 674 (hereafter cited as *CP*).

14.   Harold Strauss, "Conrad Aiken's Story of a Criminal," *New York Times*, 29 September 1935, 60.

15.   Malcolm Cowley, "Biography With Letters," *Wake* 11 (1952): 29.

16.   Aiken, likewise, had been a Harvard tutor for one year, from 1928 to 1929. For a fictional account of this experience, see George Anthony Weller, *Not to Eat Not for Love* (New York: H. Smith & R. Hass, 1933).

CHAPTER 2: Freud and the Psychoanalytic Foundation

1.   *Blue Voyage* was actually begun before the first volume of short stories, *Bring! Bring! and other Stories* (published in 1925). According to Houston Peterson in *The Melody of Chaos* (New York: Longmans Green & Co., 1931), Aiken wrote the first chapter in 1922 and 1923 and then put it aside. During 1924 and 1925, he wrote chapters 2 through 4 and again dropped it. In January 1926, he quickly wrote chapter 5 and stalled again trying to get into chapter 6. He wrote to Robert Linscott that he was "turning and turning over in my poor mind, night after night in bed, the conjectural variants for it, vainly (so far) trying to decide on the best tone for it: I hope it's not going to result in another hiatus of a year. A chapter per annum! this would never do. They would bury my body in the egypt garden long before it was done——" (8 February 1926, Washington University Library Manuscript, St. Louis, Missouri; hereafter cited as WUL MS.) Later in the month Aiken again complained to Linscott: "My novel is stuck again. . . . My dialogue chapter now looks very bad. Very bad. All my little creative energy seems to have gone pfluuuump. No brains. No instinct. No rhetoric even. Just a few tired commas and semi-colons, and here and there a staggering parenthesis with his arms around nothing at all" (23 February 1926, WUL MS.). In his preface to *Three Novels*, Aiken admits that after starting *Blue Voyage* he needed a "trial-run in short form" and turned to the short story (n.p.).

2.   R. H. Wilbur, "The Art of Poetry IX: Conrad Aiken—an Interview," *Paris Review* 11 (Winter-Spring 1968): 118.

3.   The "real" Cynthia was Reine Ormond, niece of John Singer Sargent. The heart of the conflict, which Aiken was to set forth in *Blue Voyage*, appears substantially complete in a letter Aiken wrote to Robert Linscott: "Do you remember Reine Ormond, whom I met on the boat a year ago? Well, she turned up on the boat again, with her mamma and her huge black ruffian of an uncle, John Sargent. I prowled onto the first cabin deck one night early in the voyage. And there she was. But when it was discovered (1) that I was travelling 2nd Class, and

sneaking thru into the lst; and (2) that my family was going to be in London for the winter (and might be a social nuisance), they proceeded thenceforth to 'cut' me! . . . Really, of all the disgusting bad manners, provincialism, conceit and snobbishness I've ever encountered, this is the worst. Sick transit glory Ormundi! I thought better of the lady than that" (3 December 1921, Joseph Killorin, ed., *Selected Letters of Conrad Aiken* [New Haven: Yale University Press, 1978], 64; hereafter cited as *SL*).

4. Malcolm Cowley, "Biography With Letters," *Wake* 11 (1952): 30.

5. Mary Ross, review of *Blue Voyage*, by Conrad Aiken, *New York Herald Tribune*, 13 July 1927, 5.

6. Manuscript in the Conrad Potter Aiken Collection at the Henry E. Huntington Library and Art Gallery, San Marino, California (hereafter cited as HHL).

7. Conrad Aiken, *The Collected Novels of Conrad Aiken* (New York: Holt, Rinehart & Winston, 1964), 24 (hereafter cited as *CN*).

8. Houston Peterson, *Melody of Chaos* (New York: Longmans Green & Co., 1931), 48–49. Aiken wrote of this same fear in a long narrative poem, "Punch: The Immortal Liar" (1921). The poem is deterministic throughout, and in the epilogue, Mountebank—the puppet master—must admit that even he is "a puppet drawn out upon strings" (Conrad Aiken, *Collected Poems*, 2d ed. [New York: Oxford University Press, 1970], 360; hereafter cited as *CP*).

9. Burton Rascoe, once describing Aiken in "Contemporary Reminiscences," *Arts and Decoration* 20 (March 1924), might well have been describing Demarest: "He is a short, stocky, sandy-haired, freckle-faced, youngish chap who might pass ordinarily as a grocer's assistant or as a college athlete who nourished an ambition to become a successful bond salesman. He is excessively shy and diffident and gives me the impression of someone greatly burdened with fears and inhibitions" (12).

10. Aiken was interested in the psychology of the inferiority complex, having assured Wilbur, in "Art of Poetry," that he was greatly influenced by Adler. It was in 1923 (available in translation in 1924) that Adler wrote *The Practice and Theory of Individual Psychology*.

11. Conrad Aiken, "Answers to an Enquiry," *New Verse* 11 (October 1934): 13.

12. Conrad Aiken's personal library (now part of the HHL Aiken Collection) included Freud's *Interpretation of Dreams*, trans. A. A. Brill (1922), and *Beyond the Pleasure Principle*, trans. C. J. M. Hubbard (1922); Alfred Adler's *The Neurotic Constitution: Outlines of a Comparative Individualistic Psychology and Psychotherapy* (1917); and Ernest Jones's *Applied Psychology* (1923).

13. Among his good friends were psychologist Henry A. Murray, Director of Harvard Psychological Clinic; George Wilbur, psychiatrist and long-time editor of *American Imago*; and Grayson P. McCouch, a neurophysiologist.

14. Henry A. Murray, "Poet of Creative Dissolution," *Wake* 11 (1952): 101.

15. Murray, "Poet of Creative Dissolution," 101.

16. Letter to Frederick J. Hoffman, *Freudianism and the Literary Mind* (Baton Rouge: Louisiana State University Press, 1957), 288.

17. Conrad Aiken, *Ushant: An Essay* (New York: Oxford University Press, 1971), 141 (hereafter cited as *Ushant*).

18. Hoffman, *Freudianism and the Literary Mind*, 283.

19. Ashley Brown, "An Interview with Conrad Aiken," *Shenandoah* 15 (Autumn 1963): 36.

20. Even as late as 1952, Alfred Kazin, in reviewing *Ushant*, echoes such simplistic criticism: "For this is the story of a man still imprisoned to the nightmares of his youth, of a writer who in his conventional reiteration of Freudian doctrines never sees enough beyond the self to reach that blessed isle which lies on the other side of determinism" (review of *Ushant*, by Conrad Aiken, *New York Herald Tribune*, 12 October 1952, 26).

21. Conrad Aiken, *A Reviewer's ABC* (Connecticut: Meridian Books, Inc., 1958), 18 (hereafter cited as *ABC*).

22. Hoffman, *Freudianism*, 111.

23. Brown, "Interview," 36.

24. Alden Whitman, "Conrad Aiken, 80, Discusses Dislikes," *New York Times*, 5 August 1969, 26.

25. Although Aiken never published a play in his lifetime (he revised an adaptation of "Mr. Arcularis" when the author, Diana Hamilton, became ill during the production), he was always interested in writing drama, and there are several manuscript fragments of plays in the HHL Aiken Collection. In one untitled, unfinished play—with loud echoes of Pirandello—the charater who is the Producer calls people out of the audience and interrogates them: "Yes, that is the real question I was going to ask all of you. What is it you really want? Have you ever stopped to ask that question of yourselves—I mean seriously? Do you really know what you want? Which is another way of saying, do you really know who you are? That's very important, you know. Some people—looking at me right now—spend their whole lives without knowing in the least who they are or what they want. In the end, and it really seems pretty sad, they die just as anonymously as they lived. I might even go so far as to say that really they don't die at all, they don't experience death, since they never really lived, or experienced life: they vanish like shadows. . . . " (HHL MS. Aik 3502).

26. Richard P. Blackmur, "Conrad Aiken: The Poet," *Atlantic* 40 (April 1932): 41.

CHAPTER 3: The Evolution of Consciousness

1. Conrad Aiken, *Collected Poems*, 2d ed. (New York: Oxford University Press, 1970), 1018 (hereafter cited as *CP*).

2. Conrad Aiken, *A Reviewer's ABC* (Connecticut: Meridian Books, Inc., 1958), 130 (hereafter cited as *ABC*).

3. This preface was written in 1948 to replace the original one that had been lost, but Aiken assured his readers that "the present one however is a fairly accurate summary of it" (*CP*, 1021).

4. Malcolm Cowley, "Conrad Aiken: From Savannah to Emerson," *Southern Review* 11 (Spring 1974): 248.

5. R. H. Wilbur, "The Art of Poetry IX: Conrad Aiken—An Interview," *Paris Review* 11 (Winter–Spring 1968): 119.

6. Soren Kierkegaard, *Fear and Trembling and the Sickness Unto Death*. Trans. Walter Lowrie (New York: Doubleday Anchor, 1954), 210–11.

7. Jay Martin, *Conrad Aiken: A Life of His Art* (Princeton: Princeton University Press, 1962), discusses Potter's influence on his grandson (209–10). This study is primarily concerned with Aiken's poetry, but it includes some incisive information on each of the novels and *Ushant*. Although written in 1962, it remains the single most important book on Aiken.

8. Robert Wilbur, "George Santayana and Three Modern Philosophical Poets: T. S. Eliot, Conrad Aiken, and Wallace Stevens," Ph.D. diss., Columbia University, 1965. Aiken, years earlier, had written to Eliot that he was of the opinion that "all philosophy should start with a study of biology, morphology, and such 'literature' as The Origin of the Species. From the last in particular would I have philosophy spring" (14 March 1913, Joseph Killorin, ed., *Selected Letters of Conrad Aiken* [New Haven: Yale University Press, 1978], 30; hereafter cited as *SL*).

9. William James Potter, *Twenty-five Sermons* (Boston: George H. Ellis, 1885), 312.

10. Conrad Aiken, *Ushant: An Essay* (New York: Oxford University Press, 1971), 111–12 (hereafter cited as *Ushant*). The importance of this memory to Aiken is reflected, for instance, in his incorporation of it in his poem "Hallowe'en" (1949):

> O you who made magic
> under an oak-tree once in the sunlight
> translating your acorns to green cups and saucers
> for the grandchild mute at the tree's foot,

> and died, alone, on a doorstep at midnight
> your vision complete but your work undone,
> with your dream of a world religion,
> "a peace convention of religions, a worship
> purified of myth and dogma:"
> dear scarecrow, dear pumpkin-head!
>
> (*CP*, 896–97)

11. Wilbur, "George Santayana," 156.

12. Martin, *Conrad Aiken*, 209.

13. In the twilight of his career, Aiken reiterates very nearly the same idea in "Thee" (1966):

> Self-praise were then our praise of THEE
> unless we say divinity
> cries in us both as we draw breath
> cry death cry death
> and all our hate
> we must abate
> and THEE must with us meet and mate
> give birth give suck be sick and die
> and close the All-God-Giving-Eye
> for the last time to sky.
>
> (*CP*, 1009)

14. I am indebted to Malcolm Cowley for this observation in "Conrad Aiken," 255.

15. Rosalia Ruffini, ed., "Due lettere di Conrad Aiken," *Studi Americani* 14 (1968): 454.

16. In an obituary essay that Aiken wrote on Eliot, "T. S. Eliot," *Life* 58 (January 1965), he speaks of his being "a convert to the Anglican Church (from which I, a Unitarian, tried vainly for a while to dissuade him)" (92). This appears to be the only time that Aiken so labeled himself; just two years before, in an interview, he had flatly stated: "I'm not a Unitarian. I'm profoundly religious—but I wouldn't give it a name. I'm nothing" (Andrew Sparks, "An Hour with Conrad Aiken," *The Atlanta Journal and Constitution Magazine*, 5 May 1963: 46).

17. Aiken remained enthusiastic his whole life about the seminar he took with Santayana, out of which subsequently came *Three Philosophical Poets*. In an interview in 1966, Aiken acknowledged that the course was "one of the best things I ever had anywhere" (Tom Fleming, "Please Continue Mr. Aiken," *Phoenix* 1 [1966]: 20. The learning environment was ideal, since the admiration was mutual; see George

Santayana, *The Middle Span: Persons and Places*, vol. 2 (New York: Scribners, 1945).

18. Manuscript in the Conrad Potter Aiken Collection at the Henry E. Huntington Library and Art Gallery, San Marino, California, Aik 2503, circa 1933 (hereafter cited as HHL MS.).

19. Conrad Aiken, "A Plea for Anonymity," *New Republic* 84 (September 1935): 155, 157.

20. Conrad Aiken, *The Collected Novels of Conrad Aiken* (New York: Holt, Rinehart & Winston, 1964), 24 (hereafter cited as *CN*).

21. John Gould Fletcher, "Conrad Aiken: The Metaphysical Poet," *Dial* 66 (May 1919): 559.

CHAPTER 4: The Dilemma of the Artist

1. Conrad Aiken, "Poetry and the Mind of Modern Man," *Atlantic Monthly* 214 (November 1964): 80.

2. R. H. Wilbur, "George Santayana and Three Modern Philosophical Poets: T. S. Eliot, Conrad Aiken, and Wallace Stevens," Ph.D. diss., Columbia University, 1965, 137.

3. Conrad Aiken, *The Collected Novels of Conrad Aiken* (New York: Holt, Rinehart & Winston, 1964), 116 (hereafter cited as *CN*).

4. Conrad Aiken, *A Reviewer's ABC* (Connecticut: Meridian Books, Inc., 1958), 64–65 (hereafter cited as *ABC*).

5. Richard Poirier, "The Difficulties of Modernism and the Modernism of Difficulty," in *Images and Ideas in American Culture: The Function of Criticism: Essays in Memory of Philip Rahv*, ed. Arthur Edelstein (Hanover: Brandeis University Press, 1979), 125.

6. Aiken himself had considered writing just such a play and had asked for advice on it from psychiatrist G. B. Wilbur, his Harvard classmate and lifelong friend. In a letter to Wilbur, Aiken sketched his proposed hero: "But, unlike Christ (on whom in many respects he is founded) he is also intensely conscious of the deterministic nature of things, and, with the help of a psychoanalytic friend, glimpses the harrowing possibility that his belief in himself is of psychotic origin, and not only that, but that his 'doctrine' is equally so, and might well retard the progress of man by a thousand or two years. Learning this, he faces a dilemma: to yield to his psychosis, thereby saving himself at the possible expense of man; or to go mad.—I wish you would give this a thought, and let me have a little guidance" (5 May 1924, Joseph Killorin, ed., *Selected Letters of Conrad Aiken* [New Haven: Yale University Press, 1978], 89; hereafter cited as *SL*).

7. Aiken had obviously written to G. B. Wilbur about this dilemma, and Wilbur replied: "Whether it is better to BE or TO DO? Is it sufficient compensation for living to know oneself that one is an

interesting personality with an extensive experience (albeit some of it vicarious) or must one objectify it in work so that others may take over the knowing. . . . the point comes when something of this sort is necessary to get beyond a point of arrest in one's own ability to experience i.e., to gain new experience. . . . and perhaps that after all is the decisive factor. . . . in short is it more 'mature' to be a narcissist directly or indirectly, by displacement and identification with the worshipping Other. . . . the rewards of 'doing' seem to me increasingly less worthwhile . . . perhaps I should qualify that by limiting it to what others call doing" (20 December 1930, Manuscript in the Conrad Potter Aiken Collection at the Henry E. Huntington Library and Art Gallery, San Marino, California, Aik 2215; hereafter cited as HHL MS.).

8. As one of the major American literary critics of his day and one of the most prolific writers, Aiken compounded his own confusion by occasionally reviewing his own work, and he could be devastating. For instance, he reviewed his *Nocturne of Remembered Spring* for the *Chicago News* ("Schizophrenia," 23 January 1917): "It is difficult to place Conrad Aiken in the poetic firmament, so difficult that one sometimes wonders whether he deserves a place there at all. Mr. Aiken himself seems to be somewhat uncertain as to his role—he comes to the rehearsal, so to speak, still fumbling in his pants for his part. Sometimes the radicals please him and he plays with the radicals; sometimes he plays with the shell-backs. And even when apparently most single-minded he carries on clandestine flirtations. . . . In *Turns and the Movies* he willfully sacrificed his ability to write in smoothly involute curves for a dubious gain in matter-of-fact forcefulness. In *The Jig of Forslin* he recanted, and, with occasional sops to downright and rigid realism, abandoned himself to a luxuriation in romantic virtuosity. And now, in *Nocturne of Remembered Spring*, he is more clearly than ever a schizophrenic. . . . Furthermore, Mr. Aiken displays here a tendency to take refuge in an emotional symbolism which lies perilously close to the vague" (*ABC*, 120–21).

9. Houston Peterson, *Melody of Chaos* (New York: Longmans Green & Co., 1931), 29.

10. Suetonius, *The Lives of the Caesars* (Cambridge: Harvard University Press, 1960), 461.

11. Considering Aiken's acknowledged interest in Jung, it might be worth noting Jung's explanation of the psychological significance of the crucifixion: "Christ, as a hero and god-man, signifies psychologically the self; that is, he represents the projection of this most important and most central of archetypes. The archetype of the self has, functionally, the significance of a rule of the inner world, *i.e.*, of the collective unconscious. The self, as a symbol of wholeness, is a *coincidentia oppositorum*, and therefore contains light and darkness simultaneously.

In the Christ-figure the opposites which are united in the archetype are polarized into the 'light' son of God on the one hand and the devil on the other." C. J. Jung, *Symbols of Transformation*, trans. R. F. C. Hull, vol. 2 (New York: Harper, 1956), 368.

12. Conrad Aiken, *Ushant: An Essay* (New York: Oxford University Press, 1971), 177–78 (hereafter cited as *Ushant*).

13. Robert Lovett, "Blue Voyage," *New Republic* 51 (August 1927): 316. Harold Bauer told fellow psychiatrist G. B. Wilbur that he had been reading *Blue Voyage* and that it was "by all odds the best of the stream of consciousness books, not excepting Joyce" (12 September 1931, HHL MS. Aik 2117).

14. "Blue Voyage," *Outlook* 147 (September 1927): 26.

15. Kenneth Burke, "A Decade of American Fiction," *Bookman* (August 1929): 565.

16. "Blue Voyage," *Outlook* 147 (September 1927): 26.

17. "Blue Voyage," *Times Literary Supplement*, 26 May 1927, 372.

18. Conrad Aiken, Preface, *Three Novels: Blue Voyage, Great Circle and King Coffin* (New York: McGraw Hill, 1965): n.p.

19. "Blue Voyage," *Spectator* 138 (28 May 1927): 957.

20. Malcolm Cowley, "Biography With Letters," *Wake* 11 (1952): 28.

CHAPTER 5: The Recurring Betrayal

1. Conrad Aiken, *Ushant: An Essay* (New York: Oxford University Press, 1971), 167 (hereafter cited as *Ushant*).

2. Richard H. Costa, "The Lowry/Aiken Symbiosis," *Nation* 204 (June 1967): 825.

3. Joseph Killorin, ed., *Selected Letters of Conrad Aiken* (New Haven: Yale University Press, 1978), 179 (hereafter cited as *SL*).

4. This timetable makes problematic Clarissa Lorenz's insistence that the "best-kept secret" was that *Great Circle* was prompted by her affair with Henry Murray, Aiken's psychiatrist friend (*Lorelei Two: My Life with Conrad Aiken* [Athens: University of Georgia Press, 1983], 177).

5. Manuscript in the Conrad Potter Aiken Collection at the Henry E. Huntington Library and Art Gallery, San Marino, California, Aik 3477 (hereafter cited as HHL MS.).

6. Conrad Aiken, *The Collected Novels of Conrad Aiken* (New York: Holt, Rinehart & Winston, 1964), 251 (hereafter cited as *CN*).

7. Earlier in her account of life with Aiken, Lorenz maintained that he was jealous of her relationship with their friend, English artist Paul Nash. Speaking of a particular quarrel in which Aiken became angry and stormed off to a pub, Lorenz writes, "He seemed to be goading me into being unfaithful" (*Lorelei Two*, 134).

8. David M. Rein, "Conrad Aiken and Psychoanalysis," *Psychoanalytic Review* 42 (1955): 406.

9. Rein says that this definition of love is based not on Cather's relationship with his wife but on his relationship with his mother ("Conrad Aiken," 408). In light of the entire novel, it would appear that the comments grow out of both relationships. Aiken wrote in *Ushant* about his affair with Amabel, the Kensington blue-stocking, in very much the same way: "he had taught the poor woman how to love, but at the expense, to her, of heartbreak, and, to himself, of a fearful complex of pity and guilt, but mostly pity, which had made him physically and morally ill. It had given him a new concept of the terrible—almost evil—power of love, its power for destruction and horror. One could not witness such suffering, such a depravity of suffering, and ever be quite the same again" (308–9).

10. Bill lectures Andrew quite explicitly: " 'In every one of your love affairs, you've tried to make your sweetheart your mother. That's why they've all been unsuccessful. Why do you want to do it?—that's the question. It won't work. That's why sooner or later you reject or abandon them all, or they abandon you—they have to. You force them to. Bertha is no exception' " (*CN*, 251). Andrew responds with textbook resistance: " 'You're damned unpleasant. Let's talk about something else!' " It is not surprising that one of the women Andrew seeks out during the several days of his great turmoil is "old Mary," who had mothered a fair share of the Harvard male faculty through crises (*CN*, 248–50).

11. Taking the boat out in the face of a major storm undoubtedly stems from David's wild adventurousness. There does not seem to be any evidence to support Arthur E. Waterman's suggestion, in "Evolution of Consciousness: Conrad Aiken's Novels and *Ushant*," of suicide—at least not in any way similar to Aiken's family tragedy (*Critique: Studies in Modern Fiction* 15 [1973]: 67–81).

12. The first, hasty account in the previous evening's paper (*The Savannah Evening Press*, 27 February 1901), 1, has the child informing the sergeant only that "his father had shot his mother" (which may accurately reflect an unconscious emphasis).

13. Conrad Aiken, "Prologue to an Autobiography," *American Scholar* 35 (1966): 626; also *Ushant*, 43.

14. Dr. Aiken frequently wrote poetry, and among the papers found on his desk the morning of the fatal shooting was a poem significantly titled "Isolation":

> When my naked soul shall feel
> Primal darkness softly steal
> Closer, closer, all about—

Blotting all the light of living out.
Like a garment soft and warm,
Grateful to my shrinking form—
Promise of the welcome sleep,
Free of dreams and oh, so long and deep!
When the mother angel, Rest,
Gently folds me to her breast—
How far off and dim will be
All these joys and pains 'twixt' thee and me!
Naked then my soul shall feel
Primal darkness softly steal
Closer, closer, all about.
Blotting all the light of living out!
(*The Savannah Evening Press*, 27 February
1901, 1)

15. Malcolm Cowley, "Conrad Aiken: From Savannah to Emerson," *Southern Review* 11 (1974): 245–59.

16. It is interesting to note that Aiken did not return to Savannah for thirty-five years, but when he did, he moved into 230 E. Oglethorpe, next door to his parents' original home at 228.

17. Conrad Aiken, *A Seizure of Limericks* (Canada: Holt, Rinehart & Winston, 1963), #36.

18. Richard P. Blackmur, "The Day Before the Daybreak," *Poetry* 40 (April 1932): 38.

19. Ashley Brown, "An Interview with Conrad Aiken," *Shenandoah* 15 (Autumn 1963): 38.

20. Conrad Aiken, Preface to *Three Novels: Blue Voyage, Great Circle and King Coffin* (New York: McGraw Hill, 1965), n.p.

21. Letter to Robert Linscott, 9 November 1932, in Washington University Library, St. Louis, Missouri (hereafter cited as WUL MS.).

22. Graham Greene, "Fiction," *Spectator*, 20 October 1933, 538.

23. Ted Spivey, *Writer as Shaman* (Macon, Ga.: Mercer University Press, 1986), 104.

24. See, for instance, Robert E. Carlile, "Great Circle: Conrad Aiken's Musico-Literary Technique," *Georgia Review* 22 (Spring 1968): 27–36.

25. Conrad Aiken, *A Reviewer's ABC* (Connecticut: Meridian Books, Inc., 1958), 155 (hereafter cited as *ABC*).

26. Eliot wrote an early letter (19 July 1914) to Aiken in which he referred to him as "Prof. Dr. Krapp" and as "scholar extraordinaire" (HHL MS. Aik 482).

27. Robert Humphrey, *Stream of Consciousness in the Modern Novel* (Berkeley: University of California Press, 1968), 28.

28. Sigmund Freud, *An Outline of Psychoanalysis*, trans. James Strachey (New York: Norton, 1949), 91, 92.

29. Sigmund Freud, "The Interpretation of Dreams," in *The Standard Edition of the Complete Psychological Works of Sigmund Freud*, trans. James Strachey, vol. 5 (London: Hogarth Press, 1953): 354.

30. This sentence appears as a fragment of verse (with a telling variant in the last line) in Aiken's college notebook in the HHL Collection: "Here lies the winged pig / Feared and befriended by man / [illegible] and loved by one" (4–5 January 1912, HHL MS. Aik 3588).

CHAPTER 6: The "Queer" Book

1. About the novel, Aiken wrote to Robert Linscott on 7 September 1934: "Whether it's balderdash or not I haven't the courage to decide. . . . Of course my heart's not really in the book, which is against it, but on the other hand I actually find it rather interesting simply to have to do a thing against the grain, and as if to order; the fun will perhaps be in seeing how good a piece of mere carpentry, given the shoddy materials, I can manufacture. But it won't be funny if when it comes out (if it ever does) the critics dismiss it as precisely that and no more. . . . there's always the little chance that later it might really get hold of me and turn into something unexpected?" Washington University Library, St. Louis, Missouri (hereafter cited as WUL MS.). Several months later, Aiken gave a progress report to Linscott: "don't know just how bad or good it is—it's obviously outgrown somewhat its potboiler outline, and taken on a sort of something or other goodish, but whether in the upshot it's fallen between the stools I can't guess. I just look at it from a great distance and, as I say, moan softly like the bulgarian weasel to its young. It never answers me, so I suspect it's dumb" (15 February 1935, WUL MS.).

2. Manuscript in the Conrad Potter Aiken Collection at the Henry E. Huntington Library and Art Gallery, San Marino, California, Aik 3815 (hereafter cited as HHL MS.).

3. Jay Martin calls Jasper Ammen "diseased and abnormal" (*Conrad Aiken: A Life of His Art* [Princeton: Princeton University Press, 1962], 149), and Arthur E. Waterman calls him "a paranoid. . . . A personality distintegrating into madness" ("Evolution of Consciousness: Conrad Aiken's Novels and Ushant," *Critique: Studies in Modern Fiction* 15 [1973]: 74).

4. Herbert Leibowitz, "Aiken as a Novelist," *New Republic* 150 (May 1964): 26.

5. Vincent McHugh, "The Monstrous Tree," *New Republic* 85 (December 1935): 109.

6. Martin, *Conrad Aiken*, 149.

7. Conrad Aiken, *Ushant: An Essay* (New York: Oxford University Press, 1971), 213 (hereafter cited as *Ushant*).

8. R. H. Wilbur, "The Art of Poetry IX: Conrad Aiken—An Interview," *Paris Review* 11 (Winter = Y-Spring 1968): 118.

9. Alfred Kreymborg, *Our Singing Strength* (New York: Coward-McCann, 1929), 433.

10. Houston Peterson, *Melody of Chaos* (New York: Longmans Green & Co., 1931), 48.

11. Conrad Aiken, *The Collected Novels of Conrad Aiken* (New York: Holt, Rinehart and Winston, 1964), 308 (hereafter cited as *CN*).

12. Calvin S. Hall and Gardner Lindzey, *Theories of Personality*, 2d ed. (New York: Wiley, 1970), 120, 121.

13. Ammen is surely an exceptional Aiken character in this regard. Frederick C. Crews accurately assesses most of the central personae in Aiken's novels as "sex-obsessed." Review of *Collected Novels, New York Times*, 12 January 1964, 1.

14. Alfred Adler, "Individual Psychology," in *Psychologies of 1930*, ed. Carl Murchison (Massachusetts: Clark University Press, 1930), 400.

15. "Overtaken Pioneer," *Time* 83 (January 1964): 72.

16. Adler, "Individual Psychology," 398.

17. The usual explanation for the hero's name is that it suggests his isolation: a-men. Jennifer Aldrich claims that the tragedy in *King Coffin* is that Jasper Ammen, "isolated in his refined and individualistic awareness, refuses to recognize concomitant participation (suggested by his punning name, 'Am men') in humanity, as symbolized by Jones, whom he wishes to kill" ("The Deciphered Heart: Conrad Aiken's Poetry and Prose Fiction," *Sewanee Review* [Summer 1967]: 505). Mary Martin Rountree thinks that the hero's name reflects his purity: "The unusual name 'Jasper' does not seem a haphazard choice on Aiken's part, especially since the black jasper is used as a touchstone for testing the purity of precious metals" ("The Fiction of Conrad Aiken," Ph.D. diss., University of Pittsburgh, 1965, 79). She does not comment on his surname. Jay Martin accepts Aiken's much too facile explanation of the name: "The protagonist was named after 'a singular character in my apartment house in Cambridge, odd name something like Ammen!' " (*Conrad Aiken*, 85). Then, too, given the political background of the subplot, "Karl Jones" must be heard resonating "Karl Marx."

18. Conrad Aiken, Preface to *Three Novels: Blue Voyage, Great Circle and King Coffin* (New York: McGraw Hill, 1965), n.p.

19. Peterson, *Melody of Chaos*, 34.

20. Friedrich Nietzsche, "Zarathustra," in *The Portable Nietzsche*, ed. Walter Kaufmann (New York: Viking Press, 1954), 225.

21. Friedrich Nietzsche, *Human, All Too Human: A Book for Free Sprits*, trans. Alexander Harvey (Chicago: C. H. Kerr & Co., 1915), Aphorism #426.

22. Nietzsche, "Zarathustra," 329.

23. Karl Jaspers, *Man in the Modern Age*, trans. Eden and Redal Paul (London: Routledge and Kegan Paul, 1951), 171.

24. Jaspers, *Man in the Modern Age*, 45.

25. Malcolm Cowley, "A Remembrance of the Red Romance," *Esquire* 61 (April 1964): 78–81.

26. Conrad Aiken, "A Plea for Anonymity," *New Republic* 84 (September 1935): 156.

27. Nietzsche, *Human, All Too Human*, Aphorism #579.

28. Aiken, "A Plea for Anonymity," 157.

29. Crews, review of *CN, New York Times*, 12 January 1964, 1; Rountree, "The Fiction of Conrad Aiken," 68.

30. Reuel Denney, *Conrad Aiken* (Minneapolis: University of Minnesota Press, 1964), 21.

31. In *Ushant* Aiken comments on the marriage: "after all, it had been a marriage of cousins: his mother's surnames had merely, after the marriage, been reversed. And thus, here too, again had occurred that fusion of inheritance" (106).

32. *Savannah Morning News*, 28 February 1901, 10.

33. Wilbur, "Art of Poetry," 117.

34. Conrad Aiken, "Smith and Jones," *Dial* 64 (January–June 1923): 369–78; "No, No, Go Not to Lethe," *Scribner's Magazine* 86 (July = Y-December 1929): 151–63.

35. Martin, *Conrad Aiken*, 147.

36. The narrator assesses Babcock: "And when opportunity afforded for a longer and more careful scrutiny, as with his pupils and his colleagues, he cherished with the nicest care his gradual peeling of layer after layer from the unsuspecting soul. It gave him a special ecstasy, in such cases, if, while thus reaching to the very ore-seams of another's soul, he could maintain his own soul's silence unbroken. An overwhelming sense of power came over him when he saw that soul's defenses going down, one by one, under the minute blows of his searching and surgical curiosity" (Conrad Aiken, *The Collected Short Stories of Conrad Aiken* [New York: Schocken Books, 1982], 428; hereafter cited as *CSS*).

37. Aiken's choice of his title from Keats's "Ode on Melancholy" suggests that he made a particularly astute observation on that poem— that there is an unhealthy indulgence in Keats's speaker, not unlike that in Babcock. The speaker suggests that one go not to Lethe, or to poison, or to yew berries when seeking melancholy, but, among other

less voyeuristic suggestions, he says: "Or if thy mistress some rich anger shows / Emprison her soft hand, and let her rave, / And feed deep, deep upon her peerless eyes." Aiken did not choose titles casually.

38. Martin, *Conrad Aiken*, 147, 148.

39. Knowing Aiken's great admiration for the German poet and in light of the sensitive role that Gerta plays within the novel, one wonders if the woman's name is not Aiken's punning on "Goethe," who once said that there wasn't a crime he couldn't imagine himself committing.

40. It is a consistent misreading to see Ammen calmly welcoming his death by suicide: "The book ends with his suicide, performed, appropriately, with the indifference with which he had expected to murder Jones" (Martin, *Conrad Aiken*, 154). Similarly, Waterman claims that Ammen finally realizes "that only in death will he find the peace he wants, that King Coffin's home is the grave. He returns to his apartment, turns on the gas, and lies down to die" ("Evolution of Consciousness," 74). Like all the other reviewers, Leibowitz for the *New Republic* accepts Ammen's death as fact: "At last, discovering that the stranger is himself, Jasper can only annihilate his own personality" ("Aiken as a Novelist," 26). Rountree points out that Ammen has invited the couple living downstairs to come by for a drink the following evening with the intention that when they arrive, they will find that this "host had committed suicide on the preceding evening" ("Fiction of Conrad Aiken," 84). Since we know that Ammen has taken great pains to be discovered no later than eleven o'clcok in the morning by Gerta, we know that there is a good chance that he will yet be alive—but even if he is dead, it is not likely that she would let the corpse remain in the kitchen until evening! In a CBS adaptation of the novel for a Studio One production in 1953, Ammen—here a professor—shoots himself in the end as the dean of his college and the police chief are about to enter his room.

41. Joseph Killorin, ed., *Selected Letters of Conrad Aiken* (New Haven: Yale University Press, 1978), 135 (hereafter cited as *SL*).

CHAPTER 7: The Fictional End

1. Conrad Aiken, *Ushant: An Essay* (New York: Oxford University Press, 1971), 341 (hereafter cited as *Ushant*).

2. Alden Whitman, "Conrad Aiken, 80, Discusses Dislikes," *New York Times*, 5 August 1969, 26.

3. Conrad Aiken, *The Collected Novels of Conrad Aiken* (New York: Holt, Rinehart & Winston, 1964) 460 (hereafter cited as *CN*).

4. Whitman, "Conrad Aiken," 26.

5. Aiken was convinced of the possibility of treating a potentially sentimental topic without resorting to the contemporary cynical posture. In his important essay "Back to Poetry," published originally in the *Atlantic* the year after *A Heart for the Gods*, he finds such cynicism one of the failings of the poetry of the day: "That a poem should be simple, sensuous, and passionate—passionate, above all things!—it is for them not merely inconceivable, it is disgusting. To betray feelings in a poem, to run the risk of being charged with sentimentality—oh no, anything but that. And so a little cynicism must be injected; or a little irony, like so much precautionary iodine; and if the taste is bitter, that won't matter, for at all events we shall have avoided vulgarity" (Conrad Aiken, *A Reviewer's ABC* [Connecticut: Meridian Books, Inc., 1958], 100; hereafter cited as *ABC*).

6. Such specific phrases as "the plumed serpent" and the more general descriptions of the Mexican landscape call to mind D. H. Lawrence's novel *The Plumed Serpent*, written more than a decade earlier. Both novelists concern themselves with the close relationships between modern man and his ancestral heritage, but *A Heart for the Gods* lacks the full panoramic scale of Lawrence's work and makes only glancing use of the world of the occult. There are also useful comparisons to be made between Aiken's novel and Malcolm Lowry's *Under the Volcano* (1947), set in Quauhnahuac between the two volcanoes of Popocateptl and Ixtaccihuatl.

7. [Kathleen Raine], "Answer to the Sphinx," *Times Literary Supplement*, 19 April 1963, 258. The novel was not even published in America until 1964, when it was included in *The Collected Novels*, and then it was consistently discounted except by very few critics.

8. "It looked almost disconcertingly easy: it looked like the ripe fruit ready to drop into one's receptive hand. It looked as if one would scarcely need to touch it. . . . No such thing. It had proved to be no more than a fatal temptation to fine writing" (*Ushant*, 343).

9. Aiken's enthusiasm for romantic affirmation is reflected in his choice of *The Cloud Messenger* for Noni's diversional reading on the train trip. It is a very lyrical fourth or fifth century Sanskrit poem written by Kalidasa, the great lyric poet of India. It is an extravagant love tale written by an exiled lover and sent by way of a cloud to his loved one. At one point Aiken had considered calling the novel *The Cloud Messenger* or *The Cloud Message* (Letter to Robert Linscott, 3 December 1937, in the Washington University Library, St. Louis, Missouri; hereafter cited as WUL MS.).

10. Hayden Carruth, "Heart for the Gods," review of *The Collected Novels of Conrad Aiken*, *Nation* (February 1964): 172.

11. Jay Martin, *Conrad Aiken: A Life of His Art* (Princeton University Press, 1962), 158.

12. Mary Martin Rountree, "The Fiction of Conrad Aiken," Ph.D. diss., University of Pittsburgh, 1965, 110.

13. Noni has a number of spiritual sisters, such as Cynthia in *Blue Voyage*; Caroline Lee, the young girl who dies in "Strange Moonlight"; and Reine Wilson, who is also dying of a bad heart in "Your Obituary, Well Written." Of Reine Wilson, the narrator says: "I think I was first struck by the astonishing fragility of her appearance, an other world fragility, almost a transparent spiritual quality, as if she were already a disembodied soul" (Conrad Aiken, *The Collected Short Stories of Conrad Aiken* [New York: Schocken Books, 1982], 403; hereafter cited as *CSS*).

14. Aiken had not always been so critical of his novel. He had tried to convince Robert Linscott, his American agent, that the novel was good: "Linsk . . . I am saddened by your indifference to Mexico, which myself I think good, say what you will . . . and classical in form—this is one of the days when I feel confident about it, after many, many more, when I viewed it with a somber blue lacklustre stale-oyster eye—so forgive me if in defense I lay on the self-praise with a golden trowel. Not that I think it great, or profound, or vast, or anything like that—but it's a genuine poem for all that, and so much better than 99% of the labored trash that passes as fiction that I will wager you a purple bible against a decayed molar that ten years from now it will be ensconced in a nice little glass-lined niche of its own, when all the best sellers and books of the month and pseudo-literary works of this day are long since pulped" (31 December 1938, WUL MS.).

15. Harvey Breit and Margerie Bonner Lowry, eds., *Selected Letters of Malcolm Lowry* (Philadelphia: J. B. Lippincott Co., 1965), 15.

16. F. C. Crews, review of *The Collected Novels of Conrad Aiken*, *New York Times*, 12 January 1964, 30.

17. Rountree, "The Fiction of Conrad Aiken," 110.

18. Martin, *Conrad Aiken*, 160.

19. It is interesting that each of Aiken's novels is given a more intense title in *Ushant*: *Blue Voyage* becomes *Purple Passage*; *Great Circle* is *Dead Reckoning*; *King Coffin* is curiously omitted; *A Heart for the Gods of Mexico* becomes *A Heart for the Barranca*; and *Conversation* is escalated to *The Quarrel*.

20. Aiken admitted to Ashley Brown in an interview that he had occasionally overemphasized musical forms in his works: " 'I went up that alley a little too far, simply under the influence of Richard Strauss, who absolutely intoxicates me. I fell under his spell, and I think you can trace it all the way down to my novel *Conversation*. This musical

preoccupation, or obsession, took me too far at times; but there is some justification for it' " ("An Interview with Conrad Aiken," *Shenandoah* 15 [Autumn 1963]: 35).

21. Once again Aiken had drawn heavily on a specific event in his own life. In a 1920 letter to Robert Linscott, Aiken had lamented: "John Coffey [the professional fur thief] and Max Bodenheim and Mrs. Bod., and one Louise Bogan . . . who has her infant (the offspring of a lawful wedlock now in process of dissolution) have all blown in in the last 24 hours, rolling in money, and have hired a house not far away. . . . Jessie is frantic, and as for me I don't know what in the hell to do" (Joseph Killorin, ed., *Selected Letters of Conrad Aiken* [New Haven: Yale University Press, 1978], 49–50; hereafter cited as *SL*).

22. Aiken, as usual, was recycling his actual experience, in this case of having purchased a Japanese print, Hiroshige's "Kiso Mountains Snow-clad" for $100, a "frightful extravagance" (Letter to Robert Linscott, 6 March 1922, WUL MS.).

23. Martin, *Conrad Aiken*, 86.

24. Martin, *Conrad Aiken*, 164.

25. Jim's initials are also those of the real-life model, John Coffey. Aiken, according to Jack Moore, in *Maxwell Bodenheim*, met Coffey originally through Bodenheim, when Aiken and Bodenheim were working together in the Others group: "The first visit [1916] was, according to Aiken in letters to me, after Bodenheim had assisted John Coffey (the professional fur thief and ultimately the model for the hero of Bodenheim's *Crazy Man*) escape from Blackwell Island Jail. The three lunched together in Cambridge after the escape" (New York: Twayne, 1970), 28. But Aiken, writing in 1924 to G. B. Wilbur, comments on Bodenheim's portrayal of Coffey: "Yes I have read Max on John, with interest. . . . I think what surprises me most is to find Max believing in the christmotif so extensively, and so little interested in uncovering its particular causes—i.e., giving so little emphasis to John's early history, the sexual influence, the ambivalence of theft and fornication and then the later translation of these two factors, mingled, into the 'philosophy' (which called for 'free wealth,' in order that there might be a maximum of 'reproduction,' to wit, sexual indulgence; at any rate, that's the way it always looked to me). . . . I may do the coffey story myself one day: with max thrown in for good measure!" (21 September 1924, *SL*, 97–98). In *Conversation*, Aiken allows Tip to digress into speculating on Jim's original motives—that is, whether he was really a compulsive thief and whether the anarchism was merely a rationalization. But Tip assuages his own misgivings: "It all came down to the question of motive, of course, and of priority of motive. If the mere pleasure in stealing came first—but did that even make any difference? There could be no question, anyway—none at all—of his honesty: his sincerity was

unmistakable. The circle of logic was complete" (*CN*, 545). In *Conversation*, Bodenheim appears as Karl Roth, the cynical man with the "dirty raincoat flying capelike over his round shoulders, the white face already sneering, the queer yellow head bare to the drizzle" (537). John Coffey was also the subject of William Carlos Williams's poem "An Early Martyr."

26. This was the first book about the Plymouth Colony and was compiled in England from material sent over by William Bradford and Edward Winslow on the *Mayflower*'s return voyage. The original title was *A relation or journall of the beginning and proceedings of the English plantation settled at Plimoth in New England* but quickly became *Mourt's Relation*, after George Morton, who saw to its publication (Robert E. Spiller et al., eds., *Literature of the United States* [New York: Macmillan, 1959]).

27. Louisa, the model for Noni, had once "very nicely pulled his leg about that trace of Anglicism in turn of phrase which had briefly afflicted him, and which, thanks largely to her, he had got rid of—? 'Seventy miles and a bit—! Seventy miles and a bit, from London—! Now aren't you ashamed? You mean, dear D., a little over seventy miles, don't you?'" (*Ushant*, 345).

28. Aiken always felt a peculiarly close relationship to the houses in which he lived. At one time, he had thought of calling *Ushant* "Rooms, Streets, and Houses," a phrase that becomes one of the refrains in the autobiography. Frequently, Clarissa Lorenz, unhappy with the financial burden of keeping up Jeake's House in Rye, complained about Aiken's devotion to it.

29. Manuscript in the Conrad Potter Aiken Collection in the Henry E. Huntington Library and Art Gallery, San Marino, California, Aik 3831 (hereafter cited as HHL MS.).

30. Aiken explained to Linscott: "The sub-title refers incidentally to the fact that I've interleaved the four sections with page-long quotes from the Journal of the Pilgrims, passages describing Cape Cod, indian huts, etc.—a rather nice device, making a pleasant little ironic commentary" (20 May 1939, WUL MS.).

31. The original lilac bushes were a gift to the Aikens from Robert Linscott. Aiken writes from South Yarmouth to thank him: "The roots were prodigious. They arrived on a rainy day, so we immediately dug up our peas, which were at last on the point of rendering us a tributary pod or two, and thrust the roots at random into the earth, thus being spared the necessity of watering" ([1920]; *SL*, 49).

CHAPTER 8: The Consistent View

1. Twenty-five years before writing this preface to *Three Novels: Blue Voyage, Great Circle and King Coffin* (New York: McGraw Hill, 1965),

Aiken, depressed over the reception of *Conversation*, wrote less euphorically to Malcolm Lowry that he was "fed up" but "girding myself slowly and rheumatically for another go, probably this time at a sort of fictionalized haughty biography, *Rooms, Streets, and Houses*; it somehow seems to be essential that no year be allowed to pass without another book sent spiraling down the drain" (21 May 1940, Manuscript in the Conrad Potter Aiken Collection at the Henry E. Huntington Library and Art Gallery, San Marino, California, Aik 2555; hereafter cited as HHL MS.).

2. Minna Littmann, "Cape Poet's Autobiography Executed in Unusual Form," *Sunday Standard-Times*, 5 October 1952, 15.

3. Aiken, with his admiration of Melville, was undoubtedly aware of the character Ushant in *White-Jacket*, whom Melville calls a "sea-Socrates," a remarkable sailor but also a philosopher: "Nor was his philosophy to be despised. . . . For this Ushant was an old man, of strong natural sense, who had seen nearly the whole terraqueous globe, and could reason of civilized and savage, of Gentile and Jew, of Christian and Moslem" (*White-Jacket* [New York: Grove Press, 1850], 332).

4. John K. Hutchens, "One Thing and Another," *Saturday Review* 52 (December 1969): 25.

5. Conrad Aiken, *Ushant: An Essay* (New York: Oxford University Press, 1971), 211 (hereafter cited as *Ushant*).

6. Conrad Aiken, *The Collected Short Stories of Conrad Aiken* (New York: Schocken Books, 1982), 287 (hereafter cited as *CSS*).

7. This is the central theme of Clarissa Lorenz's *Lorelei Two: My Life with Conrad Aiken* (Athens: University of Georgia Press, 1983).

8. The responses of both writers, specifically to their appearances in the autobiography, make a curious contrast. T. S. Eliot replied to Aiken's gift: "I am writing to thank you for *Ushant* which has just reached me, and the inscription which I shall value. It is certainly a very remarkable book. After the first few pages, I said to myself, this is all very well for a short distance, but can he keep it up through 365 pages without the style becoming oppressive? Anyway, you have done it, and I have read the book through with unflagging interest and I hope that it will have great success.

I was, as a matter of fact, somewhat shocked to find myself described as having a streak of sadism in my nature! I haven't the faintest recollection of the two incidents on which you base this diagnosis, but if it was like that, then it seems to me I must have behaved very badly. I hope in that case that I have been forgiven. Ever affectionately, Tom" (7 November 1952, HHL MS. Aik 536). Malcolm Lowry replied: "*Ushant* is a knock-out—ow, how it hurts! A great book, in many ways, technically, a marvel, in plain words a Masterwork. . . . And when I think of what gobbets of Hambo you might have chosen for display I can only affirm that in the matter of forebearance Clive of India has nothing on you" (14 September 1952, HHL MS. Aik 2534).

9. Lewis Nichols, "Talk with Conrad Aiken," *New York Times*, 26 October 1952, 26.

10. Littman, "Cape Poet's Autobiography," 15.

11. Howard Nemerov, *Reflections on Poetry and Poetics* (New Brunswick: Rutgers University Press, 1972), 96.

12. Conrad Aiken, *A Reviewer's ABC* (Connecticut: Meridian Books, Inc., 1958), 109 (hereafter cited as *ABC*).

13. Joseph Killorin, ed., *Selected Letters of Conrad Aiken* (New Haven: Yale University Press, 1978), 270–71 (hereafter cited as *SL*).

14. Nemerov, *Reflections*, 92.

15. Jay Martin calls D.'s former novels his "spiritual shipwrecks," which must be reviewed in order "to learn the perilous navigation of the soul and succeed in his prospective novel. . . . By sifting out his failures, he hopes to achieve full honesty of consciousness" (*Conrad Aiken: A Life of His Art* [Princeton University Press, 1962], 235).

16. Littman, "Cape Poet's Autobiography," 15.

17. Manuscript in Washington University Library (hereafter cited as WUL MS.).

18. Littman, "Cape Poet's Autobiography," 15.

19. R. H. Wilbur, "The Art of Poetry IX: Conrad Aiken—An Interview," *Paris Review* 11 (Winter-Spring 1968): 102.

20. Aiken wrote to Lowry: "and I ponder the three levels of reality novel which I dreamt of on the voyage back from Spain eleven bright years ago" (22 August 1944, HHL MS., Aik 2559).

21. Edward Dahlberg, "A Long Lotus Sleep," *Poetry* 81 (February 1953), 313, 320.

22. W. T. Scott, "Now, Afar Off," *Saturday Review* (October 1952): 26.

23. Malcolm Cowley, "Conrad Aiken's Autobiography," *New Republic* 127 (October 1952): 22, 20.

24. Mark Schorer, *The World We Imagine: Selected Essays* (New York: Farrar, Straus and Giroux, 1968), 261.

CHAPTER 9: The Circle Completed

1. Mark Schorer, "For Aiken Reparation," *New Republic* 126 (March 1952): 19; Henry Popkin, "The Bumbling of Timid Souls," *Saturday Review* 43 (December 1960): 15.

2. Malcolm Cowley, "Biography With Letters," *Wake* 11 (1952): 30.

3. Louis Untermeyer, "C. A.: Our Best Known Unread Poet," *Saturday Review* 50 (November 1967): 28–29, 76–77.

4. Malcolm Cowley, "Conrad Aiken: From Savannah to Emerson," *Southern Review* 11 (Spring 1974): 250.

5. Thomas R. Whitaker, "*Ushant*: Conversation as Design," paper delivered at Modern Language Association Conference, December 1988.

6. Even as an undergraduate, Aiken, with youthful arrogance, had written in his notebook: "Critic do not seek to impose your view of poetry on me! Do not try to alter me! Let my peculiar poetry impose itself on you; and thank God that this world is so full of uncontrolled vanity" (4–5 April 1912; manuscript in Conrad Potter Aiken Collection at the Henry E. Huntington Library and Art Gallery, San Marino, California, Aik 3588 [hereafter cited as HHL MS.]).

7. Joseph Killorin, ed., *Selected Letters of Conrad Aiken* (New Haven: Yale University Press, 1978), 264 (hereafter cited as *SL*).

8. James Dickey, "That Language of the Brain," *Poetry* 103 (December 1963): 187, 190.

9. Conrad Aiken, "The Technique of Polyphonic Prose," *Dial* (November 1918): 346. The following year Aiken reviewed Lowell's *Pictures of the Floating World*, and his opinion of her talents remained unchanged: "These are not poems, but the simulacra of poems. With what desperation Miss Lowell, in her determination to be original, flogs her poor vocabulary, rifles Roget for epithets, chops her lines to a sort of poetic mincemeat, resorts to effeminate expletives!! And all to achieve only a sterility somewhat oddly freaked and brindled" ("Miss Lowell Abides Our Question," *Dial* [October 1919]: 331–33).

10. Aiken had the further misfortune of bad timing: he wrote a devastating review of Lowell's two-volume biography of Keats for the June 1925 issue of *Dial*. Learning of her death in May, Aiken tried to retract or soften his remarks, but his review had already gone to press. His opinion of her work was typical of the honesty that had marked his career: "Her biography [lacking a genius for biography] becomes, therefore, a triumph of engineering, a miracle of dimensions; like the Great Wall of China or the largest potato at the fair" ("John Keats," *Dial* 78 [June 1925]: 475–90). Aiken wrote to his friend Robert Linscott about the unfortunate circumstances: "And then and there I saw that my old enemy was dead, Amy, noble Amy. . . . I was surprisingly moved and saddened, and still am. A damned shame. How did it happen? A lot of colour will go out of american letters with Amy; for all her vanities and faults a magnificent creature. . . . Last night . . . I dreamed that Jessie complimented Amy on a certain poem. 'Yes', said Amy, 'I like that poem too—it has a lovely golden-yellow sunrise

translucence, hasn't it!' And climbing into a monstrous cab, she rolled away down the hill, her round face looking out of the window like the moon. She sang, as she rolled away, and then I realized that I had failed, alas, to take off my hat. Nothing could more accurately symbolize my feeling" (manuscript in Washington University Library, St. Louis, Missouri [hereafter cited as WUL MS.]).

11. Patricia R. Willis, "Unabashed Praise of a Poet," *Georgia Review* 21 (Fall 1967): 378.

12. Alden Whitman, "Conrad Aiken, 80, Discusses Dislikes," *New York Times*, 5 August 1969, 26.

13. Conrad Aiken, "London Letter," *New Yorker* 12 (May 1936): 69.

14. James Atlas, "The Word Becomes World," in "For Conrad Aiken at 80: Three Tributes," *Harvard Advocate* 103 (1969): 28.

15. In one of Aiken's unpublished limericks, he gets his revenge:

> Whoever sent Jarrell to school
> Was wasting his time: he's a fool.
> What could be patheticker
> Than this ars poetica
> Incessantly going to stool?
> (HHL MS. Aik 3539)

16. Cowley, "Conrad Aiken," 258.

17. Willis, "Unabashed Praise," 378.

18. Conrad Aiken, *Ushant: An Essay* (New York: Oxford University Press, 1971), 276 (hereafter cited as *Ushant*). Aiken's similar sentiments are heard in *Conversation* in Tip's response to Enid's stated preference for County Street, New Bedford, friends, "And as for picking out my friends merely because they might be useful, good god, Ee, I never heard anything so revoltingly cynical and selfish and utilitarian in my life! You ought to be ashamed" (Conrad Aiken, *The Collected Novels of Conrad Aiken* [New York: Holt, Rinehart & Winston, 1964], 492 [hereafter cited as *CN*]).

19. Cowley, "Biography With Letters," 30.

20. Publishing records in Charles Scribner's Sons Archives, Princeton University Library, Princeton, N.J.

21. Unpublished letter from Aiken to Maxwell Perkins in Charles Scribner's Sons Archives, Princeton University Library.

22. Conrad Aiken, "A Note," *Wake* 11 (1952), n.p.

23. Willis, "Unabashed Praise," 378.

24. Conrad Aiken, *A Reviewer's ABC* (Connecticut: Meridian Books, Inc., 1958), 199–200 (hereafter cited as *ABC*).

25. Conrad Aiken, ed., *American Poetry 1671–1928* (New York: Modern Library, 1929), vii.

26. Stanley Edgar Hyman, *The Armed Vision* (New York: Alfred A. Knopf, 1947), 14.

27. Maxwell Bodenheim, "American Novels," *Saturday Review* 3 (March 1927): 673–74.

28. Harold Strauss, "Conrad Aiken's Story of a Criminal," *New York Times*, 29 September 1935, 6.

29. Houston Peterson, *The Melody of Chaos* (New York: Longmans Green & Co., 1931), 17–18.

30. Donald Davidson, *The Spyglass, Views and Reviews, 1924–1930* (Nashville: Vanderbilt University Press, 1963), 23, 24.

31. While it is true Aiken never sought celebrity status, it is also true that his near-total neglect took its toll as well, as can be heard in his anger over Robert Linscott's guarded approval of *Great Circle*: "GOD DAMN IT ALL TO HELL. I'm fed up with dropping my works like so many faeces into the Cosmic W. C. Voiding myself. Not even, apparently, a very good or interesting shitter. What goes on? Is it secretly being said that I'm no longer any use? . . . are there so many better writers of verse or fiction. . . . or am I disapproved of . . . because my work is too close to the autobiographic?" (10 December 1932, WUL MS.).

32. Malcolm Cowley, "Commemorative Tributes of the Academy: Conrad Aiken, 1889–1973," in *Proceedings of the American Academy of Arts and Letters and the National Institute of Arts and Letters*, ser. 2, no. 24 (American Academy, 1974).

33. Unpublished letter from Aiken to Everett L. Getchell (15 November 1940), Colby College Library, Waterville, Maine.

34. Mark Schorer, "Heroic Exploration," *Atlantic* 229 (February 1972): 98–100.

35. Unpublished letter from Cowley to me (17 January 1976). To my suggestion that Viking Press contract Cowley to edit a Portable Aiken, the response was almost exactly as Cowley had predicted: "Before we invest in the considerable expense of a new Portable . . . we have to be pretty certain of a large adoption in schools and colleges, and, unfortunately, this would not be the case for Aiken" (unpublished letter from Barbara Burn, editor, to me [26 February 1976]).

36. Aiken's influence on other poets as well might lead to a reevaluation of his importance. Eventually the Aiken-Eliot relationship will have to be put in a more accurate perspective than it is at present, with the erroneous stress on Eliot's influence on Aiken. There have been several articles moving in the opposite direction: Joseph Warren Beach, in a long article entitled "Conrad Aiken and T. S. Eliot: Echoes and Overtones," *PMLA* 69 (1953): 753–62, illustrated, for instance, the

use Eliot had made of Senlin in *The Waste Land*. An anonymous article attributed to Kathleen Raine strongly suggested that Eliot exploited Aiken ("Answer to the Sphinx," *TLS*, 19 April 1963, 258). It will be some time before the literary critics will be ready to accept Aiken's judgment: "Of course Eliot and I were so close we could be said to have swapped juices" (Bill Winn, "America Going to Dogs? Poet Aiken Says No," *Atlanta Journal*, 21 January 1968, 6A).

37. Douglas Day, *Malcolm Lowry, A Biography* (New York: Oxford University Press, 1973), 102.

38. Richard H. Costa wrote an informative article tracking the mentor role that Aiken played for Lowry and speaking of their relationship as a "maelstrom union of coeval geniuses" ("The Lowry/Aiken Symbiosis," *Nation* 204 (June 1967): 825). Like all the others, Costa speculated on the possibility "that a major Aiken revival is under way" and also that literary history would reveal Aiken as a major literary force, "the discoverer of, and catalyst for, other talents" (826). Aiken, the father figure, would appreciate the irony of his being "born" through Lowry, the son.

39. Henry A. Murray, "Poet of Creative Dissolution," *Wake* 11 (1952): 102.

40. Hayden Carruth, "Heart for the Gods," review of *The Collected Novels of Conrad Aiken, Nation* 198 (February 1964), 172.

41. Foreword to Thomas Hardy, *Two Wessex Tales* (Boston: International Pocket Library, 1919).

Selected Bibliography

Primary Sources: Works by Conrad Aiken.

The Collected Novels of Conrad Aiken. New York: Holt, Rinehart and Winston, 1964.

Collected Poems. 2d ed. New York: Oxford University Press, 1970.

The Collected Short Stories of Conrad Aiken. New York: Schocken Books, 1982.

A Reviewer's ABC. Connecticut: Meridian Books, Inc., 1958.

A Seizure of Limericks. Canada: Holt, Rinehart & Winston, 1963.

Three Novels: Blue Voyage, Great Circle and King Coffin. New York: Mc-Graw-Hill, 1965.

Ushant: An Essay. New York: Oxford University Press, 1971.

Secondary Sources

Adler, Alfred. "Individual Psychology." *Psychologies of 1930*. Edited by Carl Murchison. Massachusetts: Clark University Press, 1930.

Breit, Harvey, and Margerie Bonner Lowry, eds. *Selected Letters of Malcolm Lowry*. Philadelphia: J. B. Lippincott Co., 1965.

Butscher, Edward. *Conrad Aiken: Poet of White Horse Vale*. Athens: University of Georgia Press, 1988.

Day, Douglas. *Malcolm Lowry: A Biography*. New York: Oxford University Press, 1973.

Denney, Reuel. *Conrad Aiken*. Minneapolis: University of Minnesota Press, 1964.

Freud, Sigmund. "The Interpretation of Dreams." In *The Standard Edition of the Complete Psychological Works of Sigmund Freud*. Translated by James Strachey. 5 vols. London: Hogarth Press, 1953.

———. *An Outline of Psychoanalysis*. Translated by James Strachey. New York: Norton, 1949.

Hall, Calvin S., and Gardner Lindzey. *Theories of Personality*. 2d ed. New York: Wiley, 1970.

Hoffman, Frederick J. *Freudianism and the Literary Mind*. Baton Rouge: Louisiana State University Press, 1957.

Jaspers, Karl. *Man in the Modern Age*. Translated by R. F. C. Hull. New York: Harper, 1956.

Kierkegaard, Soren. *Fear and Trembling and Sickness Unto Death*. Translated by Walter Lowrie. New York: Doubleday Anchor, 1954.

Killorin, Joseph, ed. *Selected Letters of Conrad Aiken*. New Haven: Yale University Press, 1978.

Lorenz, Clarissa M. *Lorelei Two: My Life with Conrad Aiken*. Athens: University of Georgia Press, 1983.

Marten, Harry. *The Art of Knowing: The Poetry and Prose of Conrad Aiken*. Columbia: University of Missouri Press, 1988.

Martin, Jay. *Conrad Aiken: A Life of His Art*. Princeton: Princeton University Press, 1962.

Moore, Jack. *Maxwell Bodenheim*. New York: Twayne, 1970.

Nietzsche, Friedrich. *Human, All Too Human: A Book for Free Spirits*. Translated by Alexander Harvey. Chicago: C. H. Kerr & Co., 1915.

———. *The Portable Nietzsche*. Edited by Walter Kaufmann. New York: Viking Press, 1954.

Peterson, Houston. *Melody of Chaos*. New York: Longmans Green & Co., 1931.

Potter, William James. *Twenty-five Sermons*. Boston: George H. Ellis, 1885.

Spivey, Ted. *Writer as Shaman*. Macon, Ga.: Mercer University Press, 1986.

Suetonius. *The Lives of the Caesars*. Translated by J. C. Rolfe. Vol. 1. 1913; reprint, Cambridge: Harvard University Press, 1960.

Unpublished Material

Conrad Aiken and Robert Linscott correspondence. Washington University Library, St. Louis, Missouri.

Conrad Potter Aiken Collection. Henry E. Huntington Library and Art Gallery, San Marino, California.

Maurer, Gertrude. "Ushant: Form and Meaning." Ph.D. diss. University of Notre Dame, 1974.

Rountree, Mary Martin. "The Fiction of Conrad Aiken." Ph.D. diss. University of Pittsburgh, 1965.

Index